THE STRANGE TOOLS OF HUMAN COMMUNICATION

The Strange Tools of Human Communication: The Voice, the Pen, and the Lyre is a thought-provoking exploration of the everyday tools of communication that weaves together history, art, and science to reveal how the voice, hand, and mind shape our shared experiences.

Through a blend of scholarly research, personal insights, and field experiences – from the oral tales of Sierra Leone's Limba storytellers to ancient cave art and modern iconography – this book offers fresh perspectives on how we connect across time and cultures. Challenging the idea that spoken language alone defines humanity, it emphasises the crucial role of hands, gestures, and artistic forms as the foundation of human communication. Readers are invited to consider the possibility of an ancestral, shared consciousness and the mysterious similarities in ancient art worldwide. Through vivid examples and personal insights, the book redefines communication as a blend of conscious expression and subconscious influence, inviting readers to consider the hidden connections that unite us across cultures and time, and to contemplate the future of communication.

The Strange Tools of Human Communication is an ideal supplement to upper level undergraduate and graduate courses in cultural anthropology, sociocultural linguistics, and cultural studies.

Ruth Finnegan OBE is Emeritus Professor at the Open University, UK.

THE STRANGE TOOLS OF HUMAN COMMUNICATION

The Voice, the Pen, and the Lyre

Ruth Finnegan

Routledge
Taylor & Francis Group
NEW YORK AND LONDON

Designed cover image: NASA, ESA, and STScI

First published 2025
by Routledge
605 Third Avenue, New York, NY 10158

and by Routledge
4 Park Square, Milton Park, Abingdon, Oxon, OX14 4RN

Routledge is an imprint of the Taylor & Francis Group, an informa business

ISBN: 9781032802169 (hbk)
ISBN: 9781032799049 (pbk)
ISBN: 9781003496007 (ebk)

DOI: 10.4324/9781003496007

Typeset in Sabon
by Deanta Global Publishing Services, Chennai, India

For David
With me in my travels, here and always.

Man could not have attained his present dominant position in the world without the use of his hands, which are so admirably adapted to the act of obedience of his will.

Charles Darwin

The human animal is a social being.

Aristotle

CONTENTS

FIGURES

PREFACE

This book follows on from my *Communicating: The Multiple Modes of Human Communication* (2023), a companion volume rather than a sequel. It deals with the same themes of communication and expression but this time focuses on human activities, saying little about those of other animals. It is, essentially, about the *tools* that we human creatures develop and manipulate to express ourselves and interact meaningfully with each other.

It, thus, has a different perspective from the previous work, though it does not contradict it. It has brought me to the same conclusion, that of querying a long-established tale of the early history of human communicating. Further, as well as attention to the familiar tools of the voice, the pen, and musical instruments such as the lyre, considered in comparative perspective, this book also brings in some new topics, in particular our often unawares communicative use of numbers and colours, a greater attention to music, and some thoughts on communication in the earliest era of human history.

As well as documentary sources, it builds on my own research and has turned out a more personal take on the subject than I had planned at the outset. I have, in particular, from time-to-time, cited examples from my own experience or observation – I prefer primary evidence to hearsay. I hope you can accept this intrusion of the personal.

I have greatly enjoyed and learned from my work on this book. Thank you, my readers and my publishers, for giving me the opportunity. I had no idea, even after my earlier book, that communicating was such a wide and historically situated subject.

ACKNOWLEDGEMENTS

This book has led me back to some of my own researches, especially that seminal, first experience of fieldwork, and reminded me of my debt to those who helped me then. So, may I, above all, express my sincere acknowledgement to the long mourned 1960s Limba speakers of northern Sierra Leone, and, from later, to the amazing musicians and storytellers of Milton Keynes and of Fiji. From more recent times, let me thank the remarkable local taxi drivers who graciously shared so much of their lives and their stories.

I am grateful, too, to the many friends and colleagues in all continents of the world, especially Africa, who helped me understand the wondrous subjects of communication and its tools; to the teachers and fellow students who introduced me to the great civilisations of the ancient world, with its astonishing literary and scientific creations; and to those during my first period of fieldwork when the Sierra Leonean Limba taught me so much about the arts of communication through storytelling.

I have used, mostly in heavily revised form, some material from early publications for which, again, I am very grateful. The book also returns to earlier, mostly unpublished, thoughts and presentations (many from the COVID-19 period), for which I wish to make grateful acknowledgement here. These include the Hidden Musicians Revisited conference, Open University 2016; the John Blacking Memorial Lecture (Royal Anthropological Institute), 2018; the Orality conference, University of Sienna, 2020; and stimulating thoughts on "voice" and on "transitional texts" with Sarali Gintsburg. Sincere thanks to these colleagues who challenged my thinking with new questions but allowed me to share some of the results. For less formal communication, I wish to acknowledge all those I have interacted with, especially here in Milton Keynes, but also in many continents of the world, my sincere thanks.

Let me also thank my many good friends and colleagues for their personal inspiration and support, among them David Wilson for sharing his knowledge of the ancient Middle East and saving me from some horrible errors; Evelyn Glennie for her insights into vibration and rhythm; Rachel Murray for introducing me to functional magnetic resonance imaging (MRI) (I had no idea); and, for help over many years, the amazing John Hunt, wizard with design and illustration. Also, thanks once more to the fine team at Routledge, not least the incomparable Meagan Simpson.

For the specific illustrations, my thanks again to John Hunt for his clever editing and arranging, to Louise Langley for her photography, and to those credited for their creation or ownership. For those without explicit attribution by name, some are in my own ownership or the public domain, but for the rest, may I sincerely thank Wikipedia for their images, used under their Creative Commons copyright license (indicated by Wikipedia Creative Commons) and the stunning photographers of Unsplash, Pixabay, and Freepick who so generously allow free unattributed use of their images.

Finally, and as always, I thank my family to whom I owe everything: my astounding parents, Tom and Agnes Finnegan; my knowledgeable and ever-supportive husband, David Murray; and my three wonderful daughters Rachel, Kathleen, and Brigid.

Ruth

Shenley Wood Village,
Milton Keynes,
September 2024

1

A STRANGE, MAGICAL, LANDSCAPE

Communicating – how do we do it? Why and for what, and when and where did it start? There are many questions, and for some, there are no certain answers.

But we are humans, noted for curiosity, and the questions are worth asking. This book endeavours to describe the things that we do know, which, in some cases, is quite a lot. We know of the basic resources used by humans and other animals (sketched out in my earlier book (2023)). We can explore the tools we do know of and point to those we do not understand – in some way, like insects swarming, we communicate without using our regular senses, or somehow walk, sharing, in the ether, things I come to near the end of the book.

So, for now, dear reader, permit me to enter into what I cannot but think of as a magical, elusive space. For what could be more risky-precious than the arena where we separate, yet social-reaching, animals meet and communicate together in some way. That is where we seek to fly, looking onward from the shoulders of others.

"Tools"

The subtitle of this book refers to "tools". This is an everyday term that can introduce the high arts of human communication and expression through the things we use to survive in the short yet, perhaps, also eternal span of human life. As the butterfly, they say, tells us, "My life is short – but it is long enough".

DOI: 10.4324/9781003496007-1

Language is there, reached and created through the resources of the voice and the pen. Contrary to widespread assumptions, it is not necessarily the dominating one of the many arts we humans have found, invented, or developed over the ages. All the same, speaking and writing are indeed human crafts that necessarily receive much attention here. Other arts, too, are considered, particularly those of music and, always with us, the work of the hand.

It is through these tools that we humans engage in the interaction – the communicating – that is both natural and necessary for us as social animals.[1]

Why do humans need tools?

Imagine a scattering of units of some kind – of any kind – each going its individual way, unconnected to any of the rest. Or a jumble of robots. Or a cloud of ants or birds. Could anything order them or bring them into touch with each other? And if so, what could be used to make it happen, and coming from where?

Above all, how do humans and other social animals manage to interact with each other as, it seems, they do in some way?

That was the question that started this book.

It soon grew and led to other questions. If, indeed, humans are social, interacting, communicating, animals – and we pretty much know they are – how is it that they can interact and in multiple ways; in peace as well as war, in both liking and disliking, in many lands and across thousands, no hundreds of thousands, of years?

For sociality is not automatic. Humans might not have been like this. Remarkably, the majority of animals are solitary and, apart from the act of mating to continue the species, live independent lives; can you imagine snakes in a coordinated assembly or assisting each other, koalas gathering in the treetops for a council, or *any* reptiles cooperating?

Most species are solitary. No surprise really, as a solitary life has benefits. It means there is no need to share scarce resources, swifter movement than if travelling with others, and no groups to attract the attention of predators.

And yet humans, the minority, are social beings. This too has benefits. Individuals in groups can assist others and be assisted when in danger and in everyday tasks; they can share knowledge and discoveries and learn from others – such as in the development of specific tools; a group is more able to defend itself and to care for younger and weaker members than individuals; and, an important point, division of labour is possible with all the social cultural, economic, and aesthetic aspects that this can lead to.[2]

So, humans live in groups and interact with each other. Like other animals, they have the means to do so, chiefly through the senses of hearing,

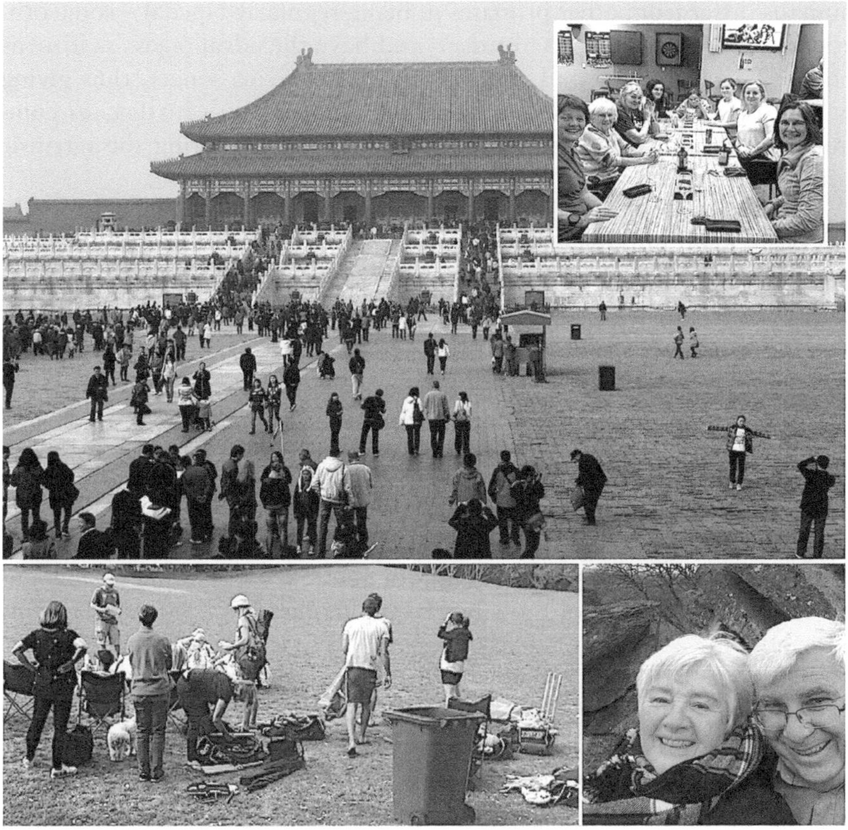

FIGURE 1.1 Social humans.

sight, touch, and smell, together with certain material objects and human made artefacts, and, for all their puzzlement, extrasensory communicative channels.[3]

These are resources that, to varying extents and in differing ways, we broadly share with other animals and are treated, in general terms, in my earlier book on communicating. But there is more to say. For humans, though not exclusively distinct from other living creatures, especially birds, primates, and perhaps some insects, are notable for creating and using a range of tools, including some external to their bodies, to communicate and express themselves,and to enhance and share their lives in this earth.

It is the skill of the hand that, guided by human will and aspiration, makes, creates, and uses many of these prime tools. This was made possible by humans' adoption of a upright, bipedal (two-footed) gait.

This is an important and pretty much unparalleled characteristic. For humans differ from other primates in being regularly bipedal – some others are, but just from time to time – and have the advantages, as it turns out, of longer infancy and adolescence and of living longer, thus giving greater opportunities to experiment and to learn and, further, to communicate their learning and their ideas while still sharing the intrinsic sociality of primates.

It is uncertain why and exactly when hominids became bipedal (I will not try to enter into the wide-ranging debates on that), but it is clear that the adaptation had advantages. Some were of a physical nature, such as the upright stance shielding the body better from the radiation of the sun and being cooler during locomotion. More relevant for communicating was that bipedalism freed the upper limbs and especially the hands for other functions than walking. They can be used for gesturing and signalling, as the upright stance enables easier mutual sighting of each others' gestures than for four-footed creatures. The hands could also now be used for tool manipulation, the more effective with the specifically human opposable.

So "Man, the Tool Maker", who, for some, is the epitome of humanness, and the creation of tools marks the moment that humans became truly human.

The term "strange", together with the general approach in this book, may seem puzzling. It is true that the tools considered here are a familiar and regular part of human life, so, in that context, they are not at all strange. But they are not usually gathered together as "tools" or treated from the perspective of this book.

I describe them as "strange" for a reason. When I think back to early human history, I start to wonder: was there any automatic reason why humans developed the things they did and not others? What about the way they did create them? Certainly, a visitor from Mars would find them unfamiliar and unforeseen, as if entering a strange and magical land – a perceptive stance to take (indeed, a typical anthropologist's way), for how can we appreciate the interest and (in a way) uniqueness of things we know so well that we just don't notice them?

So, let me explore these tools of human usage not as something given but as if something new and in that sense strange – something, therefore, of interest to investigate.

I imagine that there was, in fact, nothing automatic or predestined about what was being used or discovered at the start of human history (whatever or whenever that was). By hindsight, it all looks inevitable and predictable, part of what is too often, if only subconsciously, seen as a kind of predestined upward progress to where we have now reached in the long progression of human life through the millennia. It is tempting to talk about human "destiny". In a way, this is apt. But it was not some automatic outcome: the tools were not just "there" waiting for us to use. We had to discover them – dis-cover – and adapt them, unlock the vault, open the doors, and use them. We had to uncover them, develop them, work on them, *use* them to a purpose. It was human intentional *agency*: the actions of *individuals,* generation after generation after generation, building on the enterprising intelligence that enabled us to walk in the paths where we are.

We can remind ourselves that humans, not after all *totally* unlike other animals, have other resources that we might, instead, have built on. We have olfaction, not as of now a strong human resource but there as a potential and, to some extent, actual sense for communicating and interaction through the receiving and and transmitting of smells. We might have built on that potential and developed tools around that (why not? Some social insects have done so with astounding outcomes). Maybe in some other time or place that might have been so; it might, indeed, have gone equally well for us. Or again, as in *Dogman* (Pilkey 2017), the children's book about a little boy who took on the senses and capacities of a dog, we might have benefited from canine abilities.

But we did not. We developed as primarily audio-visual creatures, making much of the typically human tools of the voice, the pen, the lyre, and, beyond that, the hand. They are tools in which, when we look at our past and our present, we may, indeed, rejoice.

Again, I call them "strange", as if a mystery story. That term is apt, for our early history truly is a mystery, and there are no handy detectives to unravel it for us. Far from definitively pinning down *who dunnit*, the best we can do is to speculate from what evidence we have about what happened in those early early years and how we came to be as we are. We must just do our best to put together what has been accumulated, bit by bit and across many disciplines, and the theories, plausible and implausible/impossible, that have been put forward. In fact, we know quite a lot. And where we are uncertain, we can at least try to avoid the worst nonsense and winnow the results as best we can.

In the event, however, this book is not, first and foremost, a mystery story or totally a work of speculation. Communicating is something that happens here and now, right here among us. True, there are cultural variations and specificities, which, for any scientist, is a given. But there are also identifiable patterns worth pointing to. And while detailed interpretation may be difficult, we can, overall, have a good degree of confidence in what we observe and experience in our own selves and hear from those whose evidence we have found to be reliable.

This book, then, despite the openly speculative nature of some sections, is primarily a work of science detailing the evidence about the tools that humans use to communicate. Its general message is that while other animals have their own ways, human creatures too have their own special tools. These enable us to express ourselves – to be truly ourselves – to engage with and build on the riches of the earth, and to communicate with each other.

The human toolbox

We immediately, and rightly, think of speaking and writing – products of the voice and the pen. It is only right to start with these because, for all our multimodal potential, we humans are primarily, unlike some other animals, audio-visual creatures.

So, the first substantial chapter focuses on *the voice*, something always intrinsic to human beings, and so, in many views, the first, greatest tool of human communication and expression. Its use, it is true, has gone through many variations and historical vicissitudes (to be sketched out as this book progresses), but it always with us.

Then the pen, a remarkable tool, which, through its products, we humans are able to attain the kind of survival through time via our communications, which was not, at least until very recently, possible with the unaided voice.

It is the tool for writing, that continuingly important mode of human communication. I should make clear at this point that when I say the pen, I could equally have said the brush, the plume, the blade, the chisel, the fingers – any implement, that is, that humans use to inscribe or engrave marks on a surface so as to communicate in ways that through continuous habit have acquired meaning. "The pen" is shorthand for all the devices that humans use to make relatively fixed and permanent marks on a surface.

Thus, there is the brush and other devices for producing calligraphy, for pictographic writing systems, and, above all, for pictorial expression. The pen also points us to the knife, a handy term that covers a plethora of sharp and pointed implements – tools that, in their various forms, go back for generations untold. It leads further into the heavy, solid, objects that humans have, as with the knife (in its large sense), employed to shape material objects.

Behind these is always *the hand* – both the hand that wields the pen and brush (I will get to that), the hand that signs and gesticulates, and the hands that sound the lyre in music – whatever music is, that is, and wherever it first came from.

These are the central tools to considered here. We know them well.

Then there are the tools we are not really aware of but that we use often, such as the hidden spells of language, of numbers, of colours, of

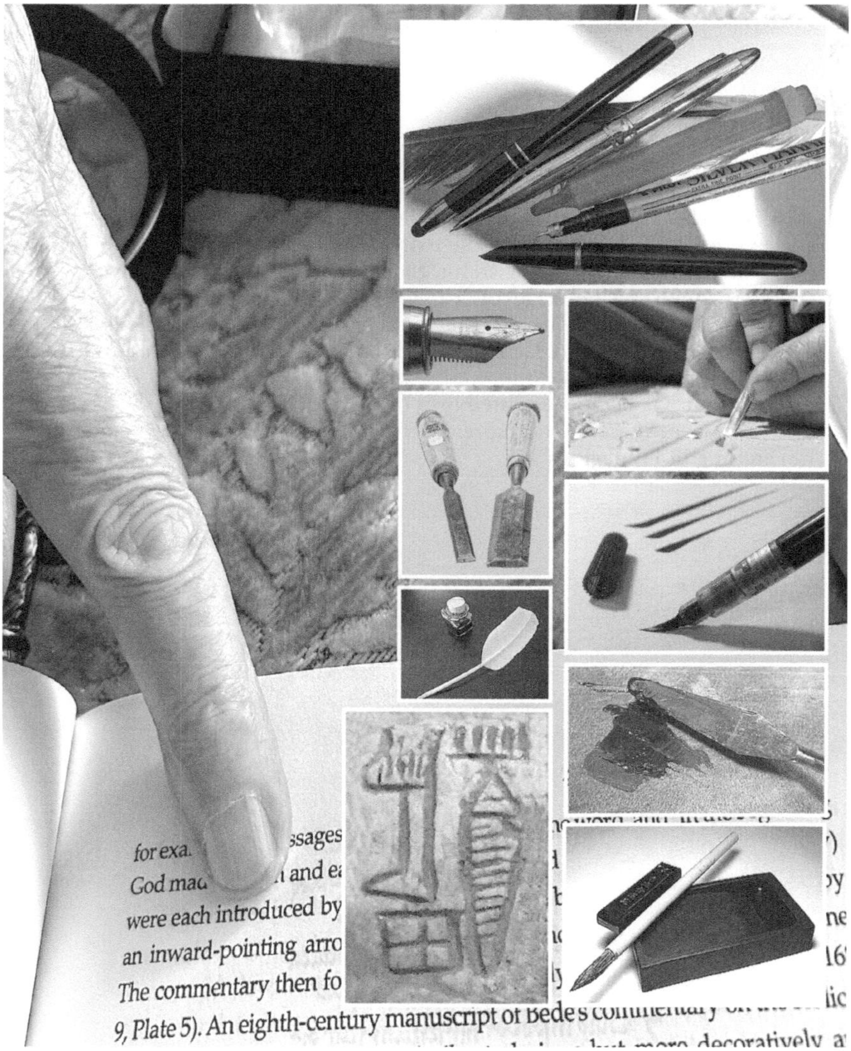

FIGURE 1.2 The pen.

the involuntary gestures of the hand and body. At first sight, these sound unconvincing as channels of communication, given that, for many and, perhaps, most people, they work largely below the level of consciousness. But they can be extremely powerful and have been over the ages and, surprisingly, across the world. In Chapter 5, I explain something of their working even as, at a surface level, they are commonly unnoticed.

Beneath and behind all that, there is the human will and intelligence: the bedrock.

Notes

1 When I speak of "we" or of "human beings," I am aware that I am generalising; there will always be individuals who have issues with one or other of the tools treated here. All the same, it is amazing how people whom some might classify as disadvantaged or disabled deploy alternative tools to communicate and express themselves. Given the existence of these gifted human beings, I feel I have no need to apologise for generalising, but please forgive me if, as you go through this book, my wording around this in any way offends.

2 On sociality see, for example, McGlynn 2010, Smelser 2001, Sussman and Chapman 2004, Figure 1.1, and examples in several other figures in this book (and all around).

3 An area that has been devastated by a disastrous civil war, so it is likely, alas, that Limba speakers are no more. Further details of the background and the storytelling in Finnegan 1967.

2

IN THE BEGINNING WAS THE VOICE

I begin with the voice. Always with us, it was perhaps the first main human communicating tool (or perhaps not, we will see). Its use with music, arguably one of its allies, has been claimed to be the supreme human art. At the least, it is the tool for some of our most used and most skilled human activities.

Let me for a moment, however, switch the focus from voice to hearing and to sound more generally. Audition is, together with its close twin, touch, the first and the last sense of human beings. We hear while still in the womb, and it is the last thing we are aware of as we are dying. We hear through vibration, through feeling, through clapping, through playing, through vocalised speaking. We communicate in sound using our breaths and our vocal cords: through the voice.

Sound is everywhere. Even those who are deaf to the kinds of sounds familiar to others are aware of vibration which, we might say, is essentially the same thing. In nature, too, sound abounds in the air, the wind, the sea, the storms, and the thunderclap. And it is in our body: our heart beats, breaths, rhythm. It has been there from the beginning, and there is no way that it is diminishing. Indeed, we could say that we now rely on sound for communicating even more than in the past, given that it is now possible to record and preserve sound and convey it over a distance of both time and space. Overall, sounds can be powerful, and their soundings be felt to have powerful human consequences.

Though we do, indeed, have other products for conveying messages, a key and initial tool for communicating meaning in sound is the voice. Now, let me emphasise that the voice stands alone, for vocalised speech is

DOI: 10.4324/9781003496007-2

a multi-modal tool. Along with its sound, we also see, feel, and sometimes touch. There is usually – not always but most often – a visual setting and an audience of an individual or a group to make speech sensible. The voice does not just communicate "language" in the sense of just speaking words that can be found in dictionaries or what is captured on a written page. For we also use laughter, silence, sighs, and, as I will illustrate in more detail below, the multiple potential intensities, variations, and modulations of the voice. It is a fine and near-infinitely versatile tool.

It is true that, compared to some other instruments, the voice has its limitations ("evolution", "God's hand", or whatever, is not necessarily perfect). I.R. Titze elaborates:

> The human vocal system would not receive much acclaim if instrument makers placed it in a lineup of traditional orchestral instruments. Arranged by size, for example, the voice box (larynx) –and the airway it sits in – would be grouped with the piccolo, among the smallest of mechanical music makers. And yet experienced singers compete well with all man-made instruments, one on one, and even paired with full orchestras. Recent investigations of how our singing voice generates a remarkable range of sounds have revealed surprising complexity in the behavior of the vocal system's elements and in the ways they interact.
>
> *(Titze 2008: 108)*

If you think of it as an instrument, it needs to have three things: a sound source that vibrates in the air to generate what we hear as pitch, a resonator to maximise the strength, and a radiating surface or opening that transfers the sounds to the air and, eventually, to a listener's ear. To generate sound frequencies, a singer blows air across oscillating, vibrating vocal folds (small bundles of tissues called the "vocal cords") and then across the vocal tract (the resonator). The laryngeal vestibule, an airway passage just above the larynx, acts to couple the sound to the remaining part of the resonator known as the vocal tract. Like the bell of a trumpet, the lips radiate the sound outward. Though the vocal cords are quite small, a good singer or speaker can manipulate them to create great resonance.

And so, the voice.

Using the voice

That's it for the physical process, but more importantly, how do humans use it?

The first thing to note is that it is a highly complex, versatile, and subtle form of expression. It is not just the vocal cords in the narrow sense. It is also the eyes, the face, the arms, the whole demeanour of the body. It is smiles, frowns, sighs. It is delay or rush in the lengthening or shortening of syllables. It is a delivery style that shares specific meanings and emotions with an audience, conveying something loud, soft, gentle, sweet, exciting, bitter, ironic, unexpected, sorrowful, traumatic. There is onomatopoeia.

The voice speaks. It utters. It sings. In its vocalising, sound matters. So do the connotations, the echoes, the overtones, and then the other senses that come multi-modally into the communicating. In some areas, particularly in South America, sound symbolism is a highly sophisticated and integral part of spoken language. As always, it overlaps with, and blends into, music, here almost the essential complement and completion of the spoken word.

Recall, yourself, how words reach their fulfilment when read or spoken aloud, even just to yourself, or even reading silently, when heard with your inner ear.

I can speak from my own experience. Every now and then, I do a reading in church, and sometimes think beforehand "this is a very boring text". But then I get up and see the listeners and project the words around them and feel the immediacy of delivery and sharing. Through the voice aloud, the words grow in power.

This experience is a common one.

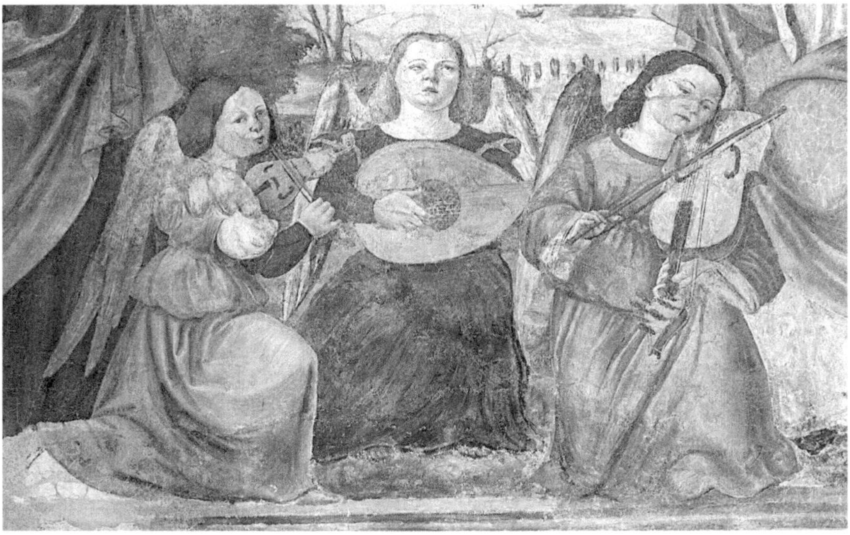

FIGURE 2.1 The singing voice.

The change is because it exploits sound: I was using my tool of the voice *aloud* to, and with, a *listening audience*. And that, of course, is the way in which the words were originally communicated and handed down, orally, through the centuries; orally, in other words, through one voice to another. The pen certainly had a place, and a significant one, but for centuries, and in some settings now too, the pen's role was often secondary to that of the voice. The voice took the lead: reading aloud (silent reading was a late invention), memorising by ear, and sonic repetitions. In the ancient classical world whose works are revered in their now-written forms, "publication" meant speaking or reading the work aloud to a gathering of friends and dependants, and only after that, then having it rendered into writing by slaves; writing was not a fit task for the cultivated creators whose high art lay in speaking, so this was a job for menials.

These sounds of the voice, the oral channel, have sometimes been ignored or downgraded in the writing-dominated scholarly literature. In the specifications of vision-preoccupied "modernity", vocalised sound is quite often pictured as something in retreat or even something of the past that we have now outgrown. In fact, nothing could be further from the truth. Quite apart from live speaking, always with us, we are surrounded by sound in the newly available forms of audio: telephones, radio, television, records, audiobooks, the web, social media. Sounds are accepted as a fit part of public events, street meetings, conferences, religious services, shopping, social media, and even sometimes a continuous background surrounding us in the home.

Whatever our conscious recognition, sound goes deep into our unconscious awareness. Even those in dementia who have lost much else are still stirred when they hear their favourite songs or music they have loved. Sounds, it seems, epitomised uniquely, though not exclusively, by the voice, can reach into us more directly and immediately than "words".

Sound and the voice have not seemed obvious subjects for academic scrutiny. Given the value accorded to the written word, it is not really strange that the arts of the voice tend to be somewhat sidelined. Typical of many, I myself grew up in a sound-rich environment and, at one level, was aware of it and knew how to "hear" and use it, but at the time, busy with written learning, I did not consciously realise it. I grew up in Ulster, where – as I now see – there is great feeling for the beauty of verbal wit and performance. I think of my mother's storytelling or my father's typically Ulster wit. But not being an anthropologist from Mars, I did not realise – nor perhaps might you – when I was in the midst of it, that those speech rhythms and cadences and gestures were there at all, far less something of significance. They were just something taken for granted as natural.

It only started to dawn on me when I went to Oxford to study the literatures of the ancient world, available in the approved form of written texts, which had to be analysed, commented on, and understood. Many students read them that way: fixed frozen on a printed page.

Permit me to continue, as my personal experience may explain a bit further some of the qualities of voice and why I want to elucidate them.

I had the luck to have a tutor who told me I should read all the (very many) Greek and Latin texts in the syllabus *aloud*, including the prose histories, philosophies, and letters. I did, and it was a revelation. That was when I began to see that these texts from the classical era, despite the long avenues of writing by which they had reached us, existed in large part in an auditory dimension. They might overlap and interlock, it is true, with scribal enscripted versions, but their roots, their true being, lay in their auditory existence (it helped that they were initially something strange to me, so I had to work at understanding these characteristics rather than not noticing them because they were just natural).

And then it went further. One of my memories from my time as an eager student is of attending a lecture by a renowned and, we thought, very dry Teutonic professor. The subject was Catullus's poem *da mi basia mille* – "Give me a thousand kisses, and then some more". The lecturer went through the text, word for word, syllable by syllable: the language, the grammar, the syntax, the structure, the transmission, the controversies. But then he stopped. "But", he said, "let us not forget, it is also – a love poem", and he read it aloud. That aloud was the true meaning, the real poem. It started a growing revelation of what it meant to be oral, sonic, auditory – to begin to understand something of the tool of the voice.

He added to my insights when, in a lecture on another occasion expounding the complex text of Aeschylus's great tragedy, *Agamemnon*, he broke into his dry lecture delivery by bursting into the bass part of the "Sanctus" from Bach's *Mass in B Minor*. That was when I and my fellow students began considering how the voice can bring language and music together in a common identity.

He also, without saying so explicitly, fed my dimly growing awareness that poetry, like music, can be seen as having, metaphorically at least, some kind of a divine origin. Certainly Homer was of that view. Both his great epics begin with an invocation to a divine goddess to "*sing*" (not *speak*) the story. Even amidst the excitement of the adventures, the echo of that invocation somewhere remains: the songs come from the muse of poetry and exist in a world of enchantment.

It is relatively easy to see how an auditory dimension was applied in the sound-aware contexts of Greece and Rome and similar cultures. But there is more. This sonic, magical world is not just something of the past. It also, to an extent, shapes the poetry and song of the present and recent past too. It is, in large part, through sound that it truly communicates and moves us. Think of the inescapably auditory nature, rooted in rhythm and, to an extent, melody, of lyrics or sayings such as:

> Fear no more the heat o' the sun,
> Nor the furious winter's rages;
> Thou thy worldly task hast done,
> Home art gone, and ta'en thy wages:
> Golden lads and girls all must,
> As chimney-sweepers, come to dust.

(Shakespeare, Cymbeline)

Or

> Just for a handful of silver he left us,
> Just for a riband to stick in his coat –

(Browning, "The Lost Leader")

Or the inescapably rhythmic and catchy

> Peter Piper picked a peck of pickled peppers,
> A peck of pickled peppers Peter Piper picked;
> If Peter Piper picked a peck of pickled peppers,
> Where's the peck of pickled peppers Peter Piper picked?

(Traditional)

Or, leaving aside song or poem or tongue twister, take the resounding, opening verses of the biblical New Testament's fourth gospel, echoing down the generations:

> In the beginning was the Word,
> and the Word was with God,
> and the Word was God.
> The same was in the beginning with God.
> All things were made by him; and without him was not any thing made that was made.
> In him was life; and the life was the light of men.
> And the light shineth in darkness; and the darkness comprehended it not.

(John 1:1–5, King James translation)

These are the kinds of things we may think of when we say that the voice is a human tool and works great riches and has done so, not perhaps from the very beginning of things, but through many thousands of years as an intrinsic, ever-ready tool of human communication and expression. We may sometimes forget it, but we humans are its prime user and inheritor.

The products of the voice, in other words, are all around us and have been for millennia, products of an inbuilt human tool of expression. They are there especially in song, more with us than we always realise. We know Shakespeare's lyrics as written forms, but they were designed to be sung, and the word "lyric" is from the Greek word for a lyre; "lyric" means words to be performed to a lyre as music. All songs, whether from Paris or New York or the Beatles or modern hip hop, are, in the last analysis, *musicalised words*, evincing the sweet overlap of language and music through the communicating expressive voice in its cadences, rhythms, repetitions, and its sonic communication of meaning.

It comes in its infinite variety of meaning and emotion, not just in sonorous phrases such as "I anoint you", "I do", or "May the wind blow soft behind you", but, equally versatile and full of meaning, even in the most familiar off-hand phrases, varied in their import by the subtle varied soundings of phrases such as "I'm so sorry", "Do come in", and "How are you?"

The sound of the voice *exists* and has reality. In the past, it was hard for analysts to study because there was no way of capturing sounds in a permanent form and setting it down as an objective thing for study. Current devices for recording and capturing sonic products has led to a revolution in the appreciation of oral forms. This was the breakthrough by Albert Lord and Milman Parry in the rightly famous *The Singer of Tales* (Lord 1960). Because they had a device to record the songs of the Slavic epic singers as auditory products, they were able to detect and compare aspects previously unnoticed even by the most diligent observers and the poets themselves. And now we have moved into recordings, broadcasts, and audiobooks to reveal more aspects of sounds that we are increasingly able to recognise and study.

Without sound how would we understand the great things the voice can communicate to us? We know that poetry communicates much in rhythm and sonic overtone not just in the surface words. It has been the great human tool that, coordinating later with the pen, has brought us the sounding cadences and rhythms of Milton's sonorous sonnets, Blake's "Tyger tyger", and Donne's resounding shout-back at death:

> Death be not proud though some have call-ed thee
> Mighty and dreadful, for thou art not so …

Thomas Trehearne's "the corn was orient and immortal, wheat, which never should be reaped", or Shakespeare's "shall I compare thee to a summer's day?". Nearer home, we can *listen* to Philip Larkin's *This Be the*

Verse, so often and so rightly spoken aloud, resonating with echoes of other poems and songs innumerable. It is right for it to be spoken aloud and heard, with its crisp opening lines, the quieter perhaps forgiving reflection as it goes on, the melodic opening of the last verse (we feel the slowing sounds of its perhaps gentling conclusion), and the final bang of its end.

Philip Larkin's *This Be the Verse*, so often and so rightly spoken aloud, resonating with echoes of other poems and songs innumerable. The text, which can readily be found on the web, needs to be read aloud and heard, with its crisp opening lines, the quieter perhaps forgiving reflection as it goes on, the melodic opening of the last verse (we feel the slowing sounds of its perhaps gentling conclusion) and the final bang of its end.

And of course, it is not only in English, though, that being my native language, I draw my examples from there. Other languages have as much: we hear it in the music-suffused tones of Italian, the love for lingering over vowels of Brazilian-Portuguese, the grandeur of Russian, the flow of Irish Gaelic, and what some would call the most acoustic of all, the beat of Greek and Latin hexameters. Once heard, who can forget the onomatopoeic sound-picture of Virgil's galloping horse as it leaves its marks in the dusty ground:

> *Quadripedante putrem sonitu quatit ungula campum*
> The hoof shakes the crumbling earth with its four-footed sound

We can translate the *words*, but the true communication is gone, for that is in the sound.

These works of that great tool, the voice, are there when we *listen*. It is not surprising that some think of sound as the supreme human quality and voice its messenger. When people speak, when they deliberately use the voice to communicate and perform, we could even say that they somehow create, some more than others, something of a sacred space in which both speaker and listeners are enclosed. The voice, furthermore, is always a strong metaphor: something human but not just human. There are the birds, ever with us to emulate; there are angel choirs in heaven – who, of any religion, imagines paradise without its singing voices?

Arts of the voice

The voice is not a tool of a passive unchanging nature. Its utterers modulate it, decorate it, show it off in a multitude of ways, complement it with gestures, movements, facial expressions, and more. Some of this can be deliberate, but much of the detail lurks below the level of our consciousness. And yet, it is this detail that makes for effective communicating, in calling, in conversation, in story.

Yes, story. We know, do we not, that stories mean more than just the surface plot: they can hold and communicate great truths, enjoyment, heritage from the past, escape, reassurance, and more. The truth in them may be enshrined in metaphor and carried by sonic as well as cognitive echoes. It is said that the number of basic stories can be counted in single figures: enough, for they are recycled and rewound in infinite different ways by myriad individual creators.

We now have a plenteous repertoire of stories to draw on and inspire us. What must it have been like in those early days of human life? And how much we owe those first story makers who, doubtless, over thousands of years, gradually at first, through the stories created in their cave paintings, began creating that rich store for us. We have inherited it but still do not know how it was started by those first humans who walked the earth.

Leaving aside these speculations, let us travel to Africa, no less a home to story than any other land, to illustrate some of the arts of the voice. I will focus on the performof stories among Limba speakers, most of them recorded in Kararima, a small hilltop village of 30 huts in the hilly uplands of northern Sierra Leone in the 1960s.[1]

The Limba people of this village were predominantly subsistence rice and millet farmers, influenced by Islam, and in touch with the nearby Muslim cattle-herding Fulani people but kept to their own traditional religion and did not themselves profess to be Muslims. Of a village population of a few hundred, three of the children had attended school but only briefly, and they were now ordinary dwellers in the village and showed no interest or ability in reading. Many of the villagers were impressively bi- or multi-lingual in nearby languages, but none spoke English and few the local pidgin lingua franca.

In their own language, *hulimba* (*hu-* being the prefix for an abstract noun), there were several individuals who were highly skilled in the arts of the voice. Everyone had some competence, but some were recognised as more expert than others. With the consent of the tellers, I tape-recorded many of the stories as they were told. This gave me a much greater grasp of the arts of the voice than if (as I did for a few) I had merely taken them down from dictation.

First, the vocabulary of the stories was much the same as that of the ordinary speech of day-to-day conversation. In this respect, the spoken narrative was in contrast to songs, both those interpolated into the stories and, even more, those sung independently; these tended to be in obscure or unusual language, the attraction lying not in the words but in the sound, rhythm, and dance. Apart from these songs, there was no specialised or esoteric vocabulary, and the syntactical structure of the delivery differed little from that of ordinary speech.

This, however, could be used to advantage in storytelling, given the frequent dramatic enactment of the greetings, remarks, and conversations of the characters portrayed. These were exactly like those heard at any hour in the village as people went about their work or stopped to greet or argue. As events were reported or discussed in real life, so too were they in the stories. The sequencing appropriate to narration, however, meant that passages in a story were sometimes longer and more drawn-out and flowing than in conversation; narrators did not need to pause for another's response or fear interruption in the flow.

The overall situation, then, was that there were no striking linguistic differences of wording in Limba stories from the vocabulary or structure of other forms of speaking.

But, and here we come to the key point, there were ways of manipulating the voice that were open to narrators and extensively taken advantage of by many, for they heightened their delivery to attract and impress their audience. These devices were extensively used by good storytellers to play on the potentialities of the language.

In keeping with the genius of the Limba language, the stories were essentially made up of short, apparently abrupt, sentences of parallel – paratactic – phrases rather than, as in English, of nested subordinate clauses. These short sentences were bound together by various connecting devices. Narrators kept the audience agog by forward-pointing words, with a pause before and after, like *wuna* ("that's why", "therefore") and *mena* ("then"); the interjection *awa* ("well") was frequently used to mark a new stage or, alternatively, a pause for thought or breath (very handy). The listeners would stay attentive, knowing that the narrator, whatever the silence, had not given up but was merely pausing to prepare for the next exciting episode.

The connection of a new sentence or move with what had gone before was also made clear by short interjections such as *huna*, *wuna* ("that is it", "that is why") at the end of a piece of direct speech to show that it was now complete. Particles such as thing, just, immediately, *nda*, already, or *nene* to introduce a new point were also used to clarify or point the sense. Another effectively used particle was *na* (and its negative *kute*), which stressed the preceding word, thus making it possible to point the meaning of the sentence more simply and effectively than can be achieved in translation.

A particularly effective device was the word *kumang*, a word common in storytelling rather than everyday converse. It could be translated as "behold", as it is used to introduce a point outside the narrative frame that is yet unknown to the characters in the story. More colloquially, it could be rendered as "and you know what ... ?", "and all the time", or just, "and wow!": a great device for adding drama and excitement. It was a kind of stepping aside by the narrator, directly involving and appealing to the audience.

Storytellers liked to use direct speech, a very simple construction in Limba. It was introduced by *na*, repeated before each clause, group of words, or even single emphatic word of the speech so that the fact that the words were still part of the speech was never for a moment lost to the listeners; even when no verb was explicitly included, there was no confusion. People were always reporting others' direct words or suppositions both in everyday conversation and in story, and, as described later, narrators made good use of this.

There were many contexts in Limba for these syntactic features. Whether in formal speeches, reporting of news, and the everyday interchange of information, speakers used this mainly paratactical form of sentences, interspersed with various connectives and the quotation of others' direct words. These features of *hulimba ha* (the Limba language) and *malimba ma* (the flowing processes of Limba ways) were all used in the stories.

Before further detail, here is a short example to set the scene. It is, inevitably, rather far from the original, not only because it was first transcribed into writing, thus inescapably missing much of the effect, but then translated. My attempt to reproduce the paratactic structure results in a rather childish sounding style in English, it so should be remembered that in the original Limba, it is a rich, expected, device. Trying to render it into the complex nested form more to appropriate English syntax would, in my view, have taken it too far from the effect of the original telling.

The background, it needs to be noted, is that oral stories, no less in principle than the more explicit communications in sermons or lessons in books, can convey ideas and thoughts about the meaning of life, birth, and death; of joy and suffering; and of humour, irony, and, as Virgil had it, "the tears in things". A story does not have to be in Latin to analogously suggest a great truth or be told in an urban setting to communicate uplifting meanings to fellow members of the human race.

Here, at any rate, is a light-hearted tale without any "deep" import, but, nevertheless, with its clever and, in fact, quite courageous indirect but understood comments on certain village power arrangements and its witty identification of humans with rats, a kind of commentary on the ways of humankind.

The tale of "the clever cat"

The story was told by a young man called Kiringkoma who had spent some time away from Limba country and had had some, but not very much, European-type schooling. It is shorter and with a less complex plot than many Limba stories but long enough to illustrate both the humour and the insight and reflection that he seemingly intended. The listeners enjoyed the plot and the irony, but the outstanding attraction was the repetitive chorus in which they energetically joined; they also loved the ridiculous name, Katingkiritangkarakatarina, that the rats/humans called their country. They picked up on the way the narrator daringly but humorously referred to the powerful and fearsome women's secret society, the Bondo, which normally was not to be mentioned except in hushed tones if at all by men, and on the ridiculous picture of its chief officer lining up the initiate rats in the exact procedure followed in the usually highly solemn and secret initiation ceremony, turning its all-powerful head with her broom symbol of office into a rapacious cat.

Typical of Limba storytellers, Kiringkoma began with a courteous salute to the chief personage in his audience, here singling out "Yenkeni" (my Limba name, meaning "a beautiful girl" – that was then!) and ending with the formulaic concluding phrase and cadencing.

***

A story for you. Kirinkoma is bringing a story for Yenkeni.

Awa, this is it.

Clever ones had not yet begun, foolish ones had not yet begun on the earth here – the cat was a very clever one. She saw that all the people on earth here were foolish, that she could trick them – they were the rats.

The rats called their country *Katingkiritangkarakatarina*. That was their country. There they came into existence. They wanted to know what was meant by the Bondo. In the Bondo, the leader was – the cat! The cat said "I agree, I accept you into the Bondo. If you wish".

The time came. That time was called The Great Monday. On that day, she was to begin the Bondo initiating for the rats.

The Great Monday came. She lined them all up. The rats who were in the bush, they had their own names. Each one had a name – Mabela, Barongko, Bakingking, Bapopo. They all came to be put into the Bondo by the cat. On The Great Monday, the cat told them, "Line yourselves up. But anyone for the Bondo, the Bondo, anyone for the Bondo, anyone – you must not look behind you. You must only look forward. Forward". *Gbang.*

They said, "We agree. We will not look behind. We will look forward. Forward".

She took the broom.

She said, "Line up!"

They all lined up, the rats. Mabela was in front; she was the clever one of the rats.

The cat sang a song.

The song I sing – when I sing you are to reply to me the same way. She meant the rats.

"We agree", they said.

Awa. And so – She sang,

"When we go, let no one look behind oh,
when the cat is free oh
o ey
o ey"
Chorus responds
"When we go, let no one look behind
oh ey
when the cat is free
fo fey..." (repeated *ad lib*)

Kumang. See? Aha, the reason for the cat doing this – see, it was to find a way to catch the rats. One by one. And to eat them. Wuh. That was the reason.

She sang,
"When we go, let no one look behind oh,
when the cat is free oh
o ey
o ey"
Chorus responds
"When we go, let no one look behind
oh ey
when the cat is free
fo fey..."

She caught the one at the back, Bapopo. She was the one at the back.

She sang again
"When we go, let no one look behind oh,
when the cat is free oh
o ey
o ey"
Chorus responds
"When we go, let no one look behind
oh ey
when the cat is free
fo fey..."

She caught the one at the back, Barongko. She was now the one at the back.

She sang,

"When we go, let no one look behind oh,
when the cat is free oh
o ey
o ey" "
Chorus responds
"When we go, let no one look behind
oh ey
when the cat is free
fo fey..."

She caught the one at the back. Bakingking. She was now the one at the back.

She sang again. Louder.

"When we go, let no one look behind oh,
when the cat is free oh
o ey
o ey"
Chorus responds
"When we go, let no one look behind
oh ey
when the cat is free
fo fey..."

She finished all the ones at the back. ALL. She finished eating them a-a-a-lll.

Awa.

And then what happened?

Awa. She sang the song. VERY VERY VERY LOUD.

Mabela, the one in front, she heard the song coming near her now. She heard. Now now now she heard. She recognised the cat's voice.

The cat sang,

"When we go, let no one look behind oh,
when the cat is free oh
o ey
o ey"
Chorus responds
"When we go, let no one look behind
oh ey

when the cat is free
fo fey..."

Mabela, Mabela now, she turned round. She looked behind her. To see her sisters – they had all been eaten up! All all a-a-a-ll u-u-up.

She saw. She saw she was the only one left. No one – *ohh* – no one left ohh.

Gbarati! She threw herself out of the way! She ran, she ran, she ran, *doing doing doing doing.*

She went off into the bush. She became clever.

Thus, are the foolish ones compared to the clever ones. No one will become clever unless someone shows them cleverness...

That is it, it is finished. *Lo-o-ontang*.[2]

***

The storyteller's voice

Kiringkoma, still young, was not regarded as among the most skilled of Limba storytellers but, though much is inevitably lost in transforming vocalised delivery to a written text, enough may remain to give a taste of the craft as typically practised by Limba tellers.

It began with Kirinkoma setting of the scene, his introduction of the story's characters (humans: represented as not-very-clever rats), the interchanges in direct speech, the repeated song in the cat's and the rats' chorus voices, respectively, which was, as he intended, taken up and sung at length by the chorus and ended each time by the narrator breaking in with a louder voice to move on to the next step in the story. Then the denouement when Mabela disobeys her orders (unthinkable in a Bondo context) and escapes, followed – one typical story conclusion – by the narrator's moralising.

Kiringkoma made good use of repetition, a common device to bring out some point in the story with extra drama and always enjoyed, and anticipated, by listeners. Here, he used it to convey the threatening feel of the cat's voice getting closer and closer. It was common in stories for questions and statements to be repeated many times and – an opportunity for pleasurable participation by the listeners – for songs to be repeated over and over by the listeners, once the narrator had sung the opening line. As often in narrations, he used the device, bringing out not only the dramatic importance of an event ("Great Monday came") but also the length of time it continued and the concentration of the story's actors (all that singing). Great excitement could be directly expressed by repetition as, for example (in a different story) in an indignant and agitated refusal by a first wife to allow another woman to join them, "No, no, no, I don't agree".

Sometimes a phrase was repeated again and again at recurring key points in a story. For example, in a story in which Kanu (God) goes round on earth looking for hospitality, his perseverance and weariness were conveyed by the continual repetition of exactly the same words after each episode – "he went on [again]".

In a less elaborate way, and one that occurred in every kind of speech, single words were themselves often reduplicated. Sometimes, this was an existing word pronounced with special expression or effect by a skilful storyteller, for example *gbokogbiko* rub in, *ngkinikini*, pity. Superlatives were commonly expressed by a word's repetition separated by a high-toned prolonged *oo*, stressed or lengthened for even more effect, especially in storytelling, to add yet more emphasis, as in *mbe ooo mbe*, "everything", *kame ooo kame*, "everywhere", *bali ooo bali*, "not a single thing", and so on.

Repeating a single word or root was also creatively used for effect by storytellers, in this way conveying a more extreme sense. Thus, *yete* meant "small", while *yetiyetiyeti* meant "very very very small"; *wunde ke* meant simply "he went", *wunde ke ke ke ke ke ke ke* in a story about a great witch painted a picture of her persevering over an immense distance for a long time without stopping even once; *piripiri* meant "all night" *piripiripiripiripiripiri* that someone continued in his struggle for absolutely the whole length of the night, not giving up for an instant.

It was not just the repetition of syllables that was effective in conveyed meaning, it was the intensity, timing, facial expression, and high or low tone, clipped or gentle, fierce or (pretendedly) shy, and the prolonged or shortened timing that created the planned effect. The subtle and skilful manipulation of the voice and its repetitions was where the narrator's skill resided.

Narrators also made frequent use of parallel phrasing: repetition of a sort, but with variation of certain key elements. The two men in a story about "the white and black brothers" were simply presented in parallel as "the one white, the one black", and the names of three twins given as "one Luseni, one Koto, one Siema". Even minor examples like these could be used in a purposeful and expressive way to set the scene or produce an impression of opposition or interdependence between those introduced.

Lists of parallel objects or events were very popular, recited with a conscious air of comprehensiveness or climax – an enumeration of exciting events, for example, as in a story about a man "killed for a banana" in which the Limba is so much more terse and rhythmic than any possible English translation: "he was seized, he was thrown down, he was killed, he was skinned" *(nde boho, nde tongo, nde koro, nde sengo)*. In another story, the care and single-mindedness with which a difficult task was meticulously completed was indicated in the list of the actions taken by a twin trying to revive his father. The parallel phrasing makes us see the son's careful attempts, one after another, then another: dripping the medicine on all parts of his father's body in turn – on his ear, on his nose, on his eyes, on his brains, in his mouth, on his arms, on the soles of his feet.

Long lists of people or objects were also heard with appreciation. These too were in a kind of parallel phrasing of rhythm, tone, or meaning. In one story, the various palm wine tapping instruments brought by Kanu (God) were carefully enumerated; in another (the comic "the stomach is chief of the body"), the various parts of the body were listed at both the beginning and the end, while in "A Story of Witches", the climax was, as often, introduced after a list of parallel phrases: the boy concealed in the cotton tree had his attention called to the witches dancing round it: "You see your mother? You see your father? You see your brother? You see all your relatives? – there to *kill* you!"

In a more extended sense, parallelIsm could also serve as part of the wider structure of a story, with the same patterns of phrases or sentences recurring over and over in successive episodes. This structural device of placing successive episodes side by side, as it were, each showing development in one aspect only while the rest remained the same, was analogous both to the common use of parallel phrasing in the more restricted sense and to the paratactical structure of Limba speech in general. It was one among the several admired means by which skilful storytellers heightened the tension and climax in their narrations.

Imitation or mimicry was also used to make the narration more vivid. One favourite was imitation of what was understood to be the sound of animals speaking: the words of an insect were pronounced in a buzzing voice, a vulture's in ludicrously high tones, dogs' growls as *krrr krrr*, and barks as *wo wo wo*. A monster's sniffing at a human was *inf inf*, followed by its breathy snuffing scary iteration of *furu yumba furu yumba* ("a human's smell, a human's smell"). Audiences were delighted when narrators imitated the stance and walk of animals, like an antelope's nervous peeping out, the staggering lopsided walk of the comic spider as he was dragged along by the ropes tying him to the bowl of rice he was trying to steal, or the ways that different animals were shown eating. Imitations of human protagonists went down particularly well. In one story, the protagonist was portrayed as tapping sharply on Kanu's knee to wake him up. In another, the teller dramatically enacted the parents of a dead boy going up in turn to the fire to save him, but each time being driven back – *oooo* – by the heat of the flames. It was not just through vocalising, for characterisation was regularly conveyed by facial expression or gesture, as in one of many examples, "The Story of a Millionaire", in which an obstinate and sulky daughter demandes more and more gold ornaments.

Narrators often used onomatopoeia to embellish their narration, interacting with the imitations mentioned earlier. In addition, there were ideophones, small words and phrases especially common in riddles and stories, but used in ordinary conversation too, that, in a instant, conveyed a sonic or visual impression: *ntirii,* for example, gave an auditory and visual picture of "flash! flash!".[3] There were also certain words that, to Limba speakers, always represented a particular sound. These included such obvious examples as bingkang, conveying the resonant sound of a shot; *prrr,* the whirr of a bird's feathers in flight; and *gbing gbing gbing gbing,* the loud beat of a chief's drum calling the people. Sometimes, the words that, to a Limba speaker, self-evidently expressed a visual sound are, to us, unsuggestive; thus, *digbi digbi digbi digbi* is heard as a noise rather like a great wind made by a spirit passing and *doing doing doing doing* as the sound of a rat running, are immensely expressive to Limba listeners. Certain adverbial (as it were) phrases could be used with great effect, as with *na tiring* and *na tirang* for the splashes made by two people as they dived successively into a pool; *na hiing,* the quiet, intent, and prolonged way in which a leopard or lion terrifyingly regarded its prey; and *na raa,* the diminishing sound of a bush cow running away. The awesome effect of a leopard scratching the ground was *na ruki ruki ruki ruki*, while *na kelethe* was the light way in which a wily spider soundlessly laid himself down, happy after successfully tricking two animals much larger than himself.

Such phrases conveyed a complex impression to a Limba listener, mainly of sound. Thus, *na kudu*, "all night", brought the whole long length of the night with its sounds and silences to the ear; *na fuu* or *na gbuu* was the slithering movement of an approaching snake; *na bide* something stealthy and quiet; and *na bis* the sudden unexpected encounter of two people face to face. *Na gbeti*, "precisely", was always uttered with a simultaneous sharp gesture and with a sharpness that suggested the sudden sound of cutting something exactly or an abrupt refusal to include one single item more – all, in Limba, definitely auditory words. Such phrases were used both in everyday speech and, to a much greater degree, in the stories, uttered with a vehemence or long, drawn-out exaggeration that brought a delighted response from listeners.

In stories, tone (pitch) was sometimes used for effect and considered highly dramatic. A clever storyteller would use exaggeratedly high and prolonged tones to represent some absolute extreme. While *wuyete* meant "a little", a high, long, second syllable in *wuyeeete* meant "very, very little indeed" and made the audience laugh. The point was clearly not referential meaning but to be amusing. *Bemandi* meant "many" people, *bemaaandi* (long, high tone) meant "very very many". In another tale, it hinted at the vast number of suitors who were, one after the other, and with no exceptions and over many years, killed by a powerful spirit. All this was vocally conveyed merely by the high, long tone in the sentence "*m-a-a-any* people were killed there". Similarly hang, meant "for a long time" or "over a long distance", but in a story, it could be heightened and prolonged so that "he went *haaang*" meant that he travelled for a long long time, he went a long, long way. *Gbeng*, "the whole day", became *gbeeeeng* to suggest the great length of the whole day, dawn until dusk, unremittingly. Special violence was also often half-comically conveyed in story by the pitch or length of such common exclamations as *ee* or *ha*, a vehemence, again, impossible to convey in a transcription into writing but, in performance, is effective in producing variety and colour, drawing listeners into shared experiential communication.

Other ways of producing effect through variety came through unexpected interpolations or exaggerations together with variations in tempo or volume. A sentence beginning with *kumang* ("behold") could be used to momentarily interrupt the flow of the narrative with an aside introducing some fact as yet unknown to the characters in the story, always with a delighted and vociferous reaction from the audience.

Variety was also produced by exaggeration or alteration in the tempo or rhythm. Speeded up delivery naturally conveyed excitement, as when the succession of dramatic events that befell a troublemaker was narrated with great speed – "he was seized, he was knocked down, he had his throat cut". The normally lengthy exchange of greetings between characters in a story was sometimes run through very quickly (as if the narrator was telling the audience "I know we have to do this because it's obligatory for humans, but let's get on to the drama"); but at other times, the words were pronounced slowly and lingered to give expression to their meaning, as in emotional phrases, such as "he wept", or the slow pathetic tones in which a man complained that however often he tried to catch Kanu asleep, he had never yet succeeded. The sad opening of Sangbang's story about the toad bringing death (told in a later chapter) was spoken very, very slowly and sorrowfully – "the toad, ah, the toad did not love us". An abrupt stop in mid-sentence could be used to violently stress the following word, riveting the audience's attention to it, as, for instance, with "he – DASHED him down", in which the violent emphasis pictured him both hitting very hard and causing sharp sudden pain – conveyed by a stress on the verb itself, but even more by the abrupt pause before it. This effect was sometimes intensified by a clap to give yet more emphasis.

Changes between loud and soft were much used in both public speaking and storytelling. A few sentences could be practically shouted with immense vehemence, then the voice suddenly dropped to little more than a whisper. Timidity, for example, was conveyed by suddenly introducing a very quiet tone into the otherwise very excited narration, as when the narrator described how the wife went and *peeped* at her dead husband or when a terrified boy replied almost inaudibly to a monster's challenge to disclose himself.

Alterations in speed or pitch were very effective in creating atmosphere. Let me illustrate this from a section of a story told by Karanke Dema, a talented storyteller, musician, and village smith.

At one point in his lengthy telling of "The Story of Deremu", Karanke gives us a picture of the hero, Deremu, standing alone on the far bank of a wide river, with all his followers now on the other side. Deremu waits isolated and in suspense for the fateful moment. The slow, quiet way in which this picture is drawn, as if with breath suspended, suddenly gives way to the loud, rapid, violent narration of the underwater struggle between hero and spirit when all is blood and turmoil and he draws knife after knife after knife in vain. At last, he uses the final magical knife that had been blessed by a "moriman", and prevails.

Then the story returns to the slow, prolonged, hushed, suspense felt by the followers waiting on the bank, how they begin to weep hopelessly, and then their sudden, breathless realisation that Deremu is safe; the tense quietness of the description is violently broken by the loud and vigorous representation of their noisy relief as "they began to dance with joy".

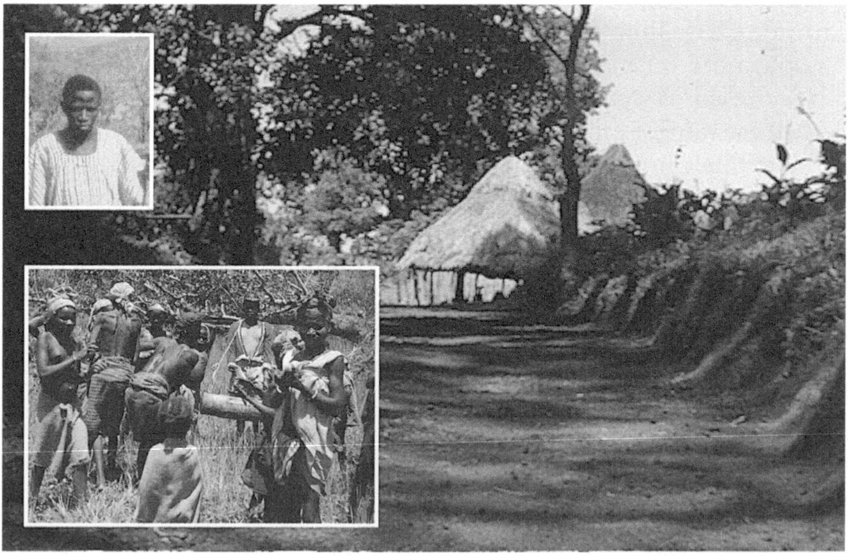

FIGURE 2.2 The multi-functional voice.

A similar contrast in speed and tone of narration comes when we are told of the sad anxiety of Deremu's mother as she waits at home, replaced first by her excitement and obstreperous happiness when she hears that her son was safe and on the way home. Then there is noisy rejoicing and dancing by the villagers and Deremu's followers. The vigour of the dance and the excited description of the mother's ecstatic, hysterical joy are momentarily interrupted by the storyteller's sad, reflective interpolation about what, due to the mother's earlier promise to give her son to be eaten by a spirit in return for its assistance, is now seen to underlie the story's tragedy. "Behold she is to die. She, the mother, was very glad. Behold she is already dying".

Here, again, it is direct speech introduced by *na*. This was popular in stories and a means by which the action could be advanced and presented through a quick exchange of greetings or questions. The voice, character, and bearing of the protagonists could be dramatically represented, and effective use made of the common exclamations of surprise, shock, or admiration – *ha, e, oh, iyo, ye* – were often delivered with great vehemence and effect by the narrator, standing, as it were, outside the events being described and looking in.

Through the simple device of merely prefacing the remarks by *na*, the action could be portrayed as drama rather than description. A character's feelings were seldom, if ever, conveyed by any direct statement about his inner experience (except perhaps for references to the heart (*huthukuma*) or to fear) but, rather, by some exclamation put into his mouth. To express surprise, the teller does not say "he felt puzzled, confused" but merely the direct and aghast exclamation *ee*! In the same way, the pleasure of meeting after long separation is indicated not by any description of emotion but by the direct exchange of greetings, such as "Father", "Oh", "Greetings", "Yes". The narrator conveys by his delivery all the drama and excitement that are missing in a written translation. The thrill of surprise and joy felt by the girl who had refused all other suitors when at last she sees her ideal husband shining in the distance is not expressed through any account of her feelings but by the uncontrolled excitement of the words she utters, ecstatically calling her mother: "Mother mother mother mother mother! The man I was talking about, the one I was talking about, he has come, it is he who will marry me; I said before that the one to marry me must have no blemish; now he has come, he is the one I want, he has come, he has come!"

As already mentioned, songs were brought into many, though not all, stories to be taken up and repeated by the listeners, sometimes as a major part of the plot but more often only at certain points in the narration, separating its successive stages. As illustrated by the cat's song in Kiringkoma's tale, they often included more or less meaningless sounds such as *o ye o, ya wo ya, woya, iyo, awaio* and the like, loved by the audience as they responded in rhythmic chorus.

The quality of the teller's *singing* was always highly appreciated by the audience, as they both listened and took part in the music, sometimes dancing or half dancing as they sang. Sometimes, quotations from characters in the story were intoned or repeated in such a way that they seemed almost a type of song. The sentence, for instance, semi-chanted by the mother to soothe her fatherless child, "hush oooh hush, your father was killed for a spinach leaf", calls to mind the songs used by Limba mothers to lull their children. In "Sira and the Monster", both the hunter's call to his dogs and their reply as they come bounding to his rescue are half sung and repeated over and over by teller and listeners, both decorating the narrative and enhancing its effect.

One could just sum the above as "he told an oral story", "He spoke", or "vocalised", and sometimes that is all we are told. But to even begin to grasp the riches of this tool of the voice, one has to try to enter into something of these modulations, the non-verbal intimations, the dramatic portrayal of the story through the artful use of voice and gesture, the experiences of audiences as they listened. Narrators varied of course but, in a Limba context at least, all has competence, and by the best – there were many of them – the deployment of this familiar tool involved highly sophisticated and much appreciated artistry.

From this, as from other elements in storytellers' style and delivery techniques, it should be clear how impossible it is for an attempted written version to convey the vivid and varied representation of scene or atmosphere evoked by the voice's enactment, particularly by a skilled storyteller.

The style and rhetorical effects in Limba storytelling were deliberate in the sense that they were uttered, and the voice modulated in accordance with the practised, learned conventions of the genre. But as with any speech genres, including those of everyday informal converse, they had become, through habitual use, a matter of learned habit rather than deliberately contrived. As with the epic singers studied by Albert Lord, the stylistic conventions – what one might call the tricks of the trade – had been absorbed from the storyteller's earliest years: the rhythms, cadences, vocal decorations and repetitions, structuring, and the full stops.

As Lord had it, "the habit is hidden, but felt" (2019: 97).

The beautiful human tool of the voice

The specific conventions illustrated in these short examples are not, of course, the same everywhere. There is the dignified intentionally undramatic delivery of the traditional Ankole praise poet, for example, the complex presentation of Zuni myth, the excited forceful push of slam competitors and their fans, the appeal of sermons delivered in the hush of a church, the voice of a dub poet competing with the noise of the crowd, and countless others. The details differ, but the overall patterns are similar: voices are modulated, intensified, and manipulated in subtle ways to communicate effectively with the listeners.[4]

It is not just in faraway research contexts that this happens. Even in recent history or in everyday settings the communicating voice of an orator can move people to what had before seemed impossible aspirations.

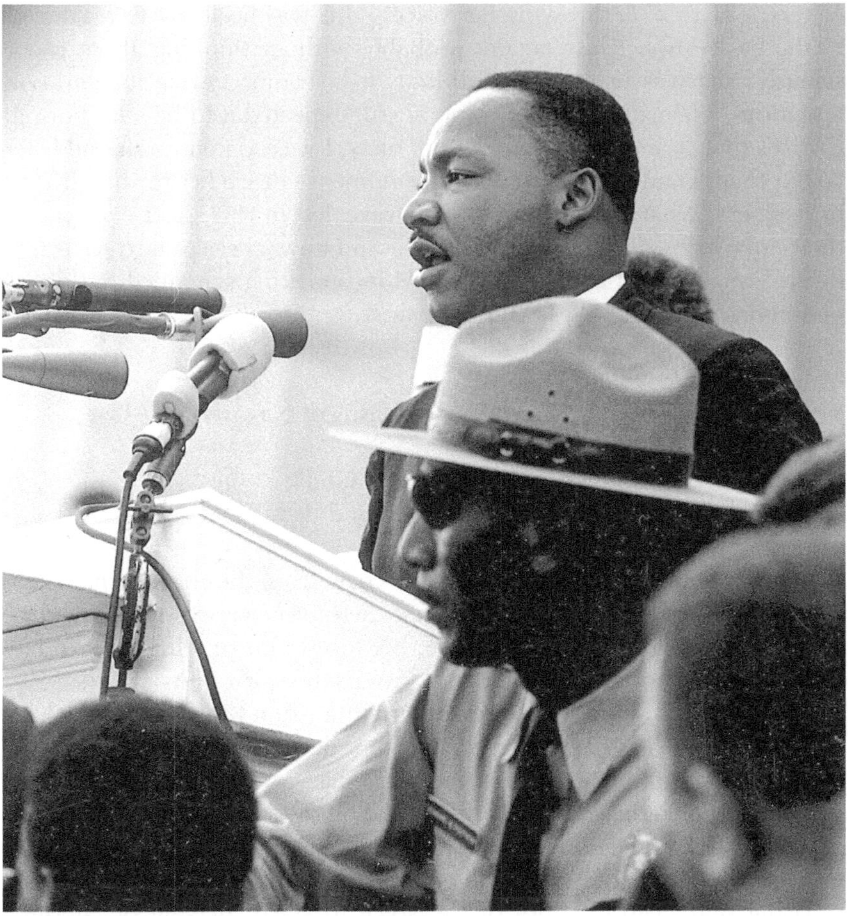

FIGURE 2.3 Martin Luther King Jr.

A speaker too can be taken by their own voice to realms unknown. A quite ordinary reading, for example, can take on a kind of enchanted quality through the exercise of the voice.

Let me give an example from of a church reading I know of from personal experience, by no means far away or long ago. A long-time church member was to read an extract from the start of Mark's gospel, a passage I had always thought of as dull but hoped the occasion and the presence of a listening congregation would lift it.

The time came, she made her way to the front and, an experienced reader, stood quietly behind the lectern. She paused (she must have internalised the importance for communicating through body language, gesture, and timing to prepare for the entry of the key communication tool: the voice). Then slowly and deliberately (she must be used to using that device too), she announced, "The Gospel Reading is from St Mark's Gospel, Chapter 1, verses 21 to 27", throwing her voice – this was needed – to reach right to the back rows. Pause (again, probably without thinking about it consciously; she was using that well-known histrionic device for gathering attention). Then she started reading. I still expected it to be a bit boring – Christ's first sermon, who cared – but okay, I was content to sit and listen.

But then, I hadn't realised until the moment I heard her reading it aloud to listeners, what a drama was being revealed in this short excerpt. For then came a passage about an evil spirit and how it cried out to Jesus from inside a man it had possessed. I heard its shocking screamed-out words, and in her reading, I felt it as it happened,

> Let us alone;
> what have we to do with thee, thou Jesus of Nazareth?
> art thou come to destroy us?
> I know thee who thou art, "the Son of God",
> Then at Jesus's command, it shrieked and fled.

I felt a smile creep up from inside me. I knew from the reading that Christ was smiling because, precisely *because*, he *loved* that evil spirit. And as I smiled, near involuntarily I suppose, because I almost felt myself to have taken on that very self, smiling with love to the spirit in its evilness.

And I felt too, I heard, the spirit shrieking round the edges of the universe forever, evil still, no doubt, and unredeemed but sustained by that one moment of glory when he, the first, the very first of all the world's people, had recognised and saluted "the Son of God".

The service continued, but it took a while for me to, as it were, "come to myself". The tool of voice had certainly been used to good effect.

Using that beautiful tool of the voice to speak or sing or, at times, imitate is creative, indeed. That aside, it has some benefits over other communicating tools. Though it is not effective at great distances or (till quite recently) have the capacity to endure over time, it has the great advantage, important to early humans and all who live in close proximity, that it works in the dark and can circumvent physical obstacles in a way that visually based tools cannot. Known from birth, a common possession of all and part of the close experience between mother and child, it often has a personal, emotional ring to it, too. Add to this, it is the vehicle for beautiful and moving works in music, poetry, and drama, the more valued and noticed now with the rapid development of audiobooks and, for some time now, in works read aloud on radio or television.

These sonic patterns of sound are created through the human tool of the voice, building on an inheritance of thought and story that has in some way reached us through the tools of both voice and pen but also, perhaps, somehow, through subconscious sonic echoes that prepare us to exercise our gift of vocal speech – in story, in conversation, in oratory, in music, in poetry. These echoes in some way come in the rhythms we are born with, not just innate but also passed on through generations from who knows how long ago – sounds to which we can vibrate and resonate and recycle for others.

And so now, many thousands of years on our human journey, it has come to be that the voice and its products and experiences are among the glories of human intercourse, communication, and art.

Notes

1 An area that has been devastated by a disastrous civil war, so it is likely, alas, that Limba speakers are no more. Further details of the background and the storytelling in Finnegan 1967.

2 This is a revised translation, differing in a few details from that in Finnegan 1967, which omitted some of song's repetitions.

3 It is often said (in fact, I think I have said it myself) that English doesn't have idiophones. Wrong - for it does have exclamations such as *whoops, wow, bang*, which have no semantic dictionary meanings, yet they communicate very effectively.

4 See also, for example, Irish storytellers (Delargy 1945), the poetry of Zuni myth presentations (Tedlock 1986), Serbian epic singers (Lord 1960), Yoruba praising (Barber 1991), and on vocal performance generally Houseman, 2002, Lehman 2017, Sell 2005, Titze 2008.

3

PEN, BRUSH, AND BLADE

And so, after that basic and beautiful tool of the voice, we come, late, to the pen and to the riches of writing. We come to the pen-wrought writings of Einstein, Ibn Khaldun, Shakespeare, Copernicus, Catullus, Achebe, Rumi, the Indian scriptures, the literatures of pre-Columbian Mesoamerica and Mesopotamia, the Bible, the Epic of Gilgamesh, and more – inscribed marks woven into our civilisation. And then on to the writings and publications of today, for even in this digital age, they too can be attributed to the ultimately hand-activated tool of the pen. Things change, but the fruits of the pen are all around us, in the present, from past ages, and, no doubt, blossoming onward into the future. Where would we be if we lacked that second great tool of humankind, the pen? By now, our world is unimaginable without it and without its works.

The pen's work of writing came late in human history, that is considering the modern pen and of writing as we think of it today. Humans date back to around 300,000 years, maybe longer, but pictographic writing to only four to five thousand years ago, and alphabetic scripts even fewer – a truly minute proportion in the long span of human history. How is it that we think the pen is so great?

It is great. But look again and consider the continuities of human history. From whence comes the pen? Was it not from biro, from fountain pen, from pencil, quill, from feather, from the brush of the calligraphers and the pictographers, the wedge of the cuneiform creators,[1] the blade of oil painters, the knife and chisel of inscription makers and relief carvers in stone, crayon on paper, chalk on a blackboard, pointers tracing charts

DOI: 10.4324/9781003496007-3

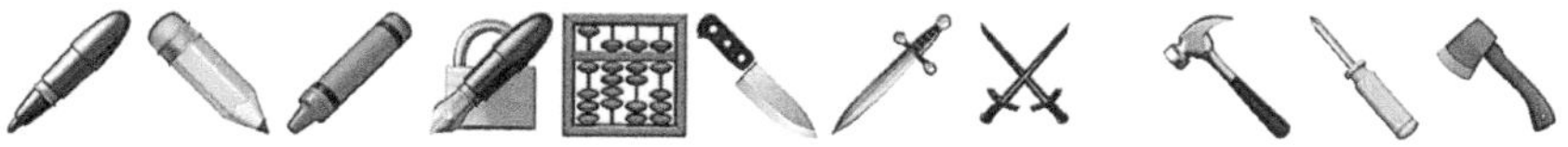

FIGURE 3.1 The multiple pen.

and images on a screen, a finger or a stick drawing in mud, a stick on a cave wall? What we refer to, for short, as "a pen" has taken many forms through many thousands of years. I will be using this broad sense of pen throughout this book.

As for the work of the pen, I will, similarly, be taking a broad sense, as in the examples above and in Figure 1.2: that of the results of any implement for making marks on a surface not only in writing in the narrow sense but in drawing, engraving, inscribing, and painting. The Greek word from which "graphics" and "graffiti" come means essentially to mark on a surface, and "glyph" (as in hieroglyphic) from the word for carve or engrave. Starting some thousands of years ago, these marks of meaning made into or onto a surface are still with us, valued and, by now, essential for our culture and, even beyond that, our nature, our deep need for sociality.

The tool we use to create these products is, to give it its short, summary title, the pen. This is our implement to make marks on, or otherwise in some way change the appearance of, a surface. It is a basic implement that, through the years, has taken multiple shapes – not just the painter's brush but also the carver's or blacksmith's chisel for inscribing shapes on stone, wood, iron; the carpenter's knife; the teacher's chalk; the conductor's baton, marking the air with its strokes; the finger drawing diagrams and pictures on a misty window, in sand, or on a computer screen; a tattooist's and tapestry maker's needle creating visible patterns by piercing into the surface to make hangings for the home or a story, as in the stunning Bayeux tapestry, for history; and more, to suit the needs and desires of specific individuals and groups in specific cultures. The inscribing, engraving pen has been a fine complement to the tool of the voice – a visual medium to match the voice's audition.

Why would humans want to create such marks? The answers might be as many as there are individuals and human needs, varying with time and place and background, but we can discern some repeated aims and functions: people's wish, for example, to make fine pictures, maps, engravings for others to see and learn from; to express themselves in written words, to serve, to administer, to negotiate, to promise, to sign, to create lyrics, to

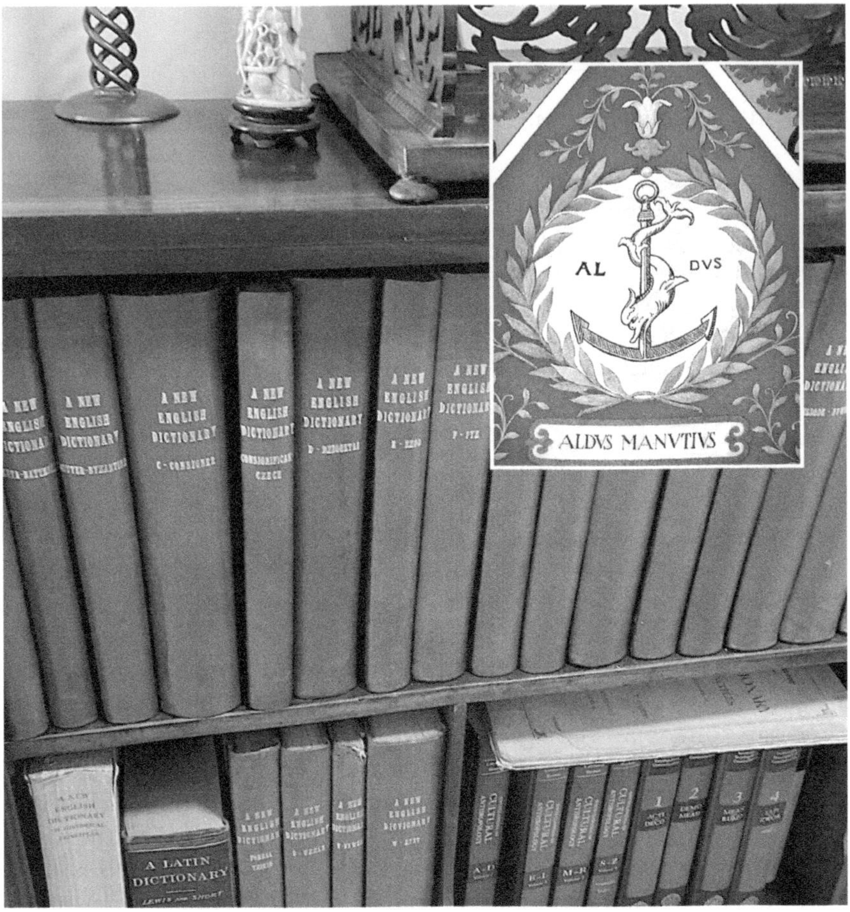

FIGURE 3.2 *Oxford English Dictionary.*

amass and store knowledge, to record law and rules; to write love letters. We use the pen to tell stories, enunciate philosophies, draw the geometric diagrams, notate music, map the earth and the sky, pen poetry that does not perish as the voice dies, treasure visually created memories of beautiful sounds, paint unforgettable pictures, and communicate their wonders to others. So, let me start with some background about this inscribing medium of communication.

First, this is, to repeat, essentially a visual medium in keeping with the primarily audio-visual capacities of human beings. The method is to use some tool like a pen – a term that, as I say, covers a multitude of forms – to inscribe marks on some surface that, again, can take many forms: pottery, stone, canvas, cloth, wood, bark, papyrus, parchment, skin – whether of living human (tattoos, brands) or dead animal (codices), sand, silk, papyrus, and most recently paper and computer screen. The process is designed, or in practice acts, to express, communicate, and give relative continuity to information, thought, or art in forms that vary with culture, becoming recognised as communicating meaning.

The resulting products can take many forms and can be kept in relatively permanent form, for example, in private homes, public places, churches, museums, and religious buildings or inscribed or engraved on the walls of buildings (or of caves), libraries, and other specialist deposits designed for the purpose: gathering, displaying, preserving, and storing information in a way that the voice cannot.

There are multiple systems of inscribing – too many to cover here – and though I will sketch some of the continuities, I will not attempt to describe them all (many others have done so, most often under the head of a history of writing, and with fine knowledge)[2]. It is, from start to finish, an amazing story – one of many – of human creativity and ingenuity. There have been contrasting and overlapping systems throughout history, and new ones are constantly being attempted.

It is actually somewhat amazing that human beings have so imaginatively created these systems for their purposes and that so many have, in some part, continued their power through the centuries.

Exactly *what* marks are inscribed vary, but basically, they are visible shapes, characters, and symbols that have, in some way, become accepted as carrying some kind of shared meaning. Often, as with Maya and other systems in Mesoamerica and the Andes, and to an extent elsewhere, the markings are pictorial, stunningly colourful, and beautiful, suggesting that the transfer of information was far from being the only point of the marks.There are many such forms, starting, as far we can tell, in the great between-two-rivers land of Mesopotamia in the fourth or fifth millennium BC. But to see how humans got there, we need to take a step back to consider how all this might have begun.

"Writing": the strange story of inscription

So, let me begin with drawing. This is because drawing, with its close twin painting, goes back to our beginnings – the first use, it would appear, of what I am calling, in its broad sense, the pen. It was there at the start. Evidence from prehistoric caves and the many examples preserved in museums worldwide indicate that the technology of drawing must be one of the most characteristic and oldest behaviours of the human species.

In essence, it seems to go right back to our evolutionary primate relatives, suggesting that, in humans too, it is an inbuilt propensity. As long ago as the 1960s, Desmond Morris made a large collection of great ape drawings. The most successful chimpanzee artist was "Congo" (1954–1964). Desmond Morris had offered him a pencil and paper when he was 2 years old, and by the time he was 4, Congo had made 400 drawings and paintings in a style described not as representational but, rather, as "lyrical abstract impressionism". This, together with the art of animals generally, especially of non-human primates (chimpanzees, above all) and of bowerbirds, has exhibited apparent parallels to human visual art, indicating, again, that this is an inbuilt propensity of human beings.[3]

This is supported too by studies of infants' behaviour that suggest the ingrained existence of drawing among humans give

> drawing behaviour in its simplest form, i.e. an active creation of visible marks that may or may not be figurative. Children start drawing what we call scribbles around their first year of age 3. At the age of 3–4 years, children begin to produce figurative drawings, i.e. they can be recognized by external observers ... completed by the progressive integration of a visual vocabulary of patterns and graphic syntax aided by the child's cultural and living environment and of course by the maturation of their cognitive skills.
>
> *(Martinet et al. 2021)*

What started it off among humans? Given the evidence on animal art, especially the non-human primates, it seems that the potential must have been there from the start. But, judging by work with other primates, not as yet the actuality. Congo was profuse and eager in his art, but only when he was offered paper and a brush. So how did it get going?

We do not know. But it may be worth making some guesses. When we look at human history, certainly it seems that the conditions have had to be conducive or, at any rate, not notably adverse. Sometimes it seems that things happen because of some external change, and adjusting to that brings about something. Sometimes it is just accident – though then there would still have to be people to follow it up.

But with all that, sometimes, it seems just a matter of one individual making one small move, which others copy and pass on – humans, it is worth remembering, probably as one dimension of their social nature, are great copiers. One person experiments, another sees and copies, then another, and another. Then, human agency continually in play, it gets taken on more generally – or not. Many must have fallen by the wayside. But some persist and become embedded into long time results.

We know such things happen, at times, with humans – we see the results around us. But, significantly, we know it can also happen with other primates. So here is an example, one to bear in mind as we read the unfolding of the story of those other primates: ourselves.

Picture a group of Japanese monkeys living undisturbed in their own ways. They are given a number of sweet potatoes that they eat very

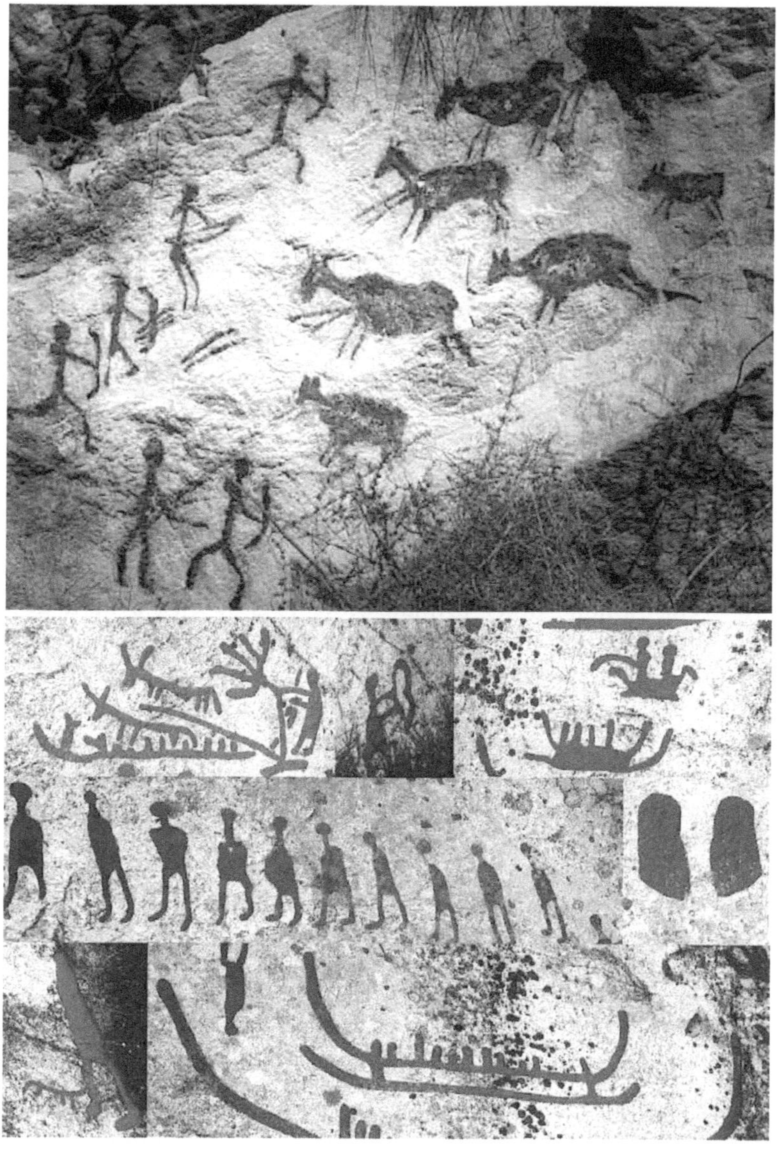

FIGURE 3.3 Cave paintings.

happily, covered though they are in sand – what did that matter? But one day, a young female, whom the researchers named "Imo", took one down to the water and washed off the sand. It was an innovation; no monkey had been seen doing this before. It worked well for Imo, so she kept doing it. Then, first, her playmates and those a year younger and a year older than her started copying her, then her siblings, her mother and her other relations, especially the younger ones. The last to join in were the adult males. In a while, the whole group had adopted the new custom.[4]

Such innovating is not unparalleled, for an analysis by a group of respected scientists (Whiten et al. 1999) showed that similar innovations had taken place among chimpanzees and been adopted into their cultures.

So maybe one gifted – or perhaps just absent-minded – individual picked up a stick of charcoal and made a line on the nearest handy surface, a cave wall. Maybe others (humans, remember are social, copying beings) noticed and then followed this example, and the process and results appealed. Over the years, which could have been thousands or just a few, making line drawings could have become an established practice. Then a gifted human – innovative like Imo – came along with red ochre and tried the effect of that and, no doubt, was applauded and copied. After quite a while, another bright spark tried white, was copied, and drawing evolved into painting.

All this, of course, is speculation; we do not and cannot have direct evidence. But it is the kind of way things happen among humans and, it now seems, among other primates too. It is at least a more credible account than believing that human beings were, from the start, born with full painting skills or received them as a gift from heaven at the time of creation.

There would, at any rate, have been attractions in such paintings. One impulse must have been to celebrate and memorialise successful hunts or just, for cave dwellers were doubtless little different from humans now, for talented artists to enjoy themselves dabbling in paint. At any rate, the impulse to make marks on surfaces seems to go some time back in evolution and to be an inherited and perfectly normal tool of human behaviour.

From painting to petroglyph, to pictogram, to writing systems

But then, how came the marks that are called "writing".

Here, the continuity of human history comes into play, doubtless interspersed and propelled from time to time by flashes of genius or experiment or even, perhaps, copyable accidents: picture the "Imos" of the human world, not monkeys, but individual human beings led by their social and mimicking nature.

Line drawing was presumably the first way of making marks on a hard surface, cave walls being the handiest for scribbling on (there were probably other surfaces and other scribbles, it is just that they have not survived for archaeologists to find). Black, the line marker, seems to have been the first colour to hand from charcoal, and what more enjoyable than experimenting with making lines on a surface. Colour painting of representational and eventually figurative art, no doubt, took many thousands of years (we too easily forget the near unimaginable timescale and the likely need for many "Imos"), but then, or perhaps alongside the paintings, there were petroglyphs: engravings, that is, incised rather than painted (and, therefore, more able to survive than surface drawings or paintings). Evincing continuity as ever, the marks had some resemblance to some of the painted shapes but, it seems, in more standardised and self-standing forms.

It is not too far a stretch (through tens of thousands of years) to imagine humans developing increasingly standardised and simplified marks of this kind and gradually putting them more and more together – genius again – into what is known as "pictographic writing".

This system of meaning-carrying pictorial marks was used in Mesopotamia from about the fourth or fifth millennium BC and, then, probably a bit later, in Egypt. This, as far as we know as of now, was the earliest writing system communicating meaning through conventionalised pictures.

This, then, was the form of writing in the civilisations of the world around the third to fourth millennium BC. The earliest example (so far), inscribed in this case on limestone, is the Kish tablet in Iraq, but there are many other examples, mostly marks on pottery, like some of those shown in Figure 3.4 (and prolifically on the internet).

In these systems, the marks resemble – more or less – in appearance the objects they represent. The symbols are their pictures, reflections, representing in a more or less conventionalised way objects in a form that viewers from that culture have learned to interpret. The marks are not attempts to represent sounds but, in a sense, like representational pictures, they mirror the objects in a way that words in phonetic-based systems cannot do.

To show it in a picture, that, indeed, is what was done in the first forms of what we now call writing. It is often not realised that the very earliest and, until quite recently (and possibly even now), by far the most extensively used form of writing took this form: standardised images in pictographic form, initially of such highly visible, striking and familiar objects as suns, moons, stars, eyes, arms, sheep, oxen, or grains of wheat;

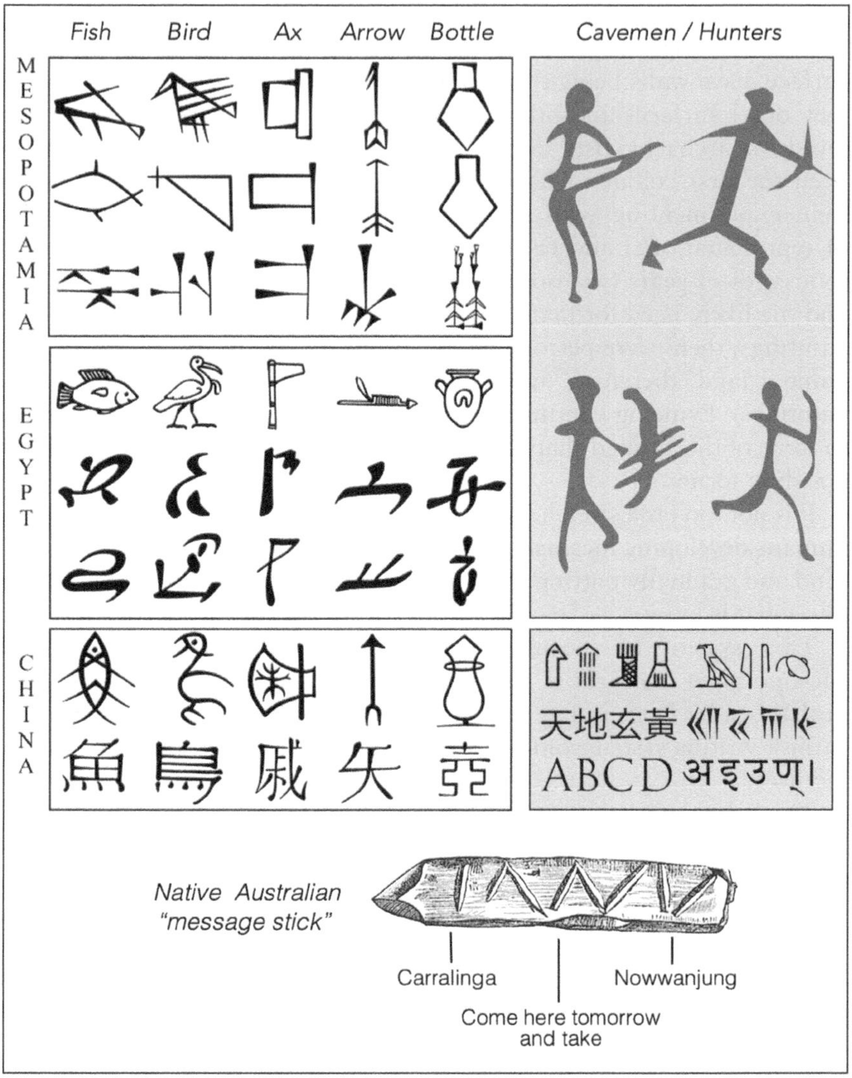

FIGURE 3.4 Pictures to pictographs.

two items could be represented by two drawings or a drawing of one with two dots – counting marks. The close-to-life representative pictures can be seen in Figure 3.5 – the likenesses to contemporary eyes, closest in the Egyptian initial images, but apparent in them all.

As well as the later, apparently independently developed Mesoamerican and Andean systems, writers in ancient Sumerian, Egyptian, and Chinese

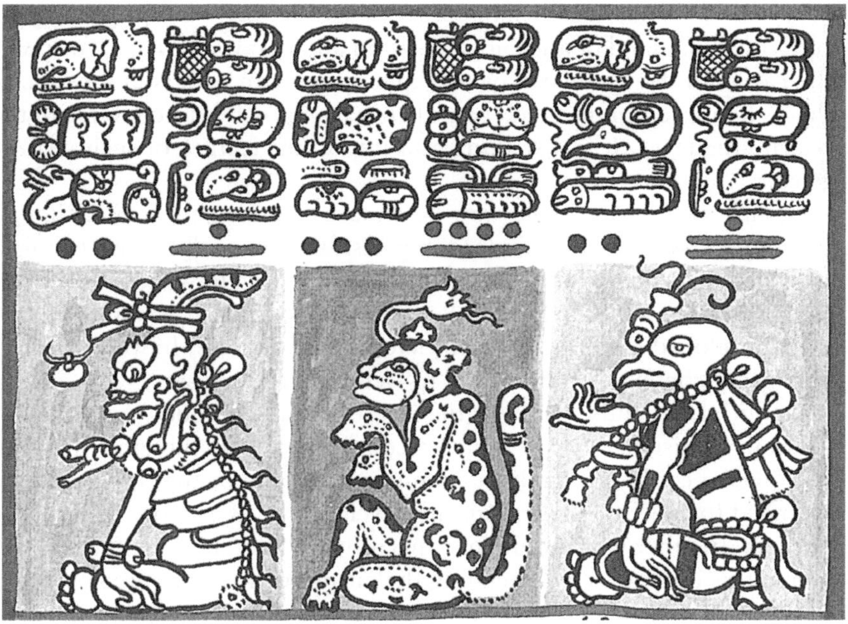

FIGURE 3.5 Maya pictographic writing.

civilisations used pictographs that they gradually, to a greater or lesser degree, simplified and standardised to represent ideas as well as visual objects.

Why was this picture-based system apparently the first to be developed? To those brought up in alphabetic systems, it doubtless looks both strange and extra complicated. But it had, and still has, several advantages, some of which we still benefit from today, for the system is actually not so very strange after all: emojis, plentifully used nowadays, are today's pictographs.

- A pictographic writing system communicates irrespective of language, transcending linguistic barriers and acting as a universal medium of communication.
- It communicates concepts directly, so it does not need explanation.
- It can convey information or a story in a simple manner, with the potential to be seen holistically – all at once – rather than in a linear fashion – word by word , line by line.
- It attracts attention, as it is composed of attractive or striking images and can make full use of colour.
- Emojis and similar pictographs can be used to share emotion in a warmer and more personal, direct way than using words/alphabetic writing.

One of the huge benefits of pictographic systems, then, is the way they transcend differing spoken languages. This has been of special importance in China, land of ancient civilisation and many languages, for those who can read the Mandarin pictographic script can understand perfectly what is being communicated even when it is impossible to converse in the spoken languages. It is a striking and important feature of such writing systems.

Against that, pictographs can be time consuming to create, though apparently less so by experienced experts, and the scripts tend to make heavy demands on learners, especially those wishing to write (in Chinese, there are about 3,000 symbols). Because they do not fit easily with currently developed digital software, pictographic systems, however powerful in other contexts, do not really fit well with computing.

An initial difficulty had been that these scripts depended on the representation of visible objects; abstract concepts such as thought, wisdom, or geometry could not easily be communicated. So pictographic systems expanded to cover them through the development of graphic symbols for concepts. In other words, humans, ingenious as ever, in time, found ways around this limitation by extending the meaning of the pictured object to a related, more general idea. In early Sumeria, for the pictograph *, meaning star, was extended to mean heaven and sky gods (DeFrancis 1989: 85); an eye to signify seeing and vision; the sun, which was extended to mean warmth or daytime; and the moon to represent night time or darkness.[11]

Signing languages, such as American Sign Lanugage (ASL), use a somewhat similar system, though their "inscribing" is through drawing shapes by gestures in the air, inscribed on an imagined rather than a physical surface. Their users have got round the limitations by deliberately devising signs for concepts. The British Royal Society regularly does this by developing and announcing signs for new scientific ideas.

Pictographic systems were not only the earliest but are still among of the world's most important communication systems. They resemble alphabetic writing in that they depend on inscribing marks on a surface for others to see and understand but differ in that the inscribing is of images or symbols, with no attempt to replicate spoken sounds. In these systems of "writing without words", as they are felicitously described in Boone and Mignolo (1994), the pen's products are not words but pictorial signs.

These systems are sometimes assumed to be outdated in the contemporary world, where it is sometimes supposed that "things have moved on". Similarly, these full systems are sometimes described as "proto-writing": this is, perhaps, based on a once popular assumption that human history has been an upward journey to a destiny only to be fully attained on reaching the pinnacle of alphabetic writing using the Latin script, with others not yet "full" systems (it is rather difficult to reconcile this implicitly disparaging judgement with the achievements of the ancient civilisations of China and the Middle East, or of the brilliantly mathematical Mayans). In fact, pictographic scripts would seem to be products of the pen and brush fully capable of carrying out all the functions expected of them.

These pictorial systems are currently widespread throughout the world, sometimes as the main medium of written communication, and, sometimes, in a fragmented way, alongside predominantly sound-based (phonographic) systems. In other words, they flourish, not just in distant ages or realms but also in sophisticated settings where they can be valued for their beauty as well as for their communicative effectiveness. Pictograms of a kind are also common on computer screens in the very visible and often highly attractive icons on computer screens, allowing communication with users whatever their language.

The main reason is that it is increasingly advantageous to use pictorial, representational symbols that can communicate directly whatever the viewers' language may be, hence their common use as visual signs in the international context of airports or the Olympics, where travellers are likely to speak many different languages. They identify by clear and easily understood symbols the location for such common needs as exit, entrance, assistance, food, toilets, and the like, signalled by such pictographs as seen in Figure 3.6.

In short, pictograms are a convenient and effective device in common use as pictorial, representational signs, instructions, or directional diagrams accepted as in no way odd or outdated.

In a different direction, pictographic displays can also be an economical and effective way to represent statistical and mathematical information. They are used to communicate on blackboards, screens, display boards, and paper as a quickly understood conspectus of, for example, how many

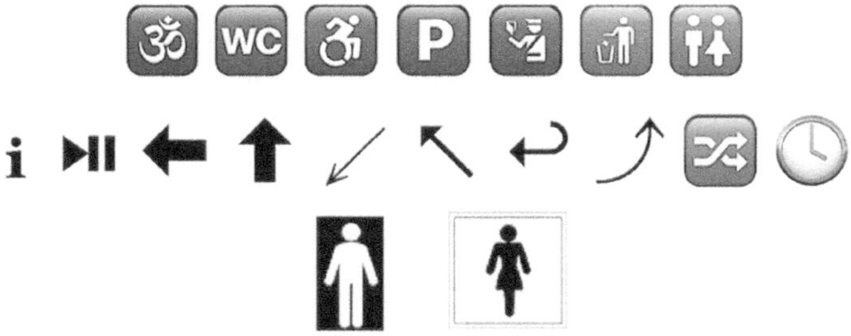

FIGURE 3.6 Pictorial systems.

items of what particular category are gathered on particular days. The information *could* perfectly well, and equally accurately, be written in alphabetic lists, but pictographic display is less complicated and time consuming to take in, just as standardised pictorial symbols on a map can often be grasped in one look. Progressive companies often pride themselves on their pictographic formulations as the most effective communication tool.

These systems, alongside the alphabetic, are still very much with us – products of the pen of great effectiveness and sometimes great beauty too.

The strange development of writing from sounds

Systems of marks based on the sounds of words (phonographic writing systems) were devised later, though still, by modern standards a long time ago. A few traces existed in the ancient stages of Mesopotamian cuneiform writing, but its consistent use started in the period after 2600 BC, the beginning of what some term "true writing" characterised by a complex combination of word-signs and phonograms – signs representing spoken sounds. These systems, in other words, were tied not to the visual representation of things but, primarily, to sound – that is, to the voiced sounds of spoken verbal language: the products of pen + voice.

Here, the graphic signs are arbitrary shapes standing for sounds that can be put together in a near-infinite series of different combinations to represent spoken words. The scripts embodying them are of many kinds, based variously on syllabic, consonantal, or alphabetic signs and displayed on many different surfaces or as three-dimensional objects and, though basically the products of the pen in its broad sense, produced by many different methods.

At first, the marks were of consonants only – still a perfectly feasible system, as in Hebrew and many mobile text messages. But then vowels were introduced by Phoenicians and used in books in the Middle East. In time, this system was taken up more widely and became the ancestor of the semitic writing systems of today. In fact, nearly all alphabetic writing today goes back to that semitic alphabet and before that to the pictographic Egyptian hieroglyphs, themselves possibly inspired by the Sumerian script of Mesopotamia. In fact, the majority of the world's living writing systems are descendants of Egyptian hieroglyphs – most prominently the Latin and Cyrillic scripts through Greek, and the Arabic and Brahmic scripts through Aramaic.

Those who so ingeniously first worked on constructing an alphabetic system based on sound seem to have begun – a hugely clever innovation – from the pictures in the Egyptian hieroglyphics.

[T]hey organized the pictures acrophonically, that is, according to their initial phonemes (sounds) or tones. For example, they selected "*alf*" meaning "ox" in their Semitic language to designate the sound "a" and *bet* meaning "house" to represent the sound "b"... We call our writing system alphabet after the first two Semitic words for "ox" and "house".

(Institute of Semitic Studies 2016)

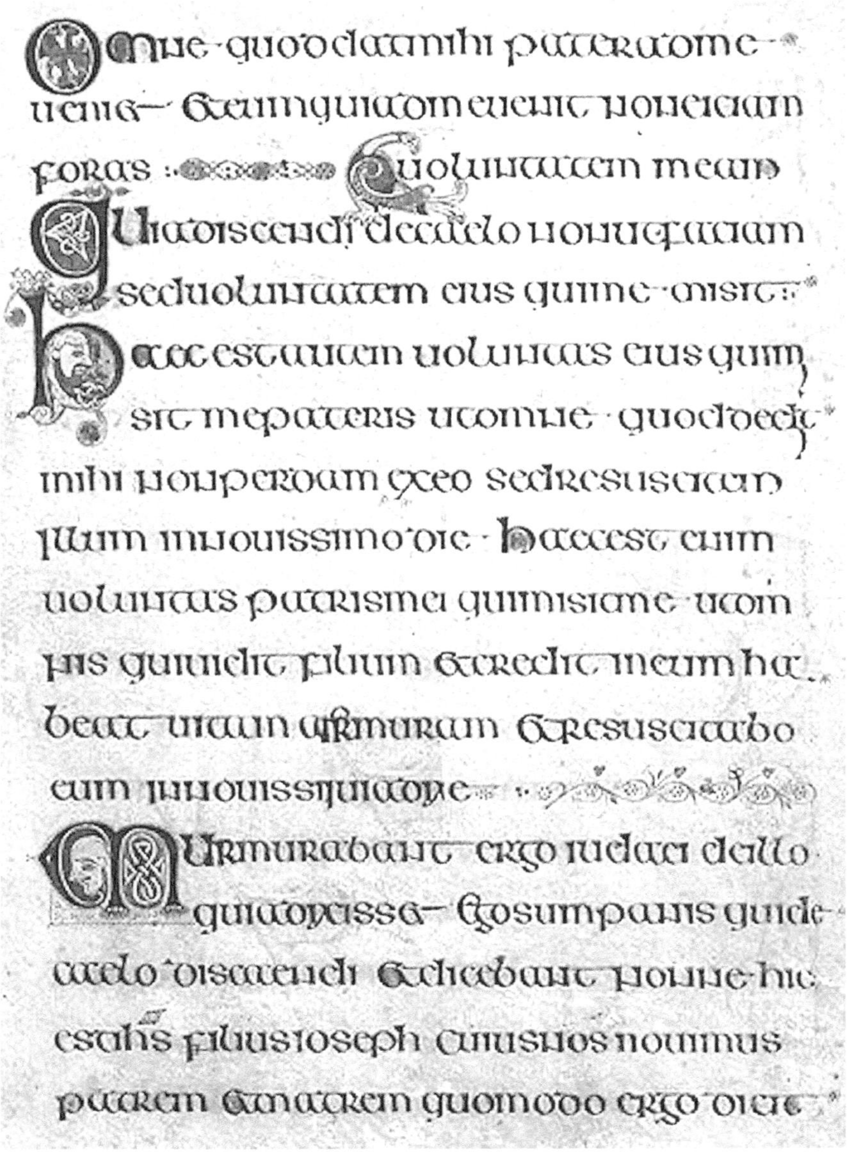

FIGURE 3.7 Mediaeval manuscripts.

Historical continuity, as ever, activated, again, as ever, through human creativity.

They have lasted up to now too. Not just *sounds* filched, then reclothed from the Egyptian hieroglyphics – garnered, some say, by Hebrew slaves seeking a communication system undetectable by their hieroglyph-focused masters – but the name and the picture too. Not just the ever-enduring name, the *alph* of the alpha-bet (not originally Greek words, as most people think, but from those iconic precursors of the Greeks, the Egyptians) but the pictorial shape too. Look at the capital A – it is the ox's head. Upend it – what but the two horned Egyptian ox. It is a shape that has endured over two millennia and more, as sound and sight lie happily together. A wonder but no wonder, for it is right for us sound–sight, audio-visual, social, communicating beings to activate, together, the voice added to the pen.

Alphabetic writing is just one sound-based variant, but it is a globally distributed and powerful one: versions of it have circulated for centuries in the West and have wide currency in the world today, deeply entrenched in modern social arrangements. Sound-based writing systems between them make up rich, standardised, and versatile visual resources for human communication, both in the present and far into the past as well as likely, for their advantages and wide acceptance, long into the future.

Pictures versus sounds

These systems are not quite as simply differentiated from other systems as may appear at first sight, however. Phonographic systems are sometimes described as "visible speech", but, in practice, no writing system is – or could be – an exact or full replica of vocal speaking. Even if all the subtle acoustic features noted in Chapter 2 were reproducible in a visual medium (and they are not), the standardised format of writing depicts only an approximation of the inevitably varying pronunciations and vocal delivery of speakers even at one period, let alone over generations or centuries. The relations between spoken sounds and their graphic reproduction may be understood by accepted conventions but are never simple.

Thus, even apparently phonological scripts contain elements that communicate visually with no direct relation to spoken words. Non-verbal elements come in all over the place: "Charts, diagrams, graphs, tables, guides, instructions, directories, and maps comprise an enormous accumulation of material ... Tens of trillions of images [are] created and multiplied the world over every year" (Tufte 1990: 9).

Book covers are a good example: there are the words and the font, which are both of importance. But the picture conveys so much about the book: it tells if it is a textbook, an abstract academic work, a reference book, a children's book, a work of fiction, a mystery, a romance, or chick lit. It's true enough that "a picture is worth a thousand words", for a picture can tell a story in a way that words cannot. Maps communicate as much by symbol as by words; similarly, the amazing pictures on mediaeval church walls or the Assyrian lion hunt frieze, communicate the strength of the lion, the courage of the men, the blood, the sacrifice, the ceremony, the glory. There is no total break between alphabetically written and pictorial representation.

The contrasts between pictographic and phonographic systems can, thus, be exaggerated. Both pictorial and acoustic elements appear in differing combinations and balances, as in the Chinese script, Egyptian hieroglyphics, or the pictographic Maya systems (sometimes referred to as "mixed" systems, as if this was somehow not quite natural). Alphabetic and other phonological systems exploit sign-based as well as phonetic principles. Picture, idea, and sound intermingle.

The preoccupation with delineating clear-cut typologies of writing was doubtless partly rooted in the long-held paradigm of alphabetic ("Western") systems as the pinnacle to which other types were leading, the most effective, versatile, and truly developed form of communication: both "simple" and 'transparent". Diringer reflected a widely held position when he asserted that "the alphabet is the last, the most highly developed, the most convenient and the most easily adaptable system of writing. Alphabetic writing is now universally employed by civilized peoples" (1968 vol. 1: 13).

This teleological model still casts a shadow, which is one reason, perhaps, for the relative lack of interest in pictographic systems in which, as in Mesoamerican pictographs or musical notations, the graphic system "communicates meaning directly" independent of language (Boone and Mignolo 1994: 15). Far from being "outdated", a pictographic dimension is, as I say, pervasive in the contemporary world. In the Chinese system, used by a large proportion of the world's population, a major element is the visual representation of ideas in the form of stylised drawings of things in combination with one another. Being relatively independent of sound, it can be read by all literate readers throughout China and beyond, even if their spoken languages differ.

The ability of pictograms to transcend linguistic barriers also means that they are crucial in modern science at every level, from advanced research to introductory science textbooks in which written text is increasingly displaced by non-verbal, visual presentation. Numerical notation and diagrammatic display are all around us, and computer generated iconic communication may be set to increasingly transcend verbal languages. Its potential for international communication may be all the more significant today in what is said to be an increasingly global and multi-cultural world, enhanced by technology's ability to digitally transfer images across space.

Phonographic scripts can, at times, partake both of the simultaneity more typical of pictures and of additional possibilities outside the apparent sequential constraints. Even if we disregard any pictorial elements in a book, there are non-verbal but definitely communicative features in the spatial layout, font, line spacing, and links to and within the text: white spaces within and around the page, paragraph indications, bold and italic print, indents, page numbers, and special layouts for "prelims", first pages, notes, bibliography, and index. In some printed works, parallel columns, marginal annotations, running heads, footnotes, and illustrations can all appear within a single page opening. End notes, diagrams, maps, or figures render the text multiplex rather than single.

There is a long history to this. The threefold format of Greek or Latin editions is familiar to classical scholars: original text at the top of one page, translation facing, and the foot of each page covered with dense notes and commentary. And, as Michelle Brown points out, the principles of computer hyperlinking were long anticipated in

> the rubrics of complex liturgical volumes [which] display an awareness of the concept of "hyper-text", whilst the 9th-century audiences of the influential Carolingian Utrecht Psalter was well able to mentally "click on" a detail of its images, relate it to a passage of text and provide a raft of underlying exegetical interpretation, foreshadowing electronic applications of intertextuality.
>
> *(Brown 1998: 90–91)*

Written forms are, thus, visual artefacts with multiple visual properties involving more than just the graphic codes for the words or letters that, from long schooling, we mostly focus on. Other visual components are there too, such as the materials used, their spatial presentation, colour, size, or overall shape. Visible signals indicate, for example, direction, proportion, or type of communication, and even within the "same" writing system, different layouts, shapes, calligraphic styles, colours, three-dimensional structures and settings, platings, or pictorial ordering can all make their visual point.

The pictorial dimensions often blend with more abstract – graphic – signs and assume comparable importance. In Maya or Egyptian forms, it can be hard to see where picture ends and writing begins. And then there are all those pictorial decorations in scripts, from pin–figure drawings or kisses in personal letters to the arts of mediaeval illuminated manuscripts or Asian calligraphy. The colours and forms in the illuminated Lindisfarne gospels or the illustrations in modern children's books are scarcely secondary to the words. The same applies in Chinese and Islamic calligraphy in which the way it is depicted can be as valued as the content.

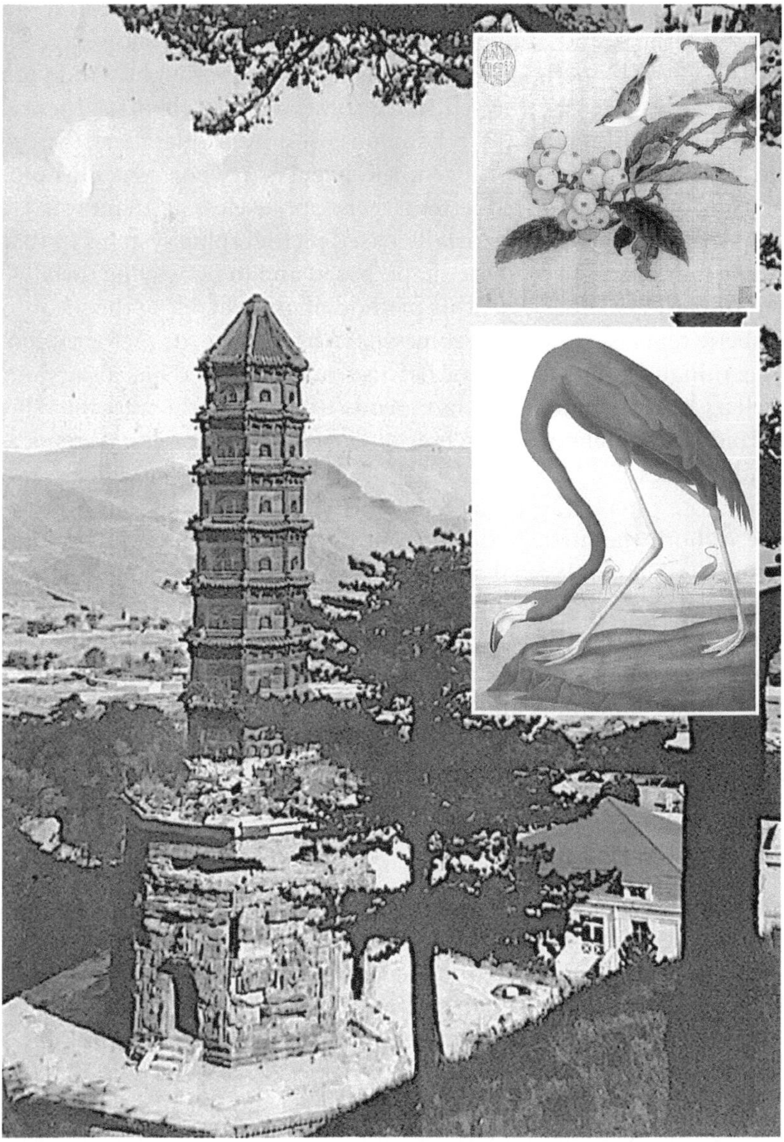

FIGURE 3.8 Beauties of the brush.

Alphabetic writing is often thought of as a linear form, fitting the dynamic linear ordering of speech and thus structuring communication in a single direction, word after word after word, in contrast to the more simultaneous and holistic qualities of pictorial display.

This is true up to a point, but the distinction can be over-stated, as in practice, this is not the only way that people read and learn to read. Many children are first taught the sounds of the letters of the alphabet and are then expected to pronounce them sequentially to, at first laboriously, reach the sound of the whole word. An alternative, however, is now the "whole word" method, which some children are taught, while others, including, I now realise, myself, have somehow absorbed for themselves and become rapid readers by relying on just a quick glance at the overall shape of word or phrase or, even, the page as a whole with little or no apprehension of the internal letters (therefore, useless at anagrams!).

This method is unlike pictorially based pictographic systems in that the meaningful signs discerned are shape-based and in no way pictorially representational. But otherwise, this method of apprehending the meaning in alphabetic texts is, in general, somewhat akin to that for pictographic systems: a mingling of both methods. This reading method has disadvantages as well as benefits but, at any rate, tends to disprove the idea that there is a sharp distinction between pictographic and phonographic systems as far as reading goes.

The more interesting point from this is that it brings out a recurrent theme in both the history and present character of human communicating. Audio-visual and social creatures ever, we rely not on one single channel but on a complementarity: both sound and sight, both drawing on the air and drawing on the wall, the genius of both voice and pain in their multiple different guises. As I concluded in my earlier study of communicating (2023), ingenious and creative creatures that we are, we make the most of our auditory and visual senses and, to an extent, of touch and, to a lesser degree, of olfaction to achieve a remarkably effective mix of arts.

Treasures from the pen

Mostly, we do not know the specifics of how these inscribing systems were started and by whom: the unidirectional narratives recounting their origins and diffusion through the millennia are doubtless over-simplified. But people are certainly capable of creating writing systems, and a number of new ones have been deliberately invented over recent centuries. Indigenous scripts using alphabetic, syllabic, or pictographic forms were devised for several African languages in the nineteenth and twentieth centuries, for example, remarkable for their originality and precision in the representation of meaning. Some, for a time, achieved some currency, especially in religious and esoteric contexts, and the names of their local creators are sometimes known.

No doubt, similar processes have happened at many other times and places. Many systems have presumably been built up and gained wider currency (or were imposed) over time. Human beings, ever inventive, ever social, are fertile in developing methods for expressing and treasuring their memories and for the far and near communicating with each other.

Using the tool of the pen and its allies, then, humans have found ways – miraculously it sometimes seems – to encapsulate and communicate and store knowledge and experience in (relatively) permanent form, which can, to an extent, transcend both space and time and, to a degree and in some cases, bridge cultural and linguistic differences too. Materialised through a series of visible and multiplex forms, the use of this essentially visual resource exploits the capacity of the human hand to inscribe and the human eye to analyse a vast range of visual dimensions and to deploy a combination of them in their communicating.

Whatever the details, these complex visual systems did not spring up of themselves or grow by some impersonal process of natural selection or teleological evolution (as some accounts still imply) but – even more amazing, in fact – were and are created and activated through the intelligence and abilities of human beings.

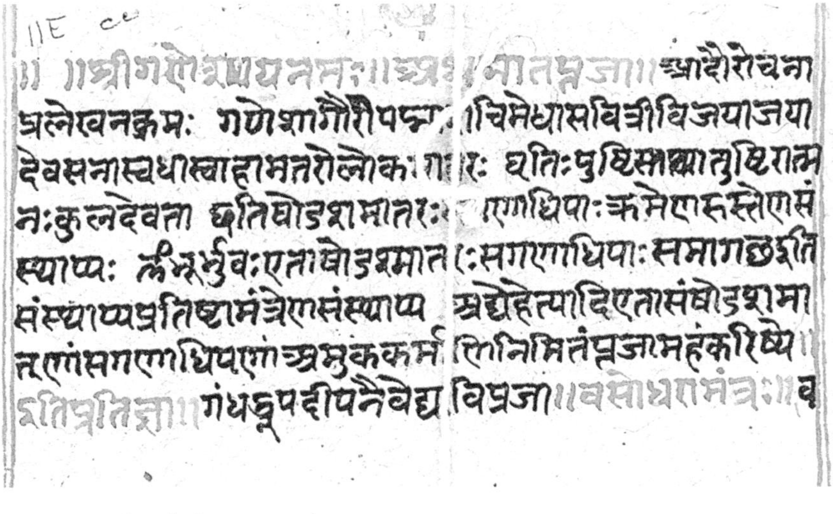

FIGURE 3.9 Sanskrit manuscript.

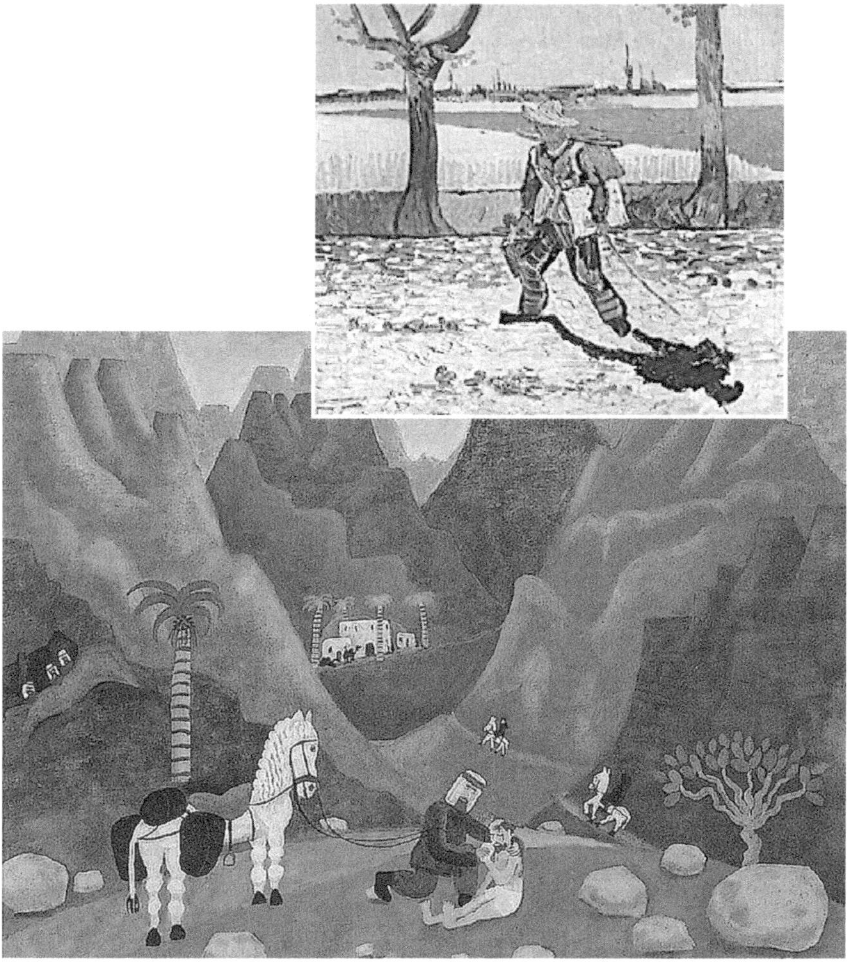

FIGURE 3.10 Stories from the blade.

These pictorial and graphic systems, finally, are themselves only one category among the many material things that humans have developed in the past and present and pressed into use in their communicating: think of drawing, painting, friezes, calligraphy, tapestries. The range of human visual artefacts is. indeed. remarkable, created in both two- and three-dimensional forms and going far beyond anything we know of organised visual communication among other animals.[5] A large part of human interconnectedness lies in this exploitation of vision, creating and using these visual artefacts – material, pictorial and graphic – in our communicating.

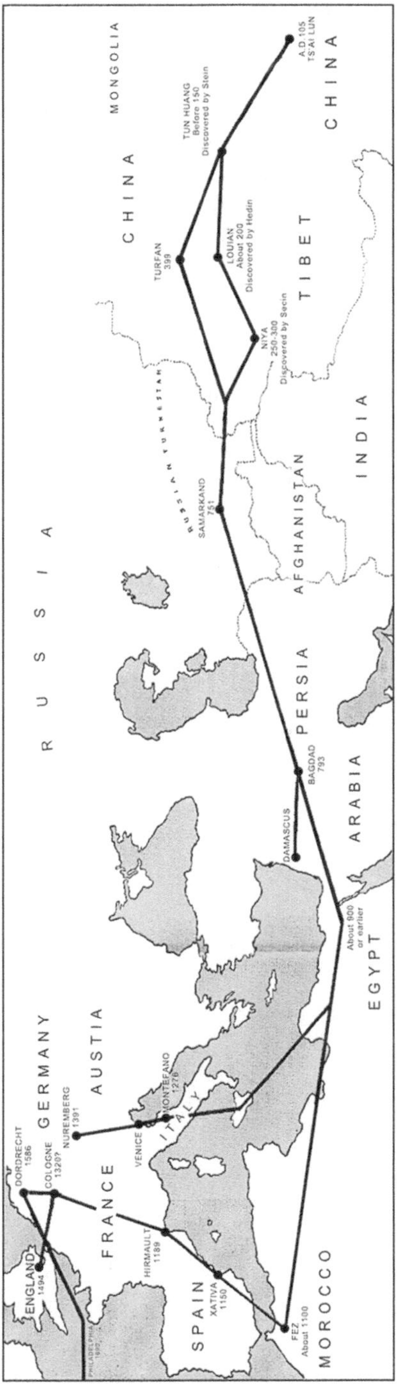

FIGURE 3.11 Print's travel.

Let us not forget that whatever the system used, the inscribing "pen" enables us to capture achievements not catchable by the fading voice, to fix and, for longer, preserve communications for the spirits, for the family, for oneself, for other humans, for posterity.

Where, then, would we be without the great tool of the pen in all its guises for drawing, for pictures, painting, inscribing, writing, enabled by humans' intelligence in innovating and copying. Throughout, it works with and complements that other great tool of human communication, the voice. The two tools are different, but we need the interplay of both.

Notes

1 For example, Coulmas 2002, DeFrancis 1989, Diringer 1968, Ferrara 2023, Fischer 2000, Robinson 2007; also https://en.wikipedia.org/wiki/History_of_writing/ and further references there.
2 See especially Madden 2008, Martinet et al. 2021, Morris 1962, Taylor 2018, Yan 2013, and https://en.wikipedia.org/wiki/Animal-made_art/
3 Hirata et al. 2008, Matsuzawa 2015.
4 See for example Bauman and Briggs 2003, Duranti 1997, Hanks 1996, Ottenheimer 2013, Tracey 1999.
5 For examples, see the discussion and, in particular, the illustrations in the previous volume (Finnegan 2023).

4

VOICE MEETS PEN

Pen and voice play closely together. It is natural, as both communicate largely, though not exclusively, through the medium of verbal language. They are not the same, follow different rules, and sometimes play on different sides of the net, but so long as each can have a bit of their own way, their encounters are mostly happy and fruitful. And to interplay and mingle with a complementarity of tools is, after all, typically human.

Pen befriends voice

The pen, in the narrow sense, has been wielded by humans for only a few thousand years. Yet in that minute proportion of human life on earth, it has had some striking outcomes. So what were these, and how did humans respond to and interact with the works of the pen – was it beneficial or the opposite?

First, the pen gave a way to express, preserve, and communicate the enduring verbal works produced by Pythagoras, Plato, Thucydides, Confucius, Gandhi, and Dante; the *Rigveda*, the epics of Gilgamesh and of Homer, Aeschylus's plays, the words of Allah preserved in the Koran, the biblical psalms of David, and the religions' books of the word; the sonnets of Petrarch and Shakespeare, poems of Browning, Yeats, Hafiz, and the poets of the world; and so much else – what treasures would have vanished if humans had depended only on the evanescent voice? We have used the pen to preserve them for us.[1]

The pen enabled the still living messages of power and glory on ancient palace walls (no matter, that the people could not read the script; they

DOI: 10.4324/9781003496007-4

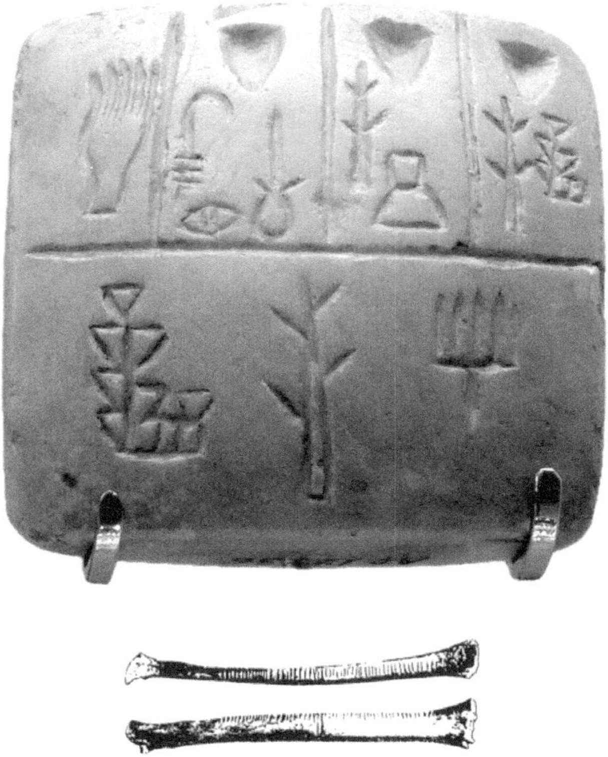

FIGURE 4.1 Cuneiform.

did not need to look, for they knew what it meant), the inscribed triumph displayed to conquered enemies and the heralded written communications for the gods. And away from scripts, but still the work of the pen, the paintings and drawings of Hokusai and Dürer, Van Gogh and Picasso, and the careful calligraphy by the meticulous talented scriptorsof the Eastern and Western mediaeval worlds.

And the personal too: the pen gives a way to write to a far-away love; to reach a distant child in the new world; to negotiate with a friend, an enemy, and a trading partner; or to correspond with a pen friend across the globe in, at first, new and different forms of communicating.

And then there was too the pen's early creating of the notated language of mathematics – so often forgotten in our obsession with the linguistic – penned on ancient tally sticks and Mesopotamian tablets and in the Hindu-Arabic symbols in use today; and the pen's capture of the swathes of musical sound in colourful far Eastern manuscripts or in the West's notated scores – might we be without the works of Bach, Tallis, or Mozart and so many others if the pen had not done its work?

It remains, of course, true that, as illustrated earlier (Chapter 2), any attempt to turn a multi-modal oral performance into a written page is going to have only limited success. In any case, a written text, whatever its ultimate origin, has limitations, as Socrates rightly commented, however many times you look at it, it always just says the same thing, implicitly drawing a contrast with the flexible dynamic of spoken communication.

The pen, then, is a tool with limitations. But it is what it is, and what we have we, and it has enabled some not insignificant results and produced some glories. Without the written works of the pen, how could the riches of the classical world have been preserved for centuries by Arabic culture and eventually reached the Western world again? How could the wisdom of China have been spread throughout the Far East? How could the Christian writings have been cherished for centuries in Ethiopia or the writings of the "religion of the book"? Or the couplets in Cato's *Distichs* remained a first Latin primer for countless generations of children and a best seller for centuries? Or modern readers been able to rejoice in the ancient *Epic of Gilgamesh*?

The voice had a role in these treasures, but without the human-activated pen, their preservation and distribution would have been, at best, unlikely. The pen contributed too to the knowledge and appreciation of the cultures whose unwritten products, above all those of Africa, Australasia, and native America, had previously been unknown to the West and risked being lost. They were not totally unknown it is true – many pioneers had open eyes and ears – but, in general, it was the work of the pen that uncovered this tapestry of treasures to new eyes.

What riches, then, that simple tool has created, protected, and revealed to the world. No results can ever claim to have no dark side, but those resulting from the pen and the brush might well be seen as, overall, a cause for rejoicing, an element of the happier side of human history.

As if that were not enough, recall the pen's contribution to human institutional arrangements.

The pen enables *documented* histories of events. People can make a detailed check on the truth of historical accounts, as the past becomes something not mythic but objective and analysable.

The pen can also introduce greater certainty. The writing down of English law in the twelfth to thirteenth centuries, for example, was that for the first time uniform written rules were applied to day-to-day legal procedures, and a bureaucracy grew up whose writings reached every bailiff and local official and, hence, potentially every village in England. As the historian Michael Clanchy comments,

> It became possible to compare different accounts of the past objectively, to some extent irrespective of contemporary claims: self-interested appeals to "immemorial custom" could be decisively contradicted when there were written records, in a way not possible in a purely oral situation. Thus, it seems that increased objectivity and uniformity in legal practice too can be attributed to the "decisive change-over from oral to written modes" in English law in the twelfth and thirteenth centuries.
>
> *(Clanchy 1970: 172–173)*

The essential characteristics of industrial society too were rooted in pen-wrought rationality and bureaucracy. Max Weber, in particular, held that modem Western institutions, both political and economic, depended on "rationally established norms by enactments, decrees, and regulations" (Weber 1958: 298–299). And this was ultimately dependent on the work of the pen.

So too was the possibility of the accumulating and storing information over time. Even single individuals can gather more information if they keep written notes; and this is vastly multiplied when the accumulation is extended beyond what one person or one generation can manage. The knowledge and experience of different periods and different cultures can be recorded in written form, to which others from quite different backgrounds can have access. And then, on from this, there was the development of Western science and technology, the emergence of specialised experts, the existence of higher education – all of these would be inconceivable without (as in Figure 3.2) the accumulation of knowledge made possible by writing.

The work of the pen allowed the communication of knowledge from one generation to another and to different cultures. It assisted the spread of religions, such as Islam, Christianity, or Hinduism, and enabled the rediscovery of the stored wisdom of the classical world during the Renaissance and the transmission of the insights of Indian wisdom to the West – here as often pen working voice.

Economic development too is linked to the pen. Writing enables systematic accounting as well as a complex of sophisticated mathematical procedures and trade with orders placed in writing. Economic and social development, they say, depends on the ability to read and write. This has been constantly stressed by the United Nations Educational, Scientific and Cultural Organization (UNESCO) and similar organisations for which literacy has long been seen as an essential prerequisite not only of economic welfare and industrialisation but also as a precondition for democracy and freedom, perhaps too for individualism, the possibility of free thought and dissent, and science.

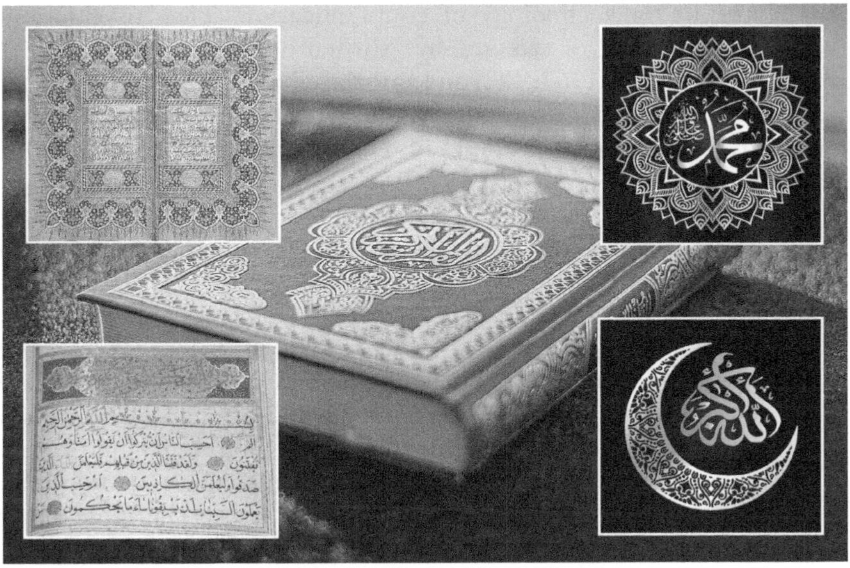

FIGURE 4.2 Koranic calligraphy.

Much the same consequences, but even more extreme, may have flowed from print, something, it has been claimed, that "reinforces and transforms the effects of writing on thought and expression" (Ong 1982: 117) and

> allows individuals to withdraw, to contemplate and meditate outside of communal activities. Print thus encourages privatisation, the lonely scholar, and the development of private, individual points of view.
>
> *(Carey 1967: 19 on McLuhan)*

Lenin was of the same view: "an illiterate people cannot build a communist state", he said, and "an illiterate person is outside the sphere of politics ... the first thing he needs is to be taught the alphabet".

Through print, the pen has also played a part in nation-building. It enables the circulation of a national language in fixed and visible form and maps it, giving a visual appreciation of the nation. The two, great turn-rounds in Europe, the Reformation and the Industrial Revolution, are often said to have been linked to print.

Pen-enabled print too – or so say thinkers such as McLuhan (1962, 1967) – led to a revolution in the way of apprehending the universe.

Humans moved from an auditory to a visual mode of knowing, the cause lying in the technology of communication. The "psychic and social consequences" of typography "shifted previous boundaries and patterns of culture" (1967: 182) and saw the emergence of "typographic man" – aloof, detached, specialised, and cut off from the psychic and emotional unity of oral culture. In his classic *Understanding Media*, he concludes that

> Thousands of years ago man, the nomadic food gatherer, had taken up positional, or relative sedentary, tasks. He began to specialize. The development of writing and printing were major stages of that process. They were supremely specialist in separating the roles of knowledge from the roles of action ... But with electricity and automation, the technology of fragmented processes suddenly fused with the human dialogue and the need for over-all consideration of human unity. Men are suddenly nomadic gatherers of knowledge, nomadic as never before, informed as never before, free from fragmentary specialism as never before – but also involved in the total social process as never before; since with electricity we extend our central nervous system globally, instantly interrelating every human experience.
>
> *(McLuhan 1967: 381–382)*

Look back at the miracles the pen has wrought for us.

Pen looks at her results

It is great to think of these results of writing. But were all these changes due, or solely due, to the utilisation of writing? The changes listed *did*, it seems, indeed, take place (though possibly not as comprehensively as sometimes implied) and, in the process, went along with human uses of the products of the pen. But does it follow that it was *writing* that, on its own, brought about these changes rather than just being there alongside them? The key term is, surely, "enabled": people took advantage, as, presumably, they always have, of the tools available at any given time.

The "all change" story also, as it seems to many, links to a somewhat romanticised and, at the same time, implicitly demeaning view of non-literate cultures that supposedly depend solely on "purely oral" means for their communicating. Such cultures were envisaged not just as those of the past but those living in the colonised or previously colonised "developing" places of the world (those once labelled "primitive"); it is to project onto them an upside-down-from-the-present concept of a culture where without the intrusion of the technology of writing and led by an oral mode of communicating, people lived natural, human, emotionally vibrant "community" lives. It was "the world we have lost" in Laslett's echoing phrasing (1965), the "oral" culture that inhabitants of the current literate world could look back on with nostalgia but with no wish to emulate. Inhabitants of the "civilised" had in this perspective moved on and up.

In these generalising accounts, it is often forgotten that this writing-led "revolution" was only there for a few. In archaic Mesopotamia and Egypt, cited as the locations where writing first started, those able to read and write would have been very few, perhaps 1% of the population. Later, the number was higher – in classical, Athens for instance, often seen as the hub of civilisation, it was probably 20% to 30% of adult males (in other words, no females, immigrants, or slaves), and even as recently as 1820, only one in ten people in the world could read and write. So the "consequences" of this ancient and supposedly shattering "writing revolution" as it has often been called, would have applied to few people, and probably directly affecting only those living near the abodes of power and able to see the writings on the palace walls.

And does "the acquisition of literacy" *always*, as implied, lead to the same results? There is plentiful evidence suggesting the opposite.

And, again, is it true, as implied by, for example, McLuhan and Ong, that in oral cultures (Africa seems always to be the place in mind), there was no scope for individuality or free thinking and that even if some people could tell stories, all they were really doing was mindlessly transmit word for word content that had been passed down to them through passive and unchanging tribal tradition from "time immemorial".

The changes noted above did, of course, mostly happen (though possibly not as comprehensively as implied). But does it follow that it was writing that brought about these changes rather than just happening alongside them? The key term seems to be "enabled": people took advantage, as presumably they always have, of the tools available at any given time. Technological determinism is an over-simplified interpretation of the complexities of human-driven history. One might also ask how deep these claimed changes really were or are when we constantly hear politicians and thinkers invoking them not as things already achieved but as aims (or menaces) for the future.

The "literacy wins" accounts were quite often built on a somewhat romanticisation but, at the same time, demeaning pictures of non-literate "oral "cultures", projecting onto them a satisfyingly upside-down-from-the-present concept of a culture where, without the intrusion of writing and led by an oral mode of communicating, people lived "natural", emotionally vibrant "community" lives. It was "the world we have lost" in Laslett's echoing phrasing (1965), the "oral" culture that inhabitants of the current literate world could look back on with nostalgia but with absolutely no wish to emulate. Inhabitants of the "civilised" world had moved on and up.

Nevertheless, the claims are not totally beside the point. In some areas, there may have been relatively few with literate skills to read and write, and yet the area as a whole was, in some ways, pervaded by communication in writing. Just about everyone might know someone who was literate and who could, when asked, read and write letters for their unlettered acquaintances, a common and comfortable arrangement in places where few were literate; religious rituals commonly involved readings, singing, or recitations from written scriptures; public institutions and the exercise of power were in part based on, and eventuated in, written records; as time went on, newspapers were scrutinised by readers, then the news spread by word of mouth; radio news was a common source of information, certainly, but its content was as like as not drawn, at least in part, from written sources; and so on and so on. Without necessarily undermining vocalisation, the tentacles of the written are everywhere; "literacy rates" notwithstanding, and in some way or another, sometimes only slightly, sometimes more pervasively, reach into people's lives.

Let me set this into the context of some of the longer stories of human history.

Just so tales

"In the beginning, dear children", goes a widely told story, we humans had a voice. It was also called speech and orality. Then, behold, came the pen that brought writing and, finally, print. This changed the world. With the expansion of the West, pioneers sallied out to take the products of the pen to the benighted natives, along with some rather strange things, but some good things too, so as to evangelise the "good news" of the products and processes of the pen, of enlightenment, as it seemed to the pioneers. The key to open the door to all this was the pen, the tool for writing and print – something new and different from anything that those "others" had ever before experienced.

The scholar Walter Ong saw the change for those moving from an oral mode as truly massive. This was due to "basic differences" between

> the ways of managing knowledge and verbalization in primary oral cultures (cultures with no knowledge at all of writing) and in cultures deeply affected by the use of writing. [The] shift from orality to literacy and on to electronic processing engages social, economic, political, religious and other structures.
>
> *(Ong 1982: 1, 3)*

This is a story widely told and accepted.

On from this is a parallel, longer story. This tells of the beginning of writing from far back, in the fourth or fifth millennium BC when there was "proto-writings" that then moved up to the "real" form, the alphabetic system and, finally, the moral and technological pinnacle: the outputs of the Western-originated (as was believed) printing press.

This chimes in with a long-told, credible story about the deep-rooted effects of writing on human ways. The concept of human history as having "reached a revolution" with the emergence of writing, leaving those without it radically behind, goes back many centuries, but the mid-twentieth century saw it acquiring a new sharpness that still, to an extent, affects us. The rampant was seen to be set up to destroy the work of the voice, removing age-old oral skills from those led or forced into literacy. Some regarded the pre-literate as the "natural" state, while others, with an inspired vision to save them from the backwater of illiteracy, saw literacy as their saving grace. Scholars wrote persuasively of the tale of Western civilisations rising out of the darkness of "purely oral culture", seen as typically located in Africa, into the enlightenment of writing and, above all, of Gutenberg-inspired print.

Set beside this is a different story. This starts from a historically situated view of the workings of the pen and, from that, of "writing". It broadens the perspective – reasonably so in the light of human development described in the last chapter – to all forms of making marks-with-meaning on a surface. This story tells of the continuity of the work of the pen, with its fellows, the finger, the brush, blade, and knife, right from cave dwelling days; of picture into pictographs; drawing and painting overlapping into other forms, cooperating with gestures, coordinating within groups, combining into the many modes of human communication and expression that, shaped as we all are by diverse cultural ways, we know today.

And "voice meets pen"? This is nothing new. These encounters and cooperations have been with us for millennia.

In the all-change story of the human history, one particular encounter between the two has been taken as of overarching interest, marking, as it were, an unprecedented apocalypse, communicated through the writings of the pen and, for a time, immensely influential among pen-immersed scholars.

To retrace our steps for a moment, this tale too centres on the particular voice–pen encounter brought about by the advent of writing. Its tellings, and the arguments these have led to, have become known as the "literacy–orality debate" or, much the same thing, the debate over the "Great Divide" between "oral" and "literate" culture. The impression given (not always, perhaps, to be fair) was of a complete and comprehensive change: at first immersion in totally oral things then the move to the literate world.

This impression was fortified by the assumption, once popular, that once writing arrived, the skills of the voice had to flee.

Pen fights voice

These accounts, in a way plausible, with some first-hand evidence, and still treated seriously by many, suggest that, to summarise, the pen, when it comes, must forever oust the voice. When literacy "arrives", society is revolutionised, and individuals' psychic and mental processes irretrievably changed.

"Revolution" seemed the obvious word for those who saw the advent of writing as setting a chasm between the mentally free individualistic ethical and scientific state of literate society as against one whose inhabitants who were illiterate and, as Marshall McLuhan (1962: 18) had it, immersed "in the magical world of the ear", forever incapable of understanding the "visual, neutral world" of modernity, individual freedom, and science.

Sometimes, the move from one to the other was envisaged as essentially in the past, at the time of the advent of pictographic writing, or, later, of phonographic and, in time, of alphabetic writing. Sometimes, it was perceived as more recent, as in Lord's study (1960) of the far-reaching effects on the oral epic singers of the then Yugoslavia of their becoming literate. The change was envisaged as profound and the techniques of pen and voice to be mutually exclusive. It had to be either one or the other, not transitional or with cohabiting elements of both.

In other words, there are just two modes of communication and expression open to humans: the oral and the literate.

Though many, perhaps most, scholars today (including myself) would probably hold that this extreme stance is not supported by the historical and comparative evidence and eventually leads nowhere, it is still worth considering. Many are still influenced by it, and, for a time, it was the accepted and unquestioned wisdom. And after all, if, as proposed, speaking and writing (or orality and literacy) are, indeed, the two great, opposed modes of human communication, then it is necessary to understand their distinctive qualities and contrasts.

The basic idea, to put it in the extreme terms used by some of its proponents, was that the invention and use of writing came as a "thunder-clap in human history ... an intrusion into culture, with results that proved irreversible" (Havelock and Hershbell 1978: 3). Walter Ong put it equally strongly when he contrasted his conception of the traditionalist, acoustic, participatory, communal, and "natural" world of orality with the new world of writing. Functionally, literate human individuals, he writes, are:

> beings whose thought processes do not grow out of simple natural powers but out of these powers as structured, directly or indirectly, by the technology of writing. Without writing, the literate mind would not and could not think as it does, not only when engaged in writing, but normally even when it is composing its thoughts in oral form. More than any other single invention, writing has transformed human consciousness.
>
> *(Ong 1982: 78)*

Such conclusions drew extra credence from that once widely accepted story of humanity as divided into two opposed kinds: primitive against civilised; rural, traditional, and unchanging, as opposed to modern, urban, and progressive; oral against literate. The romantically envisaged "other" was felt, with some nostalgia, to exist in a world defined as through and through "oral" and "traditional" – unchanging, passive, emotional, unaffected by rational thought, individual human agency, or changes through time, the opposite in every way of how we would like to picture ourselves. The key divider was writing, above all the alphabetic literacy of the enlightened West. Small wonder that a step out of the gloom of non-literacy looked like a radical one.

A crucial contribution came in the work of Albert Lord (1960). In his research on the oral mode of epic singers in the then Yugoslavia, he showed how they drew on oral resources. Relying on these, they were able to pour out their songs, newly created in each performance, for hours without hesitation. The evidence he found convinced him of the uniqueness of this "oral culture" with, it followed, a sharp break between an "oral" and a "literate mode".

Or as Lord put it in a much-quoted statement about the effects on a singer who, having previously sung in the orally shaped "composition in-performance" mode, learned to read and write:[2]

> The two techniques are, I submit, contradictory and mutually exclusive. Once the oral technique is lost it is never regained. The written technique, on the other hand, is not compatible with the oral technique, and the two could not possibly be combined, to form another, a third, a "transitional" technique.
>
> *(Lord 1960: 129)*

In other words, and with many followers, Lord saw the worlds of orality and of literacy as sharply bounded and mutually exclusive. Not so extreme but something in the same vein was Plato's "If men learn writing it will implant forgetfulness in their souls, they will cease to exercise memory because they rely on that which is written, calling things to remembrance no longer from within themselves" (Plato *Phaedrus*).[3]

This, then, was what many writers went on to suggest or, rather, with or without the benefit of very much evidence from non-European cases, to affirm as proven. There is a wealth of material on these lines, illustrating the extensive use of the "oral-formulaic" method characteristic of the epic singers' oral mode of composition, applying it to, for example, the Old English *Beowulf*, early Greek poetry, the Siberian Olonko epic, early Japanese works, and even parts of the Koran.

It is an attractive and, in a way, engagingly simple approach, both forceful and striking in its potential application to the long sweep of human history and one that still has some currency. However, outmoded though in many ways this debate is, it is significant that the work of these two interacting human tools should be considered important enough to have attracted so much passion. Clearly, the modes for human communication matter.

There is one point to note first. In the accounts of the claimed institutional effects of the discovery or the invention of "writing", it is almost always phonographic writing that is being assumed. Most of the time, it is as if pictographic writing systems had never happened. But the particular link between voice and pen evinced in phonographic writing that we now take as the taken-for-granted one is surely not set in stone. It is common to think of the voice as inextricably tied to the sound of words almost as if it is this alone that defines meaning. But humans have only created and employed inscription linked in this way to sound for a relatively short time in the span of human history. It is strange that a linkage used for (relatively speaking) such a microscopic percentage of time in human history has been viewed as if it is a forever established property of human kind, perhaps almost like the definition of being fully human.

But that aside, the key issue, as it is seen by many, is whether vocalised communicating is really radically different from written, and if so, whether this really does have revolutionary results for the individuals and/or the culture(s) involved. These are significant questions, for it is highly relevant for the patterns of human communication to consider the meeting, as it were, of the products of inscription with those of spoken language.

Starting from a wider comparative approach, proponents of an opposing viewpoint have taken issue with several of Lord's famous and often universalised statements. There are not, they point out, just two communicating modes; ways of living and communicating are vastly more complex and diverse than that, and once students of communication trust them themselves to come out of the sheltered studious study, they find plenty of evidence to prove it.

FIrst, they note that there have long been other forms of composition without writing that poet-singers could and did take advantage of. Many poets, such as those among the Inuit, Somalis, and Fijians, did not use the composition-in-performance method of South Slavic singers. They depended on long thought-out work inspiration beforehand, sometimes in trance, to compose their poem or song, which they then delivered in identical wording time after time. The same is true of many, though not all, rock singers and song composers of today.

Second, unwritten poetry has been composed and presented not just in the "purely oral" contexts envisaged in Lord's account but in many different conditions, including literate settings, with many examples of such songs and poems going in and out of writing.[45]

A third point that has attracted much passion, is Lord's claim that once a poet becomes literate, they can no longer compose in the traditional oral manner; it is all or nothing.

There are two strands here: first, the claim that poets who have learned to read and write have no choice but to rely on a written mode for creating their works; they can no longer compose orally. And second, that there is no half way point;: there are no "transitional" texts, for a poet must use either oral or written methods, so no mix is possible.

Rather than remaining at this generalised rather high and abstract level, let me, instead, move to evidence from a detailed first-hand example. It is a case of interest both for its relevance to the wider debate and is an example in its own right as a product by someone employing the tools of both voice and pen.

Let me first set this context. It is a story told in Africa – the Africa that in the all-or-nothing view can be taken as the epitome of an area existing in a natural, untouched culture without any hint of literacy (I know that sounds ridiculous, my apologies, but it is the clear impression given in the influential publications of Marshall McLuhan and his fans).

Memory meets creativity meets sociality

So let me, for a moment, turn the focus on Africa.

Here, if anywhere, we might be able to see what it is like for humans to dwell in an oral culture (as it has been pictured) and/or to move out from that into the world of literacy governed by the pen. It is an appropriate focus as, despite the comments of many well-informed writers, Africa has been presented as *the* iconic example of pure undisturbed "oral culture". McLuhan's hugely influential work speaks frequently of the African "as the epitome of someone steeped in the oral" "magical" culture, associated with the "tribal horde" and a "return to the Africa within" (1962: 45, 255). Africa was envisaged as untouched by history and, therefore, unchanging for millennia and without contact with nations outside the continent and little internal movement either beyond hunting bands and "nomadic" tribal wanderings. There, if anywhere, would surely be found the pure oral culture untouched by literacy pictured by writers such as Walter Ong, Marshall McLuhan, and their fellows – the type of culture that the newly intruding and threatening pen was seen to demolish, bringing in ways that could never co-exist with the traditional, oral, "natural" products of the voice.

If, on one side, the significance of writing in the world is sometimes overblown, the other side is rather often ignored, as if it was not until the advent of the Western moveable-print press a few hundred years ago that humans' use of writing really happened at all. But actually, it has been around and of influence for some time.

Jack Goody makes the point clearly:

> At least during the past 2,000 years, the vast majority of the peoples of the world (most of Eurasia and much of Africa have lived in the neither situation but in cultures influenced in some degree by the circulation of the written word and by the presence of groups or individuals who could read and write. They lived on the margins of literacy, though this is a fact that many observers have tended to ignore.
>
> *(Goody 1968: 4–5)*

This is worth bearing in mind when finding Africa set up as an extreme example of oral culture: unchanging, passive, and not open to contact from the "outside" world. In the great divide that envisaged two kinds of cultures – unchanging tradition versus modernity, passivity versus democratic politics, oral versus literate – Africa has typically been seen as the extreme of orality and all that was associated with that.

In fact, this picture is wholly mistaken. For centuries, much of Africa has, like Europe, been a continent of writing. Even if we disregard the ancient inscriptions of North Africa and the civilisation of Ethiopia that preserved the writings of Christianity, lost to Europe's "Dark Ages", writing flourished in sub-Saharan Africa. The reason that Africa was for so long regarded as typically non-literate (or, even more undermining, as pre-literate) was, presumably, because the writing was in an Arabic not a Roman script and was not really noticed or if noticed somehow felt not to really count.

Yet in Africa, both Arabic and vernacular works were plentifully written in this script, and new alphabets, furthermore, ingeniously invented locally and sometimes for short periods practised. As recounted in full detail in such works as *A Fistful of Shells* (Green 2020), Africa had long been in contact with Western literacy through traders, missionaries, and explorers. West African kings and princes negotiated on equal terms with European potentates (the Ghanaian royal house employed Arabic scribes to deal with their European correspondence) while in South Africa, there were ties with India and its civilisation, in East Africa with Islam and classic literature in Arabic. Explorers, travellers, hunters, adventurers, miners, and evangelists

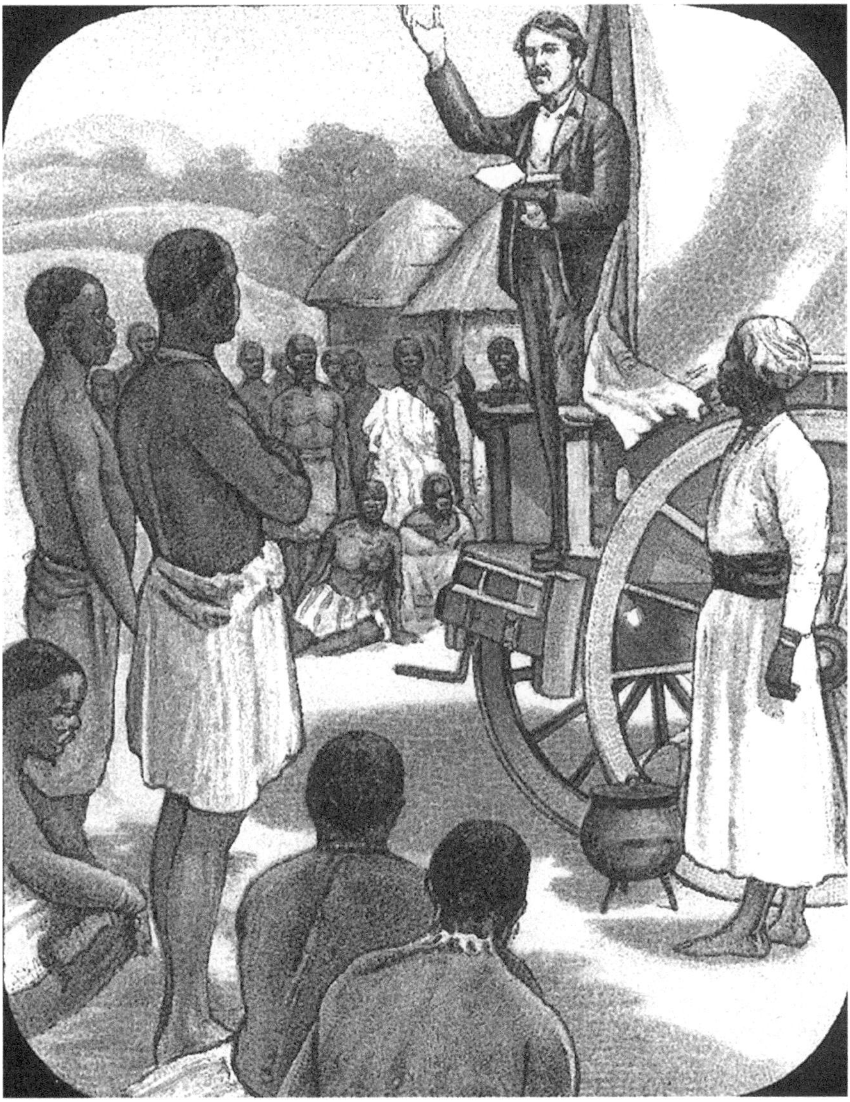

FIGURE 4.3 David Livingstone.

ranged the length and breadth of the continent not to speak of railway makers, colonialists, imperialists, and commercial hopefuls with their bureaucratic apparatuses and followers. And then, in due course, and even in the interior, European missionary educators promoted a surge of publications in the alphabetic Roman script in local languages, with many missionary-inspired translations of the gospels. Printed books, especially of the Bible and the colossally popular *Pilgrims Progress*, "the portable Bunyan" (Hofmeyr 2004), flooded the continent. And as Jack Goody rightly had it back in 1968, literacy had been around for several thousand years, why would it not have touched Africa as well as other parts of the world?

It is true that writing was, as in the Europe of not so very long ago, accessible to and taken up by only a minority and was generally utilised and disseminated on limited lines and for limited purposes. But it was writing all the same, and as elsewhere, even if in some places only lightly, tentacles of literacy touched people's lives. In Kakarima, the remote village where I spent many months and to which, well off the road, I had to walk on foot, only three children had ever been to school and didn't seem to have gained much from it.

But they *knew* of schools and of writing. They were connected up to a point with the wider economy. Young men travelled down country to make money from selling palm wine, and villagers. from time to time. visited villages on the dirt road north to buy imported cloth from roadside Lebanese traders. They were neither Muslims nor Christians. but they knew quite a bit about both, and while there. I was told of an Arabic scholar living a few miles away; I did not visit him, but he was part of the context in which the villagers lived. The larger village, the home of the storyteller Kelfa Konteh and where he had told his story to enthusiastic listeners, had an American Wesleyan Mission station where they had produced a Limba translation of the gospels.

This is not to say that they lived in the kind of literate context in which. say, an English urban dweller grows up. They did not. But even in that fairly remote village, writing was emphatically not something totally unknown or without its indirect influence on many aspects of the setting in which they lived. Given that, it is hard. indeed. to continue to class Africa, with its bustling modern cities as well as rural farmlands, as an overwhelming example of pure, untouched, "oral culture" and its people as untutored, ignorant, and "natural". And if such a culture was not, after all, characteristic of Africa, was or is it to be found anywhere?

A place of writing, a greedy chief, and a viewpoint

So let me present a product from someone living in Africa, this continent of the interaction between the written and the spoken. It is a translation of another Limba story – this a tale about trickery, always a favourite subject and cause for great amusement. It was told in Kamabai, one of the more "developed" but still relatively remote Limba villages on the main road north, by a youngish man called Kelfa Konteh, who had recently returned from the capital city where he had attended school and learned to read.

Sara and the chief who wanted everything

One day a chief lived in his country. He had very many children. The oldest son was called Sara. Sara was known for his cunning.

One day, this chief died. His property was divided among his children. Sara said that he did not want anything except one cow. He was given the cow. The other children were given the possessions that were left.

It happened that all the chiefs in the country came to the mourning for Sara's father. When they were sitting there, one chief saw that the cow that Sara had was excreting gold! It went *puri puri puri puri*. The chief asked

"Who owns the cow?"

"Sara".

He sent for Sara. Sara came. The chief asked him if he owned the cow. Sara said "Yes". The chief said, "I will give you my possessions. I will divide my country in half and give it to you".

Sara agreed.

The chief took away the cow. When it excreted – it was cow dung!

The chief said, "Hey! Hey! Sara has tricked me! The cow does not excrete gold!" This angered him. He said, "I will go, I will *kill* Sara".

He got ready his warriors. As soon as Sara saw them, he thought – *ti!* – a plan. He filled a bladder with blood. He hung it on his mother, on her neck. When the warriors and the chief came, Sara said, "Wait a little now". He called his mother. He killed her – *fa ka ha!* The bladder was burst! The blood came out splashing – *porobosi!* – from her neck. The people said, "Hey! Hey! He has killed his mother!" Sara said, "Wait for me a little. I will waken her". He dipped a broom in water. He hit her with it – *peng!* His mother woke – quite, quite well.

The chief said, "I will not kill you now. If you show me the medicine to kill someone and cure him, I will give you many possessions and give you many horses". Sara agreed. He gave him the broom and taught him. All nonsense! The chief gave him those things. He went.

When the chief reached home, he met his mother. He killed her. He killed his father. He killed the sub-chiefs in his country. He was left with only a few people. When he said that he would waken them, when he hit them with the broom – the flies went *ooooooo*. He said, "Hey! Hey! Sara has deceived me. Now I will go and kill him".

When he went, he found Sara. He tied him tightly – *thebing thebing* – he put him in a basket. He carried him on his head. When they had gone a little way, the chief said that he was going to the bush [to defecate]. Sara was put down near the road.

It was a short while, then a Fula man came along. He said, "Sara, what is it that you are bound for today?" Sara said, "Alas! I am to be taken up to be chief. But I refused, that is why they bound me, taking me up to be chief by force". The Fula man said, "Well, bind me. You take the things – the headdress, shoes, Fula gown, and the staff".[signs and possessions of chiefship].

The Fula was bound, tightly – *thebing!* Sara took the things. He went off. When the chief came now with his followers, they took up the Fula. The Fula man began to talk, "e fotho yai e dorotho fotho yai" [a ludicrous imitation of clipped Fula speaking, found very amusing – and familiar – by the listeners!]. The chief said, "Even if you speak Fula today – today we kill you!" The Fula man was put into the pool – *pokeng!*

Not long after Sara came back to the chief. He said, "E! chief! The place where you threw me – it is a good place. My father is there, my mother is there, see, my brother is there. See these possessions – everyone there has these in peace and happiness". The chief said, "Bind me. Let us go to where Sara came from".

The chief was tied up. He was put into the pool – *pokong!*

His followers said, "We will go where our father the chief went".

They all went. They threw themselves into the pool.

Sara said, "All the ones who hated me – they have all died. Bring me the chief's drum. Beat it". They beat it – *gbing gbing.*

Sara was raised to become chief.

*****

There are several points of interest about this tale and how Kelfa told it.

First, Kelfa's literacy had in no way diminished his inclination to tell stories in the full oral performance Limba genre, and he was still (rightly, in my opinion) regarded as one of the best storytellers around for his dramatic performances and vocal skill. He was particularly applauded for his vivid onomatopoeia and his extreme and effective depiction of the cheated chief's surprise and anger, also for his clever imitation of the Fula man's ludicrously clipped way of speaking – a delight to the mimicry-loving listeners. Like many of the best Limba storytellers, he did not include singing, instead making the most of his extended linguistic content. In short, it had the characteristics, as described in an earlier chapter, of a typical

Limba story – the gestures, the skill of the voice, the interactions with the listeners, and so on.

And yet, to repeat, Kelfa could read and write and showed no hesitation about accepting the invitation to tell a story.

This case – and there are many many parallels – runs counter to Lord's conclusion about the impossibility of an individual being able to function in both oral and written modes. In this context, it seems that the pen can coordinate with the voice and to good effect.

Second, the final twist will be not unfamiliar to Western readers. It is a recurrent theme in the *Arabian Nights*.

This is, in fact, no surprise. The plots of many stories in Africa are similar to those of stories told elsewhere. On the face of it, Kelfa's story ultimately originated (though who can tell really about such presumably far-off roots) from the rich store of Middle East folklore from which we may speculate that the overlapping *Odyssey* and *Sinbad the Sailor* also came. Kelfa's tale and the many others like it has, if this presumption is true, an honourable origin shared with other tales of high esteem.

And basic plots that ultimately come from written sources or have in the course of their travels been, at some point, written (as all stories move back and forth between vocal and written tellings) are and have been present in plenty in Africa (as anywhere, my own home country included). Tellers use themes from varied origins, coming through many links both (currently) orally told and (currently) written, such as the *Arabian Nights*, Aesop's Fables, or the Bible – oral to written and back again in constant recycling of the versatile cooperating tools of the voice and the pen. Something of this kind happens everywhere.

Africa is not just the recipient – witness the proliferation of trickster spider stories from an African origin plentifully told (now in multiplying print form too) in the Caribbean; the Negro spirituals arriving by the same route; the inspiring works of writers such as Achebe, who used the language of Europe to write about lore learnt orally as a child in a Nigerian village; or the musician storytellers and dancers visiting Europe.

It might be argued against that Kelfa had probably not progressed very far in his education and had, after all, chosen to come back to his Limba home and had not "really" moved out of immersion in his original order culture. So, relapsed back into it, he was still able to tell stories in the oral mode.

Another of my field research experiences, however, is relevant here. One my vivid memories is of hearing a multi-lingual Limba pastor, who had trained as a free church minister – a demanding course – conduct a service in the Limba church in Freetown, the capital city. First, he read a passage from the New Testament, then preached, without notes on its theme – both, perhaps needless to say, in fluent English. The striking thing was the vocal style of his sermon. It could have a been Limba story performance in that remote village of Kakarima. It was told in that same style, with a similar concluding moral and all the drama and Limba vocal artistry – repetition, parataxis, direct speech, intensifying of the voice – that I had noted with the best Limba storytellers. His listeners reacted and joined in in the same way too. Clearly, his mastery of writing had, in no way, as Lord and his followers would have expected, destroyed his ability to compose in vocal performance, using the tool of the voice with drama and artistry. His knowledge of the pen's products had, in no way, undermined that of the voice.

There are many similar examples of literate poets and narrators deploying oral skills honed by tradition and expertly too. Learning to read had, in no way, undermined their craft.

Take another set of examples. The most famous genre in African oral art is that of the panegyric (praise poetry), the most striking and elaborate of African traditional genres. It has always been richly used in African cultures and evident in many settings – public and private ceremonies, rites of passages, self-praises for individuals, eulogies, poems for animals and natural objects, and warnings for leaders, including the most powerful – as a vehicle for poetic expression and performance and a great art of the voice.

The basic style is to pile up great panegyricising epithets – "praise names" – for the person or thing chosen, often a traditional king or chief, often in metaphorical terms, likening them, for example, to an eagle, leopard, or the like to bring out their great qualities. The famous and terrifying Shaka, for instance, was praised as

> His spear is terrible.
> The Ever-ready-to-meet-any-challenge!
> The first-born sons of their mothers who were called for many years!
> He is like the cluster of stones of Nkandhla,
> Which sheltered the elephants when it had rained.
> The hawk which I saw sweeping down from Mangcengeza;
> When he came to Pungashe he disappeared.
>
> He invades, the forests echo, saying, in echoing,
> He paid a fine of the duiker and the doe.
> He is seen by the hunters who trap the flying ants;
> He was hindered by a cock in front,
> By the people of Ntombazi and Langa [mother and father of Zwide],
> He devoured Nomahlanjana son of Zwide;
> He devoured Mdandalazi son of Gaqa of the amaPela;

He was lop-eared. He devoured Mdandalazi son of Gaqa of the amaPela;
He was lop-eared.
The Driver-away of the old man born of Langa's daughter!
The Ever-ready-to-meet-any-challenge!
Shaka!

The Eagle-which-beats-its-wings-where-herds-graze!
He drove away Zwide son of Langa,
Until he caused him to disappear in the Ubani;
Until he crossed above Johannesburg and disappeared;
He crossed the Limpopo where it was rocky;
Even though he left Pretoria with tears.
He killed the snake, he did not kill it in summer,
He killed it when the winter had come.[6]

In South Africa, in particular, the genre was especially developed as a great traditional genre of oral performance. By the second half of the twentieth century, the towns, with their popular newspapers, were intershot with literacy. Did praise poetry fade away or its singers lose their ability?

The quick answer is that they did not – in fact, far from it.

The pen was doing its work well, for praise poetry continued at every level. Expert poets appeared at great ceremonies of state, university events, and international conferences (I had my praises declaimed at one and had to dance in response), young manual workers interspersed their guitar songs with self-praises (a long-established sub-genre), and newspapers ran a regular column for printing the many praise poems submitted to them. Oral and written overlapped, as the same poem could appear in both modes.

Some of the subjects treated in more recent poems were similar to the older ones, eulogising new types of adventures, distinguished visitors, wedding feasts, and self-praises and were treated with similar solemnity and metaphor to the earlier ones. A notable example was the flood of praise poems for Nelson Mandela (himself a notable praise poet). Other poems drew on traditional style and imagery to praise (for example) racehorses, a political party, a football team, or a successful politician.

The traditional style came in *written* form too. Here is a praise poem in writing, about a train.

I am the black centipede, the rusher with a black nose
Drinker of water even in the fountains of the witches,
And who do you say will bewitch me?

I triumphed over the one who eats a person [the sun] and over the pitch black darkness
When the carnivorous animals drink blood day and night.
I am the centipede, the mighty roarer that roars within.

(Van Zyl 1941:131)

The style became increasingly popular – just as the traditional Western sonnet, novel, and drama as well as local folk forms have been for European writers – as a genre for written as well as performed poetry. Well-known writers studied and admired traditional praises, turning to them for inspiration for their own writing. This fitted with the long tradition of publishing praise poems in local newspapers, with a move back and forth between written and unwritten, and, today, using computers. There is no indication that the spread of writing or of print has been any obstacle to the composition or performance of praise poetry composed basically in the traditional style – on the contrary, it would seem, if anything, to have encouraged it by giving it wider channels of distribution.

Throughout Africa, as elsewhere, there is both change and continuity in the arts of voice and pen. Given that they cooperate and combine, it would scarcely be easy to say which predominates: the new builds into and out of the older forms and vice versa.

As well, both popular and high culture have seen people developing emergent forms with a mix of languages or media. There are, for example, the hymns of the Zulu Nazarite church, hip hop in Sierra Leone, South African radio drama, or the striking Sokoto Nigerian genre that uses standard Islamic vocabulary with a delivery style reminiscent of both traditional praise poetry and Indian film song – mixed, indeed. The same mingling of the work of both pen and voice is evident throughout Africa, as throughout the world.

There may (or equally may not), in some contexts, be fewer of the kind of storytelling in which Kelfa and Karanke were expert. There will always be changes as well as continuities in the details. But throughout the world, there are plenty of live performances all around: on the media; singers in pubs; the verbal and gestural wit of *craic*, as it is known in Ireland; impassioned discussion in book clubs and "sharing words" groups; slam contests; political oratory; and parents reading stories and nursery rhymes aloud or, as their parents did for them, telling them these stories without reading from a book. And that is without counting the to-and-fro creativity (as it is now recognised to be) of the ordinary conversations that most people engage in every day, the book-steeped as much as any. There would seem be no shortage today of communication that essentially makes use of the tools of both pen and voice.

The toad and the snake – a tale of death

Amidst this, however, there is still that other story circulated by the pen (rather, the pen's holders, as they do not always deliver readers what is accurate) that intimates a different and misleading picture: that in oral cultures ("Africa" and "the African" seemingly always the example) there was no true individuality and that even if some people were quite skilfully telling stories, they were merely mindlessly transmitting, word-for-word, content that had been passed down to them through passive and unchanging tribal tradition from, as it was regularly put, "time immemorial".

Well, here are some further examples from that very continent of Africa. It is a clutch of three short tales on the theme of the origin of death, all told by Limba speakers. The basic plot and characters, naturally with some differences of detail, are the same. But the tales, as delivered by three different individuals, tell us as much about their individual lives and experiences as, and are certainly more interesting than, anything about the traditional "nature" of the story's plot.

The first was by Sangbang, a late teenager whose life had been filled with disappointments. He had been chosen to go to school, which he had much wanted to do (he would have been the eagerest of students). But he contracted a long-lasting illness – no one knew from what (an ill-wishing witch masquerading as one of the women of the village, perhaps?) – and was unable to go. Further, and for him even worse, his continuing illness meant he could not join his coevals in the longed-for initiation into manhood. By now, he had lost his chance, and it would never happen. He would never be a full man, marry, or take his full place in the village.

Sangbang made his tale a tragedy and told the story of the tragic turn by which death came, unintended and almost accidentally, as it were, to human beings. He spoke with great sadness and quiet drama, with dignity too. For himself, the tragedy lay both in the toad's hatred of mankind and also in the present paradoxical reversal by which we care for the one who hated us and kill the one who would have saved us; his tone and demeanour somehow setting this in a more universal and tragic human perspective. The voice, indeed, wherever it is spoken, whether in a far-off village as here, or in a city concert hall, can convey from the right speaker overtones of eternity.

Sangbang Yeleme's **The toad did not love us**

The toad – ah, the toad did not love us. Kanu [God] squeezed out leaves to make herbal medicine. He squeezed the leaf-medicine. He wanted people not to see death. He said,

"But this medicine – who will carry it to the Limba, the humans?"

The snake said, "I will carry it".

The toad said, "No. I will carry it for them. We are near to each other".

But he – ah! – he did not love us. He wanted to kill us all.

He was told, "Here is the medicine".

He was given it, he put it on his head to carry it, he set out to go. He jumped once – *toling!* – the medicine fell off, *bukute!* [sound of the medicine spilling]. He spilt it.

Ah! It had been said that if anyone carried this medicine, he was not to spill it.

The snake who loved us, the toad did not allow him to bring it to us. The one who hated us, he was who brought it. He went and upset it.

So, if you see us dying now, it is because of the toad. The white people and we, the Limba, we would not have died but for the toad.

And now, this is how we and the toad are: where we build houses, he loves that place. That is why we drive him out. But the snake, who loved us in the beginning, he always pursues him, pursuing the toad. The toad runs to us. Well, the snake who loved us then, well, when we meet him now, we kill him. We do not kill the toad.

Well, Kanu looks at us for that.

Since you said you wanted to hear about it, that is how we are with the toad.

That is it. It is finished.

****

Sangbang told the story, as I say, with great sadness and with few effects of dramatisation or mimicry. His focus was on the present tragic situation in which people so continually die. He ended with a characteristically Limba moralising conclusion, pointing to the paradoxical reversal by which "the one who loved us then, well, when we meet him now, we kill him. We do not kill the toad. Well, Kanu looks at us for that".

Fanka Konteh, the second teller, was probably not considered to be one of the best storytellers, yet he was able to tell stories night after night, his lively delivery much enjoyed both by other members of the village and further afield. He had spent some time down country, as young men quite often did, to raise some money for themselves before returning home and fitting back into local life. Fanka , thus, had contact with urban ways but had no particular position of authority back in Kakarima. With little interest in moralising, he laid more stress on the actual course of events in the plot; he enjoyed portraying exaggerated surprise, amusing episodes, mimicry of animals, the dramatic representation of eating, hunger, or beating. His narration was effective without being loudly exaggerated. He presented his version as a piece of exciting action, even a bit comic, sharing laughter with the listeners well when it was a bit of a ridiculous situation: we could see it from his delivery, of a toad, of all creatures, hopping unsteadily along trying to hold a bowl steady on his head and then it – *ohhh!* – falling off, *bang, splash!*

Fanka's main emphasis was on the action of the story, the interchange of words between the characters, the way the toad put the medicine on his head, then jumped and spilt it. The interest was much more in the animals than in Sangbang's story, with no comment on Kanu's deeper intentions or its tragic implications. Despite its brevity, it went down well with the listeners who enjoyed the rollicking humorous manner in which it was told.

The toad *by Fanta Konteh*

Kanu once said, "I will make medicine for the Limba. But who will take them the medicine?"

The snake said, "*I* will take it".

The toad said, "It is not the snake who should take it. I will take it".

The toad took the medicine, he put it on his head to carry it. He set out to come.

He leapt once, he leapt again, he upset the medicine, he did not bring it to the Limba.

That is why the snake and the toad are enemies. Whenever the snake sees the toad, he catches him saying, "It was you who did not agree to take the medicine".

That is why the toad and snake are enemies.

That is what caused the Limba to die. If the snake had brought the medicine, the Limba would not ever have been dying. But the toad did not agree. He upset the medicine on the road. That is why the snake and the toad are enemies.

****

Karanke's story differed yet again. Typical of his way with story, he had extended and elaborated the plot and introduced an additional point: Kanu had intended that the snakes as well as humans should not die, and the snakes, in fact, did succeed in obtaining their portion of the medicine. That is why, his story explained, snakes do not die, but when they become old, merely change their skin for a new one. This version also, unlike the others, included a reference to what is a common moral in Limba stories – the unfortunate results of disobedience, in this case the toads.

The toad and the snake *by Karanke Dema*

We Limba, we would not have been dying. Once upon a time, Kanu loved us; he wanted us not to die, us and all the animals. He made *mafoi* (herb) medicine –

"I will give it to you".

He mixed it two parts. For the Limba – one part. For the snakes – one part.

He said, "Snake, you are to carry it to the Limba".

The snake said, "I agree".

The toad got up – "*I* will carry it. The way the snake goes is not good, going very quickly. He will soon spill it".

The snake said, "I will not spill it. I will go quickly. I will not spill it".

The toad would not allow it.

The snake took the one for them [snakes] saying he would take it. He carried it quickly, he did not spill it.

Now the toad – the toad took the one for the Limba, to carry it. But look, *kumang*, he was not able at all. He had just put it on his head. He jumped. When he jumped the second time, he spilt the medicine.

He took the bowl. He went back to Kanu. He said, "the medicine – it has spilt. Please find more medicine".

Kanu said, "the bowl with the medicine is empty now. I am not able to get more. I told you not to take it, you disobeyed, you went and just spilt it – I will not be able to get more now".

He did not give any more then, he Kanu. It was because of the disobedience of the toad.

You see now always – we Limba are always dying. It was the toad who caused that. He spilt the medicine for the Limba. But the snakes, those who did not spill it, they do not die except when someone kills them. But if you do not kill him, when he gets old, he bathes in the medicine which they carried then, which they were given then by Kanu.

Well, *wuna*, that is it, by grace of *Yenkeni*, that is it. *Lonthang*.

***

The words sound simple, a standard story, in spite of Karanke's individual twists, and so, indeed, they were. But of course, like other accomplished tellers, the words were not "just words", for he decorated them by the typical modulations of his voice, sudden pauses, excitement, and so on, as well as gestures, indicating, for example, how the toad hopped with the medicine on his head, then *whoosh*, spilt it together with the *bang* of the falling and breaking bowl and Kanu's resigned but not really very concerned refusal to produce a replacement, then the paradoxical conclusion with a wry smile, enhanced by the audience's gasps; their anticipation of the known conclusion only added to the drama.

So, in spite of the well-known plot of these close tellings, the tone and emphasis of the narrations were noticeably different when told by these three individuals. It is hard to see these three tellers as exemplars of the kind of unthinking pure oral communal culture envisaged by adherents of the "orality versus literacy" theories.

These tellers, like others in any country, tell their stories, both written and oral, drawing on the resources available to them as well as adding ideas from their own experience. It has been common to attribute such stories, if they are told in Africa, as "tribal tradition" passed on with no thought of individual creativity (one might ask, incidentally, how the plot, therefore, first came into being? – From some unnamed genius in the past?). The basic plot was, indeed, common in Africa (documented in Abrahamsson 1951), and one can imagine it being told and retold in multiple versions by travelling traders or from one nearby settlement to another over multiple generations until story tellers throughout the continent, remarkably, all knew the basic plot.

We will never know exactly how the process worked, and, perhaps, it is not worth trying. What is of interest is the situation depicted here of storytellers who, far from drawing passively on "age-old tradition", were actively shaping it to their own creative instincts. They were not alone; there are many many parallel cases, for their process was essentially that of any creator, verbal or musical, and whether using the pen, the voice, or both.

When I asked Karanke where his stories came from, he replied "From the dead people [*fureni be* – the ancestors, buried in the village compounds, still in a way with them] and from my own heart" (*huthukuma*, the seat of thought, emotion, and individuality). He thought for a moment and then went on, "And then, if I think I may be telling a story soon, I think into myself when I am alone and add a little bit".

His words were strikingly reminiscent of those used by TS Eliot on the relationship between a poet and the preceding literary tradition in his thoughtful essay "Tradition and the Individual Talent", scarcely in accordance with the "pre-literate consciousness" supposedly characteristic of the oral side of the Great Divide.

Oral to written to oral to ...

Stories go through many recyclings, many different channels. Kiringkoma's "Clever Cat" story performed orally was transformed, first (by me) into handwritten transcript, then English translation, then typescript (for a dissertation), and then print (in Finnegan 1967). It was then, without my knowledge but very pleasingly, taken up and edited for a children's book (MacDonald 2001) accompanied by colourful and wonderful pictures, designed, by the editor's clear wishes, to be read aloud then retold orally. Doubtless, that will not be the end, as quite likely, it will be picked up by

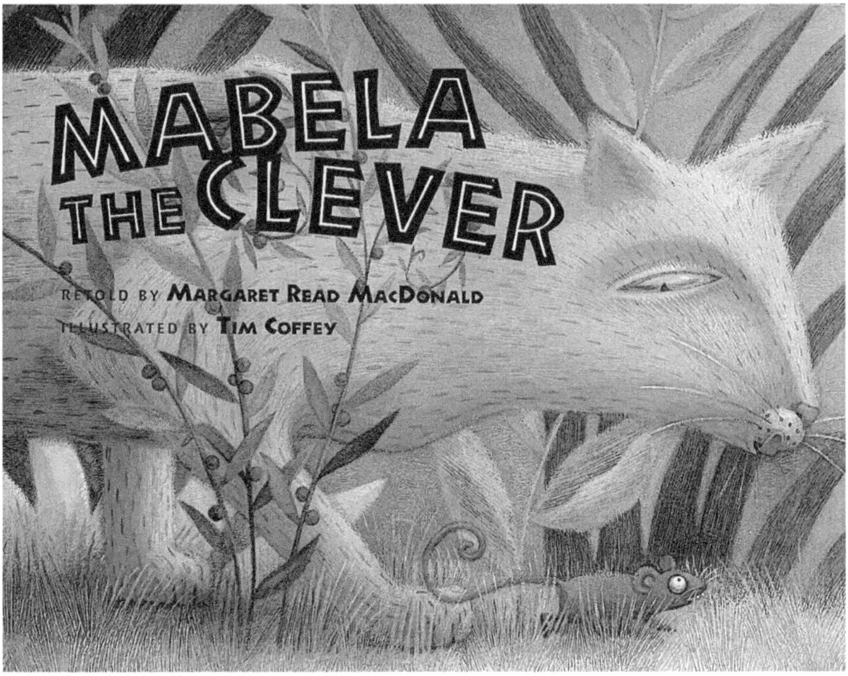

FIGURE 4.4 *Mabela book cover* (MacDonald).

a collector and published as, perhaps, a newly discovered ancient folktale. There would be nothing unprecedented about that.

This was not a one-off; there are many parallels. Such things are characteristic of the human recycling of our created arts, fruit of the tools of voice and pen. There is, I repeat, *no* necessary conflict between the two, they are human tools that are there for humans to use.

Here is another example; this time, so to speak, the other way round.

Karanke did not limit the sources for his stories – they could be from anywhere as long as he could shape them to his own individual voice. He was even happy to listen to a story from me, which I told not in the least as a research experiment but just to distract myself during a long wearying walk. It was based on the Adam and Eve story of the snake and the apple.

As it turned out, it proved an interesting instance of the interplay and recycling between written and unwritten material, for when I visited Kakarima a couple of years later, I wondered vaguely if Karanke would remember the story, and if so, what he thought of it. After all, he had such a repertoire of his own stories, he had no need to look to mine. But, I suppose like any story creator, he was open to any source that could fire his imagination. To my surprise and pleasure, he made a point of telling it among other stories he had been thinking about.

Karanke was open that he had first heard the plot from me, but that was of little interest to anyone, just a graceful way of welcoming me back. What mattered was how he told it – all the expected richness of repetitions, direct speech, parataxis, drama, and talented modulations of the voice. He had added some small twists to the action and characters that fed on typical motifs and interests, and the story was now much longer and fuller in the telling (I had told just a quick version, remember, during a hot, tiring, walk, and in my not too fluent Limba). There were all the tricks of gesture, intimation, modulation, and intensification of the voice, ideophones, snappy dialogue – and all the other vocal devices mentioned in the earlier chapter.

Far from destroying the art of his voice by drawing on an ultimately written source, the story merely extended the resources Karanke could draw in and use for his own art. It was now Karanke's story. His version was then preserved and circulated by me in writing, as products of the pen can be, perhaps to be picked up one day and "collected" by a pen scholar as an interesting example of an African myth or perhaps eventually retold multi-modally in a film.

So the re-communicating, voice-pen-voice-pen goes on, in its way, infinitely more nuanced and creative than allowed for in any stark opposition of "oral" and "literate". This was far from the only occasion that talented narrators on the margins of literacy drew on an ultimately written source to express not just a story but something of their own identity and personal experience, their philosophy. The evidence is against the idea of a sharp break between the communications of the voice and of the pen, far less of a contest between them based on a presumption of mutual exclusivity. The detail of examples such as the above, characteristic of what is, in fact, going on, can only undermine the generalised pen-ousting-oral-voice theories.

The happy cooperation of pen and voice happens in conditions of full literacy too. Winston Churchill, leading writer of the last century, received his war plans in dreams – what source could be more non-written, oral? – before implementing them and later writing about the results in his books; a bright university student in Fiji wrote her songs for celebrations using, she told me, the same trance-inspired oral method as the traditional poets; the same for me, an academic – my poems come orally, in dream mode, to be written down later; and learning to read didn't in the least stop my clever brother, great narrator that he still is, telling his brilliant stories to entranced listeners; highly as well as poorly educated musicians of the present compose their songs, un-notated, composing them while performing while interacting with fellow band members, maybe later printing the lyrics – now written – and designing attractive pictorial labels for the videos; sound-based audiobooks and multi-modal movies start off as written scripts; and my dentist told me last week about the after-care needed following an extraction – the spoken words and the smile felt personal and warm and caring, but he also handed me the exact same information in a printed pack – I knew that would be instructive, authoritative, scientific, objective and reliable, and handy to consult if I forgot what he'd said or for future occasions; they were different, the former more friendly and human, the latter more detached and scientific. Both had advantages, each reinforced the other. And so on and so on…

There is no clash. How should there be? Pen, that fine human tool, works with voice, voice with pen, and back, and around again and yet again.

Writing, and with it print, is, in essence, just a channel of communication, in principle basically like any other of the techniques that have been developed over the years. They can be used flexibly, alternately, cooperatively. We all know this from our own daily experience. And though we may continually need to adapt our communicating ways to new circumstances, as, after all, that is something that humans and other animals have been doing throughout history: new strategies to meet changing vegetation or climate conditions, for example, or steam or electricity or computers. All these must have affected human lives in various ways. But surely not a revolution of an unprecedented, colossal kind, or a radical transformation of human brains.

As I look round at my fellow human beings today, and to the evidence about human behaviour in the past, such conclusions do seem overblown. And amidst these "new" techniques of the pen (by now, not so very new, actually), we seem to have survived with ourselves and our basic mental processes more or less intact.

So, communication continues through the voice of story and moral, cooperating with gesture and music and in constant recycling with the precious tool of pen. It is so not just in Africa but throughout the world and the centuries.

Notes

1 The evidence is the whole of the world's literature. My own favourites are of poetry Shakespeare's sonnets, Rumi's gems, Wavell's *Other Men's Flowers*, and (of course) Homer; of prose – though how can anyone choose from such a treasure chest of the pen – the writings of Darwin, Erasmus, and Thucydides.

2 Implicit presuppositions, exemplified in the work of Lord himself and his prolific followers, including, among many others, Marshall McLuhan in 1962 (directly influenced by Lord), Walter Ong (1982).

3 He later changed his mind, recognising that some of his most famous singers (as was, in fact, obvious from any careful reading of his 1960 book) were, in fact, literate or had drawn on sources from literate friends, and accepted that there could, after all, be "transitional texts", a concept that has, in turn, attracted discussion (see Gintsburg 2018).
4 Amidst the huge literature around this debate, classical contributions include Finnegan 2013, Goody 1977, 1987, Graff 2010, McLuhan 1962, Ong 1977, 1982, Opland 1983, Street 1984.
5 This approach, with evidence and illustrations, can be found in Finnegan 1970, 1977.
6 Further on the background and functions of traditional praise poetry in Africa in Finnegan 1970 Chapter 5.

5

THE UNAWARES COMMUNICATING

The voice and, in its many forms, the pen are overt tools of communication. In general, we know when they are being used. But there are also ways of communicating that work below the level of consciousness. As advertisers and politicians well know, this can make them all the more powerful.

The subjects of this chapter, the significance of numbers and colours, together with some partially concealed depths in language, are somewhat problematic to present. In one way, they seem almost too familiar to mention, as most of us regularly use or are in some way touched by them. In another way, any conclusions are likely to be controversial, given that people's situations and understandings vary so much.

However, having been startled myself by how widespread and, when I thought about it, how powerful some of these things are for communicating and for moving people, I felt that omitting them would a gap in the overall coverage of the subject.

Three things we know but do not know that we know

Here are some things that have, on the one hand, been, in some cases, well considered by scholars but, on the other, have not received much attention within the study of communication.

Hidden in language

It is true that my consideration of the relative role of verbal language relative to that of other forms has, generally speaking, been somewhat

DOI: 10.4324/9781003496007-5

exaggerated in the scholarly literature on communication. I agree, however, that it is an exceedingly important part of our current communication systems. So, let me start with some brief comments on its relevance for our unawares communicating.

In his lectures on the science of language to the Royal Institution in London, the nineteenth-century philologist Max Müller spoke a panegyric of language in moving, near poetic terms. Language, he said,

> has marvels of her own, which she unveils to the inquiring glance of the patient student. There are chronicles below her surface; there are sermons in every word. Language has been called sacred ground, because it is the deposit of thought. We cannot tell as yet what language is. It may be a production of nature, a work of human art, or a divine gift. But to whatever sphere it belongs, it would seem to stand unsurpassed – nay, unequalled in it – by anything else. If it be a production of nature, it is her last and crowning production which she reserved for man alone. If it be a work of human art, it would seem to lift the human artist almost to the level of a divine creator. If it be the gift of God, it is God's greatest gift; for through it God spake to man and man speaks to God in worship, prayer, and meditation.
>
> *(Müller 1862: 13)*

In the "sacred ground" that he speaks of. we can, for one thing, dig into the history of words. That history still. from time-to-time. leaves flavours that can still affect us, communicating in ways of which we are not aware.

Take, for instance, the frequently used word "silly". It comes from an old Teutonic root meaning "sacred", as in the German *selig*. In its English form of "silly", it moved from the idea of something sacred to that of the holy humble sheep looking up, patient and not fed, and then on to meanings such as not very clever or pushy, and on to the modern meaning of "silly". The lingering flavour of its first meaning, hanging around during its gradual shifts, still sometimes comes through in the way that, despite its negative dictionary meaning, we may use the word "silly" with of tinge of warmth and a smile, "silly billy" or "You are so silly" said in an affectionate and humorous tone.

Or again, there is the word "nice". Some, at least of my (older) generation, feel it is a word not to be over-used: we had been told at school to bring it in sparingly. That slight discomfort over what, after all, is a very pleasant adjective has long roots. Earlier, it meant the opposite of its present apparent meaning, as it once had the negative sense of "ignorant" or "foolish". It began from the Latin "nescius" (*ne-scud*, "not-knowing"), then slowly moved into the meanings of "foolish, frivolous, senseless" via

Old French, then started to be used in English to describe someone who was ludicrously over-dressed, then refined and "nicely" dressed, and still has the sense of "fussy" ("he was over-nice about ..."). That background helps to explain how some (doubtless not all) have a feeling of slight discomfort about using or encountering the term.

And "nightmare". Yes, we all sometimes have bad dreams and wake up relieved. But somehow calling them a nightmare feels to be adding an extra layer of horror and hidden trauma. So, it is interesting to unpack the history of the word. "Night" is obvious. But "mare"? That originally referred to a female goblin that sits on you, suffocates you in your sleep, entangles her hair around you in a "marelock" and induces horrifying thoughts. No wonder our subconscious tells us that a nightmare is something more ghoulish than just an uncomfortable dream.

Without our thinking about it consciously in the least, there is yet something very deeply settled in our minds and emotions about the word "man". The word (originally ungendered) is our basic name. Look back. *Mâ* in Sanskrit means to measure (the origin of the word "moon"), and "measuring" is, in turn, related to craftsmanship, and so to *homo faber* – "man the maker" – a key theme in humankind's journey. But *Man*, a derivative root, also means "to think".

> From this we have the Sanskrit manu, originally thinker, then man. In the later Sanskrit we find derivatives, such as mânava, mânusha, manushya, all expressing man. In Gothic we find both man and manisks, the modern German mann and mensch.
>
> *(Müller 1862: 382)*

So. as humans. we are etymologically both *homo faber* and *homo sapiens*. It is hard not to think that, unawares, we yet in our bones somehow know this and hold up our heads.

Flavours of earlier meanings or connotations can be caught from others, doubtless down the centuries, the connotations somehow seeping through in subconscious ways through the generations even when at a conscious level we are unaware of them. Certain words can carry a feeling of, say, discomfort, reassurance, blessing, or friendship; we may sort of know we are using them in this way while not being fully conscious of it: we know, but we do not know that we know. Advertisers do know – it is their training – and make a point of building on "unconscious associations".

Not just etymologies, but sounds carrying over from the past can add an additional layer of meaning and emotive echoes. Albert Lord explains the contributions that such echoes can make in South Slavic epic composition.

> It is certainly possible that a formula that entered the poetry because its acoustic patterns emphasized by repetition a potent word or ideally was

> kept ... because the fragrance of its past importance still clung vaguely to it and kept also because it was now useful in composition.
>
> *(Lord 2019: 65)*

Sonic associations are subtle and emotive devices of human expressiveness and communication. Philologists have taught us much about words that, etymologically related through time, still carry into the present echoes from their roots. But it is also relevant to look at some that are, if I may put it this way, as it were. *horizontally* related through sound associations: ripples and waves that subliminally communicate through their echoes. Words and connotations can grow sideways through sonic similarities, and, as sound does, carry emotional overtones when heard, as our ears do, from a sonic perspective. Consider, a set of sound-related words such as *rush*, *blush*, *flush*, *mush*, *slush(y)*, *lush*, and, less directly, *rash, flash, crash, gash, lash, dash, slash, splash, brash,* and maybe *gosh.* Either singly or, infinitely more powerfully, in combination, they communicate something of suddenness or unexpectedness or that something is out of place. Or again, there is the immediacy of a run of words such as *dint, dent, daunt, dunt,* and *don't/dan't/doon't*, or, *near, dumped, dinned, demmed/damned,* and *dumbed.* As with the African ideophones mentioned earlier, the dictionary descriptions on the surface of our brains only communicate part of the story; they do not convey the emotive sonic echoes.

Whether with deliberation or with some subconscious auditory sensitivity, poets know the impact of such words, as they work with sound to create alliteration, assonance, rhyme, and rhythm or use acoustic associations to convey tone and mood. The readers/listeners may not consciously realise these poetic building blocks, but the effects are likely to be communicated all the same.

Gerald Manley Hopkins is well known for his use of sound associations. The effect is remarkable, as words and their acoustic resonances grow and somehow unite the whole through their sound echoes.

> How to keep – is this any way, is there none such, nowhere
> known some, bow or brooch or braid or brace, lace,
> latch or catch or key to keep
> Back beauty.

In poetry like this, it is easy to spot sound echoes. But in a less formalised but, nonetheless, effective ways, something like this runs below the surface through our discourse – a dimension of our communicating and a resource of which, often without being really aware of it, we make good use.

And then, have you, as we mostly do, forgotten about gestures? Sometimes these are deliberate, and some are carefully deployed by orators or actors. Mostly, however, they are involuntary, unthought about, just going along with speech even though, unless our hands are occupied with something else or we are making a special effort to appear stiff and withdrawn, gestures are a necessary part of conveying meaning through the spoken voice.

But we may be almost totally unaware of when we are using them; they just go on when we are speaking. Indeed, we gesture even in the dark, when your movements are unseen, such as when talking on the phone, or, as I caught myself doing a few days ago, on a radio programme. But they are definitely part of the meaning. Whether knowing it or not, our gestures can amplify, qualify, or even, at times, blankly contradict what our voice is saying. We have all had the experience of observing this: the body opposing the lips.

So here is yet another extremely important, near-ubiquitous kind of communicating of which we are not really aware.

There is more, such as accents, dialects, intonation, and the echoes of jointly known quotations. But that is enough for now to give a hint of the hidden potential of language of, as Müller rightly described it (1862: 13), the "chronicles below her surface".

The magic in numbers

Numbers connect intricately with how we communicate and the channels through which we do it. They have fascinated people for thousands of years, counting from the rising and the setting of the sun and the moon and the turning of the year. Augustine saw numbers as divine wisdom present in the world, while Pythagoras connected numbers to the harmony of the universe and music and held that numbers mediate between the divine and the created world.

All societies have some kind of numbering system, from the current Hindu-Arabic numbers and computer inner workings. to the amazingly transparent traditional Mayan system and the Chinese abacus. A recent blog may have it right, "MATH truly is the original and universal language" (Benjamin 2020).

However, that may be, it is true that without our being consciously aware of it, numbers play a significant but often unawares part in our expression and communication.

To start with some commonly held associations, the following may well seem familiar, though mostly not something we think about consciously.

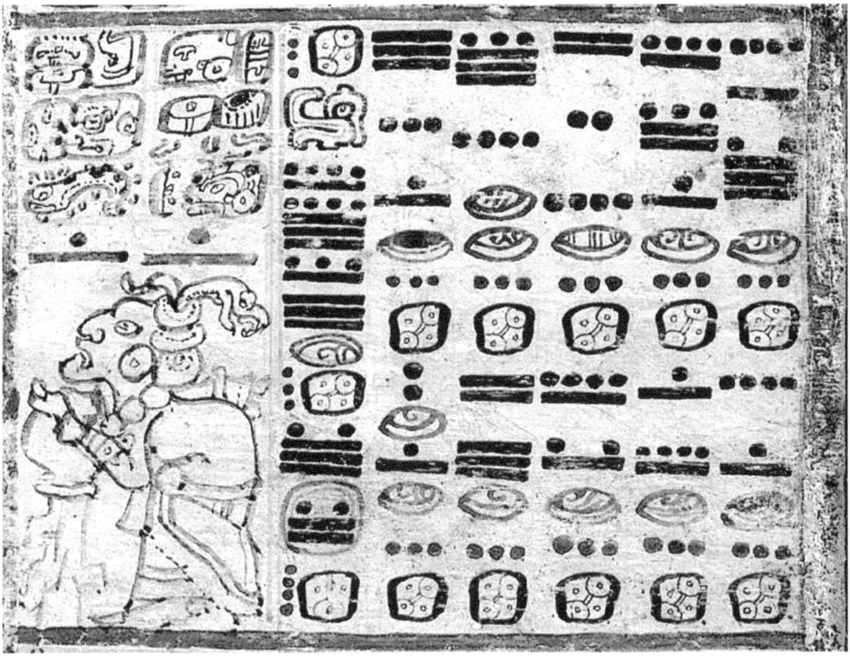

FIGURE 5.1 Mayan numbers.

0 Eternity, infinity, beginning, and end
1 Unity – a key concept in all religions
2 Duality – night and day; male and female; yin, and yang
3 Completion, spirituality, magic
4 Order in the universe – four elements (earth, air, fire, water), four seasons, four points of the compass, the Four Noble Truths of Buddhism, the four New Testament gospels.
5 Exotic and rebellious but also the five Pillars of Islam and five lawgiving prophets (Noah, Abraham, Moses, Jesus, and Muhammad).
6 The "perfect" number in mathematics; the six days of Creation
7 Mystical, mysterious, eternal
8 Auspicious
9 Amazing – three times three
10 Symbol of perfection or completeness (as in Pythagoreanism): ten fingers, ten toes, the basis of some mathematics
11 Negative, chaotic – in the Babylonian creation myth, Tiamat, god of chaos, is supported by 11 monsters.
12 Heavenly – 12 months, 12 signs of the zodiac, 12 stations of the moon and the Sun.

Let me single out two of these for a closer look: seven and three.

Seven

Consider a story that starts with a mention of someone getting a Number 7 bus or waiting for a train on Platform 7. Without further words we immediately get the feeling that there might be something slightly unusual and mysterious about this story; it will not be just about everyday doings that we can read and then forget. The same would go for the constant recurrence through the centuries of stories about the seven little pigs, the Seven Sisters, the seven ravens, the seven princesses, seven-leagued boots, the seven stars in the sky.

Seven somehow primes us just by its number to expect something a bit magical in what we are about to read – or, equally, to *hear*, for seven is a constant theme in folktales, fairy tales, and songs.

According to recent surveys, seven is the world's favourite number. Overall, it has been popular from at least the time of ancient Babylon, and in the earliest sources, there are more references to seven than to any other number. It seems to stretch across just about all cultures and periods. There are the seven wonders of the world, seven seas, seven demons (eight might, oddly, seem less threatening), the seventh heaven, and seven hills of the "eternal city" of Rome. In Greek literature, it is the number of dreams, prophecy, and the afterlife. In China, seven indicates luck and good fortune and, presumably for that reason, the jackpot on slot machines. Just about everywhere, people observe the seven-day week, fundamental to our calendar and time keeping, linked too to the biblical story of creation in which, on the seventh day, God rested, commanding that his creation do the same.

In religious thinking, seven is often thought of as conveying something spiritual. It is prominent in the Book of Revelation (seven churches,

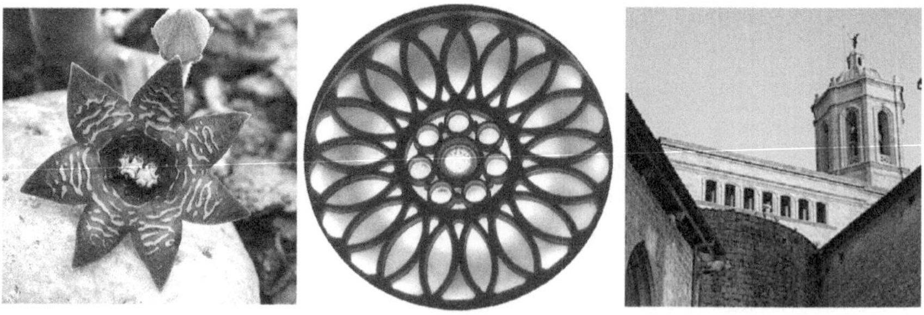

FIGURE 5.2 Sevens.

seven angels, seven seals, seven trumpets, seven stars). In Hinduism, there are seven higher worlds and seven underworlds, and in both Islam and Judaism, there are seven heavens. There are seven doors that the Babylonian goddess Ištar passes through – divesting herself of a garment at each one – when she visits the Netherworld; seven had a central place in Mithraism; we are enjoined to "Forgive seventy times seven"; and in the biblical Psalm 12 "the word of the Lord is pure, purified silver, purified seven times".

In Confucianism, seven represents harmony (yin, yang, plus the five Confucian elements), while in numerology, seven is associated with Athena, the Greek goddess of wisdom. People associated with seven are said to be especially intellectual, insightful, intuitive, and wise, likely to be gifted teachers and healers, noted for creativity and intuition. The concept of seven is common in religious contexts. In the Seven Pillars of Wisdom, 70 is the prescribed age of a human, Maya, believed to be in a seven-layered sky; the idea of a "sevenfold path" recurs constantly in religions; and in the Arabic proverb, there are seven things of which one never gets too much:

> Bread offered in kindness, meat of lamb, cool water, soft garments, beautiful fragrance, comfortable bed, and the view of everything that is beautiful.

These examples are only the start.

In Judaism, there are seven segments of the weekly readings of the Torah, a wedding's seven blessings, and the seven-branched holy candelabrum. In the scriptures, there are seven archangels, seven things that are detestable to God, seven pillars of the House of Wisdom, and, in Jericho, seven circumlocutions and seven trumpets played by seven priests for seven days were needed to make the walls fall down.

Within the Christian tradition, it is similar. In the miraculous feeding of the multitude in the New Testament: seven small pieces of food became seven baskets full of leftovers, there were the "seven last sayings" of Jesus on the cross, seven seals in the Book of Revelation, seven "Gifts of the Holy Spirit", seven virtues, the "Seven Joys and Seven Sorrows of the Virgin Mary", and seven sacraments. The Bible is full of the number seven, mentioned nearly 500 times and associated with the idea of divine perfection.

References to seven in Islamic tradition include the seven heavens, the seven doors to hell, the seven circumambulations of the Kaaba in Mecca by Muslim pilgrims, Muhammad's seven children, and the seventh day naming ceremony for babies. Hindus speak of the seven worlds in the universe, the seven sages, the seven stars of Indian astrology, and the seven wedding promises, while Buddhists recall the seven miraculous steps taken by the Buddha at birth. In ancient Egypt, there were seven paths to heaven, seven sacred cows, and seven halls of the underworld. The number seven was the fundamental number of the Rosicrucians, and was central in Mithraism whose adherents spoke of the soul rising to paradise through seven planetary spheres.

In the Indian Vedas, Agni, the god of fire, has seven wives, mothers, or sisters and can produce seven flames. The sun god has seven horses to pull his heavenly chariot. In the *Rigveda* there are seven parts of the world, seven seasons, and seven heavenly fortresses.

It extends to medicine too. In Hippocratic medicine, the number seven rules over the body, painful illnesses last 7, 14, or 21 days, and there is an extreme folk belief that a fever should be treated by taking seven prickles from seven palm trees, seven chips from seven beams, seven nails from seven bridges, seven ashes from seven ovens, and finally seven hairs from an old dog's beard.

Seven is a key number in myths and folklore, as well as in fiction, generally. Again and again we hear of seven princesses, seven brothers, seven dwarfs, seven swans, the seven nymphs (stars) of the Pleiades constellation, seven Greek warriors, and more, while the seventh son, or even more extremely, the seventh son of a seventh son, has magical powers, both good and bad. In Greek mythology, Athens had to send a tribute of seven youths and seven maidens to Crete to be devoured by the Minotaur.

Shakespeare wrote of the seven ages of man. In China, seven represents the stages of female life and the related phases of the Moon ($4 \times 7 = 28$ days in a month). Early cultures recognised seven "planets" or "wandering bodies" (Sun, Moon, Mercury, Venus, Mars, Jupiter, and Saturn). Sad or happy, once "seven" of anything is mentioned, you suspect that you may be in the land of fairy and myth.

Book titles with "seven" in them make us sit up in the way a composite abstract noun would not. There is something appealing, personal, immediate, and somehow do-able about a book with a title such as "seven things to avoid if you …", "seven tricks of the trade", "seven paths to success" that could never be said of a work covering the same ground but titled, say, "An introduction to …". It applies to fiction too in titles (imaginary so far as I know) such as 'the seventh bride", "Adam's seven years", "even winter nights". A scrutiny of Amazon entries or library catalogues brings up scores of books with "seven" in the title.

It comes in scientific work too. Consider the "seven colours" of the rainbow. In fact, the colours shade into each other, it is simply that scientists at some ancient time chose that number to distinguish them, and human culture, being as it is, what but seven? On the same principle, we delineate seven notes to differentiate the musical continuity of the classical scale (it could have been any number, really, but seven must have felt the appropriate number to those early musicologists who set this up). It feels right that there are seven seas, seven continents, seven dwarfs. We are pattern-matching beings, and the number seven is there in our minds for our use – and the more often it is used, as it has been for millennia, the more ready we are to turn to it.

Similarly we may know, at least vaguely, that the key sins in Christianity are pride, greed, wrath, envy, lust, gluttony, and sloth; in Islam they are shirking responsibility, witchcraft, usury, disrespect of parents, fornication, unjust accusation against women, and unjust murder. These, sound bad enough when listed separately, but joined as the "seven deadly sins", they have even deadlier emotional force. As Kohli says (2023) "it is as if the universe is saying, 'Hey, seven is the golden ticket to awesomeness!'".

It is hard to really justify or explain, but in each case, seven somehow feels the fitting perfect number. Seven items are easier to absorb and recall than eight. A list of seven is interesting, it sticks in our mind and ears. "Six deadly sins" or "two wonders of the world" might be equally good enumerations, but just wouldn't attract our interest: there's nothing echoing or emotional to make us sit up. It needs a special number – seven in fact – to make us remember them or think there was anything deep about the list. But with "seven" it would be memorable.

Really, when you count it up (and the above is very far from all), the number of times seven takes a leading part seems almost incredible. There must be something deeply expressive and ineradicable between humans and that number, clearly an effective force in human communicating.

Why? There have been attempts to explain it in terms of its mathematical properties. But it seems we just have to accept that we don't know how or where it began. Let's stick with seven, the key to a magical domain.[1]

Three

The number three resonates even more strongly. It is as if it is somehow built into the deep nature of the universe and of human lives – the unifying number, the number of synthesis and completion.

> The eldest of odds, God's number properly
> Heaven's dearest number, whose inclosed centrepiece
> doth equally from both extremes extend,
> the first that hath a beginning, midst, and end.

(Du Bartas 1578, English translation)

Hegel envisaged three modes of being, *Dante's Divine* comedy was in three parts, and Christ spoke of "the way, the truth, and the life".

Three is a sign of something special, not so much, as with seven, of mystery or magic but of a thing or state that is somehow complete and fulfilled, having, in its threeness, reached a kind of existential unity. The golden rule of three comes in tale after tale – the three little pigs, three

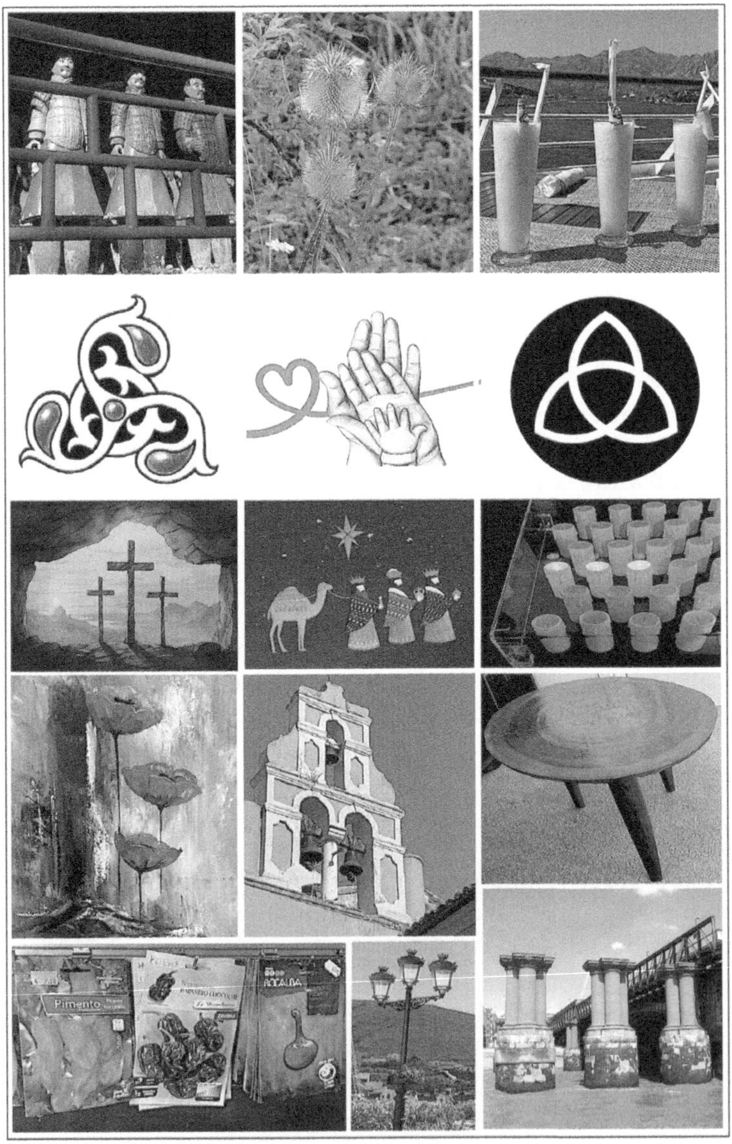

FIGURE 5.3 Threes.

wishes, three guesses, three bears, three little kittens that lost their mittens, and three billy goats gruff. In epic too: at the dramatic climax of the *Odyssey*, Odysseus's son, Telemachus, tries three times to string his father's bow, three times he fails. Twice would have conveyed the impression that he wasn't trying hard enough, four would have seemed too long drawn out, but three times tells us that he tried *just the right amount* and then withdrew so the story could move on.

Three is the smallest number we need to create a pattern or an enclosed, perfected diagram. It is a principle captured in the Latin phrase *omne trium perfectum*: everything that comes in threes is perfect, every set of three is complete.

Because three is the number of completion, it is closely associated with many religions as a divine number that represents our connection to the spiritual realm. In the Bible, words and phrases repeated three times convey the idea of significant spiritual meaning, and at the heart of Christianity is the threefold Trinity, "three in One, One in Three" where, above all, the number three represents completeness, wholeness, resurrection, and harmony.

This is only a small part of the constantly recurring threes: the three fates, the three graces, the three Shakespearean witches, and the three tests, tasks, and attempts that the heroes of fairy tales have to meet, paralleling Christ's three temptations in the wilderness, the three crosses of Golgotha, the three queries to Peter. There are three parts of the soul, the birth-life-death cycle; Freud's theory of the Conscious, the Subconscious, and the Id; the mind-body-spirit triad; and the three levels of heaven, earth, and hell or, equally threefold, heaven, purgatory, and hell. A priest makes the sign of the cross three times at certain points in a service – here, again, the threefoldness feels satisfying and right – complete. Every Christmas, we remember the three kings from the east. Three is a recurrent theme in religious contexts; its presence, as suggested by the ancient Greek philosopher Pythagoras, is because three is "the perfect number", the number of harmony, wisdom, and understanding.

The ritual repetition of "Holy, Holy, Holy Lord", comes not once. not twice. but three times (where four. which on the face of it might seem to be better, just wouldn't convey the fullness of the achievement), and there is a satisfying feeling of completion in the Hindu and Islamic threefold repetition of blessings and prayers.

The Lord bless you and keep you,
The Lord make his face to shine upon you and be gracious unto you
The Lord lift up his countenance upon you and give you peace

It is a great signal in advertising too. I often hear the rhythmically enhanced radio boast

> We're not usually ones to blow our own trumpet,
> But when we're not just,
> Once (trumpet blast),
> But twice (trumpet blast),
> But THREE times (trumpet blast),
> *the* insurance of the year, we can't resist!
>
> *(from a radio advert, 2024)*

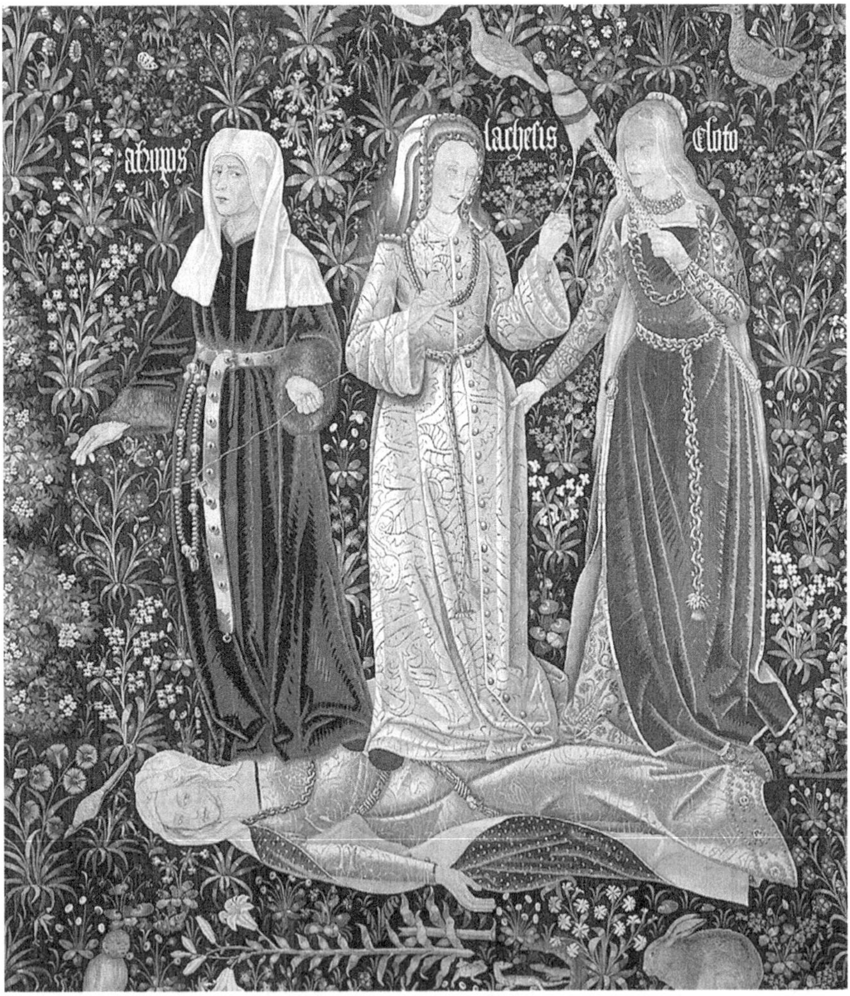

FIGURE 5.4 The three fates.

Then there is “the epic rule of three” pointed out by Olrik (1909) and the way three runs through Greek and Roman literature. The early Irish “triads” are rooted in the idea of threeness. They come, succinctly, in the names of places, but also in longer, more poetic, forms – some uplifting, some a wry comment on human ways, such as

- Three things that constitute a carpenter: joining together without calculating and without warping; agility with the compass; a well-measured stroke.
- Three things that constitute a physician: a complete cure, leaving no blemish behind, a painless examination.
- Three things that constitute a harper: a tune to make you cry, a tune to make you laugh, a tune to put you to sleep.

and

Three smiles that are worse than sorrow:

- the smile of the snow as it melts,
- the smile of your wife on you after another man has been with her,
- the grin of a hound ready to leap at you.

Similar triads come in Eastern religions and in sayings, such as Muhammad’s

The three best things:

- to be humble amidst the vicissitudes of fortune;
- to pardon when powerful;
- and to be generous with no strings attached.

and

What actions are most excellent?

- to gladden the heart of a human being,
- to feed the hungry, to help the afflicted,
- to lighten the sorrow of the sorrowful and remove the wrongs of the injured.

Not just in the past – I well remember a local taxi driver, an immigrant, asking me as I was about to alight: “What are the three most important things? His answer:

- The sun – it shines equally on all, whatever religion we call ourselves.
- The river – we all drink from it, whatever religion we call ourselves.
- The earth – we all tread on it whatever religion we call ourselves.

Those embarking on speechmaking are told to say things three times to make best use of the communicative resonance of threefold repetition. The principles have remained the same from (and, no doubt, before) the Roman Quintilian's expertise in oratory with his threefold advice that "skill in speaking is perfected by nature, art and practice"; threes run through Churchill's and Obama's speeches, and we all know, and copy, the threefold ring of Shakespeare's "Friends, Romans, countrymen, lend me your ears" and Martin Luther King's resounding

I have a dream that one day
every hill shall be exalted and every mountain shall be made low,
the rough places will be made plain and the crooked places will be made straight
and the glory of the Lord shall be revealed.

There is now parallel popular song that somehow, naturally, comes out as three stanzas, with many internal threesome lines and phrases:

I have a dream for all humanity
That we may know truth and dignity
That peace of earth becomes reality
And that one day we'll stand arm in arm, hand in hand
I have a dream.

Yes, I have a dream.
A dream for all the people in the world.
That peace, hope and freedom shall ring.
Yes, I have a dream …

It is not just in ancient or high-culture settings that three resonates. We shout "Hip, hip, hip hooray", sing "Happy birthday" three times (it *has* to be that to be properly executed), we learn our "ABCs", a keyboard (naturally, it seems) has three horizontal rows, a telephone three vertical ones. Why did all these happen to feel just right? True, threes may be the simplest for our eyes to take in, our ears to hear, but why, then, are we born like that?

We know that political parties come in right, left, and centre; a wedding is not complete without a promise of "to love, honour, and obey"; grammar divides words into good, better, and best and masculine, feminine, and neuter; clothes are large, medium, and small; music is played fast, slow, or moderato; and, worldwide, our devices are set to deliver the apparently eternal truths of low, medium, or high. Threesome parallels come in quips such as Keith Richard's "You have the sun, you have the moon, you have the air that you breathe – and you have the Rolling

Stones!" and The Commodores' "You're once, twice, three times a lady". We are "Cribbed, cabined, and confined", comedians work up our suspense till we reach the joke-words, and we hear something like

> First is worst Second the same
> But third is the best of all the game

or the great threesome advice

> Be good
> If you can't be good be careful
> If you can't be careful, have fun.

Aristotle famously pointed to the threefold nature of any complete work of art: beginning, middle, and end (the "poetic" in his title is usually taken to refer only to literary art but, though Aristotle takes his examples from there, "poetics" is actually a translation of the Greek word *poesis*, which literally means "making" or "creation", and can be taken to refer to any work of art). He is right. Many musical works are divided into three movements, and we would feel them incomplete with two; indeed, a piece of beautiful music by Schubert is described as "unfinished" because it has two not three movements. At classical Greek drama festivals, three tragedies were performed, and the first bit of advice in the myriad courses on film script writing is that all screenplays must fall into three acts if they are to be considered in any way professional. I also see, to my surprise, that at emotional points in my writing, I in some way fall into threesome wording (it just comes naturally without thinking). Indeed, so deeply is this somehow inbuilt *need* of a triadic structure that we subliminally expect any work of art to fall within it.

It is here all around us.[2]

Anything to do with *three*. in fact, communicates something to us, in deep if mostly hidden ways.[3]

Three and seven carry the greatest weight, but larger numbers can play a part too. Ten communicates the idea of ordered and commanded completeness – the satisfying conclusion. A story can end when some series eventually adds up to a hundred, while a mention of thousands or millions carries an idea of fantastic exaggeration and extravagance.[4]

Numbers "ring bells" for us, as it were, especially seven and, above all, three. Their overtones and associations, whether in story or symbolism or everyday life, carry messages beyond just a matter of quantity that communicate and convey ideas that, though they are, indeed, mostly below the level of consciousness, communicate to us. We are born, it seems, with *numbers* deeply ingrained in ourselves or, somehow, imbibed from our forebears; yet another way in which we are affected by and affect others through ever mysterious associations.

The secret messages of colour

Colour may seem an unexpected topic in this context. It surprised me too when I stumbled on the extensive work the topic. Though at first sight seemingly remote from the subject of this book, however, colours, even more directly than numbers, play a definite role in communicating.

Some would say that colours are only a trick of the light or of the way our eyes are physiologically constructed. But to us, as humans, as people, they are real enough, something with which we actively engage every day. They are used to send signals in an overt way in, for example, red underlining when correcting a script ("wrong") or black worn as a sign of mourning. The Ghanaian visual artist Joseph Awuah-Darko deliberately uses colours to cope with his bipolar condition "I'm a visual learner and I thought 'Why don't I use colour as a language?'", he says, for "the things that I can't really capture in words …. an interesting way of monitoring my life" (Dale 2024). So, he expresses his feelings at a given time through colour, red being the most depressed, blue the most positive. Colour was one of the deliberately signifying elements in the information stored in the Andean South American *quipu* devices, while in the Ersu Shaba divination pictographic script in China, colour affected the meaning:

> Writing is done with a bamboo brush or animal hair dipped in white, black, red, blue, green, and yellow-coloured ink. The colour chosen may affect the meaning. For example, the glyph "stars and moon" written in black means "dim", but written in white it means "hining".
> *(Sun 2009: 165)*

But there are hidden, less consciously noticed ways too, more influential than we mostly realise. Not that this is a simple subject. There are an infinite number of colours, and they shade into each other. Furthermore, colours are differently identified and distinguished in different languages and cultures. Classical Greeks, for example, saw the sea not as "blue", but as green or deep red – "wine-dark" as Homer called it – Akkadian doesn't seem to distinguish between yellow and green, and a number of languages do not have different words for blue and green. For the changing fashions around specific colours, you only have to look at the history of art and of personal attire during the centuries. It is people rather than nature that make colour and give it meaning – meanings that, like sunlight on a landscape, are constantly changing.

For all that, it is a remarkable fact that specific colours do tend to have particular associations throughout the world and throughout history. Without our fully realising it, they communicate certain impressions. For despite all the real variations in the associations of particular colours at different times and places, these, to a quite surprising extent, *do* tend go across cultures and eras.

The fast-developing discipline of the psychology of colour is drawing attention to the scientific evidence about the effects on colour and the way it can be a powerful communication tool to signal action, influence mood, and even shape physiological reactions. Sometimes, colours are used in deliberate communication. Football fans wear colours to match their chosen teams, people from Ireland wear green shamrocks on Saint Patrick's Day, the colours of the crosses in the Union Jack flag signify the union of the nations that make up the United Kingdom, and in the Irish flag, with its orange or gold for the north, green for the south, white signifies "the peace between them". More explicitly, in today's Russia, wearing blue and yellow shoes or dyeing your hair blue and yellow are punishable offences because this is seen as deliberately using the colours of the Ukrainian flag to communicate a political position and, hence, spread disinformation as part of the anti-war movement. And why else do organisers so often choose to carpet care homes in mauve or soft turquoise if not because they know the calming effects of these colours?

The human use of colour was started, as far as we can see, by people making outlines with charcoal and filling them with colours. More than 42,000 years ago, human painters were using the three elemental colours of black, white, and red, a chromatic triad that predominated through most of human history. These colours are still with us and still central in art and symbolism. The continuity from those early colourists is striking: why would we try to cut ourselves off from our earlier historical foundations?

And then again, where would we humans be without the symbolism and historical development of colours and colouring? We depend on colours not just for the beauty of art or as intellectual or spiritual symbols – important enough – but also for information: think of red as the widely understood signal for danger or white for a truce or a surrender.

There is something familiar, even something to be taken for granted without conscious thought, in the following associations.

- Red: energy, passion, anger, danger
- Orange: excitement, pleasure, abundance
- Yellow: joy, happiness, communication
- Pink: love and tenderness, innocence, optimism
- Green: balance, serenity, nature
- Blue: spirituality, serenity, peace
- Purple: relaxation, imagination, calmness
- Brown: comfort, resilience, security
- Gray: comfort, maturity, calmness

- White: peace, innocence, inoffensiveness, simplicity
- Black: power, strength, evil, negativity

Why should that be?

It is a puzzle, but something is obviously going on in these very common associations. We cannot tell if they arise from some event or action in the past, a build up of a series of coincidences, or even from some intrinsic, natural association. All we can tell is that given these associations, colouring is seemingly something not just of recreational or calming import but, perhaps, in some way, something of cosmic and age-old significance and, at the same time, something that, mostly without realising it, we take account of every day.

Our feelings about them go deep too and are simple, for, as will emerge, the associations of these colours, though mostly positive, also – some more than others – have a negative side. The idea of strong, blunt power at the root of black can lead, as it were, downward to evil, sin, the devil, but also up into the strength of law and authority. Red, on the other hand, is associated with energetic active force, the flaming of fire, love, or passion but also the active barring of the way, the shout of "danger", "stop". In the associations of some colours, one or the other may predominate (white is mostly positive for instance, though in a quiet rather than energetic way), but we always need to be alert to the possibility of an apparent opposite – a kind of complementary subtle balancing – in these associations. Perhaps this reflects the ambiguities of human nature and the way that every light has a shadow, every cloud its silver lining. There can be two sides to any virtue, reminding us of the classic Greek ideal of μηδὲν ἄγαν, "nothing in excess".

I will look at six of these colours in a little more detail (there is not space for all of them or for a deeper discussion, but the end note references list some excellent further sources).

We start where, as it seems, human artistic history did, with the chromatic trio of black, red, and white – a combination that for millennia underlay the human conceptualisation and enactment of colour.

The colour black

Black, linguists tell us, is one of the oldest words and one of the first colours used by the primate animals we know as humans. Burnt material such as charcoal was already to hand in early times to enable people to make marks on an inviting cave wall, probably first for drawing lines and demarcating spaces rather than a colour in the present sense of the term.

We see these black lines in the drawings of bulls and other animals by early artists. And then, on through centuries and in many different art forms, the colour black, later from a variety of sources, was used for delineating and completing human-made pictures on rock, pottery (think of the famous Greek black-figure designs), skin, cloth, silk, paper, screens, and more.

As well as its usefulness for artistic and practical purposes, black has many symbolic associations, especially with something hidden, mysterious, dramatic, and, for the most part, strongly negative. For us, it is connected to funerals, in ancient Egypt, it was part of the underworld: Anubis, its god, was pictured as a black jackal while, for the Greeks, the kingdom of death was separated from the living by the black river Styx. For centuries, it has been the colour of mourning and associated with death, evil, and witchcraft. The Latin word for black, *ater* (the root of the English words "atrocious" and "atrocity") was linked to cruelty, brutality, and evil, and in the Middle Ages, black was associated with darkness and evil. In the seventeenth century, the devil was said to appear at midnight to conduct a "Black Mass". In today's popular culture, black communicates an idea of evil or darkness and is the traditional colour of witchcraft and "black magic"; in literature and films, vampires – anti-humans – wear black and are creatures of the night. Black is thought of as the typical colour of the industrial revolution when the buildings of large cities were turned black by coal smoke; by the mid-nineteenth century, England's industrial area had become "the Black Country". In all, the colour black stands for negativity, darkness, wickedness, Lucifer, Hades, the blackness of sin, of night, and of the lack of light – in short, hell and the devil.

Like other concepts with a strong impact, the symbolism of black is complex, however, and its link with strength and power comes out in positive contexts too, sometimes, therefore, standing for opposed ideas: both authority *and* humility, sin *and* its repudiation, rebellion *and* conformity, good *and* bad. In this way, it has been a favoured colour among both priests and penitents, artists and ascetics, fashion designers and fascists. Certain skin shades were long described as "black"; for centuries, a deeply pejorative term has now been turned around and celebrated in such phrases as "Black is beautiful" and "Black History Month".

Black and white have often been metaphorically used to describe opposites such as good and evil, the Dark Ages versus the Age of Enlightenment, night versus day. In earlier years, aristocrats and the powerful wore bright colours, but since the Middle Ages, black has been the colour of solemnity, power, and authority. Court officials' black robes signified the authority of the king, those of the clergy represented the law of God and the rule of the church. Wearing black was encouraged during the Reformation and the "sin and luxury" of the traditional church's bright colours was denounced.

Black – sign of authority and objectivity – is a typical colour for uniforms, especially for police forces. It is commonly worn by judges and magistrates and the expected attire on solemn occasions from graduations or funerals to formal balls. It is the colour of official cars and of formal business dress and fashion ("the little black dress"). In fabrics, in painting, and in art, generally, black has been an ambivalent but forceful communicator of social, symbolic, and ideological meaning.

The idea of the contrast between black and white is especially effective for signifying opposites, as in a black-and-white argument, light as against darkness, good against evil. In the Middle Ages, the white knight represented virtue, the black knight something threatening and sinister. The same today – in westerns, viewers know the hero by his white hat, the villain by his black one. Black is associated with secrecy as against openness (think of "black ops"– covert acts or the "black (underground) economy") and with bad magic ("the black arts"), violence, and evil.

Black can also convey positive ideas. Devices such as telephones, wirelesses, sewing machines, steamships, trains, and early cars, such as the famous one-colour only Fords, were painted black to signify their functional roles. Black has also been the main colour of ink, clear and bold on a white page, the easiest colour to read and strikingly displayed in the black letter print of the fifteenth century Gutenberg Bible. A new kind of printer's ink, made from soot and walnut oil, made it possible to spread ideas to a mass audience through printed books and to popularise art through black and white engravings. Because of its contrast and clarity, black ink on a white surface became the standard mode for printed books, newspapers, and documents; similarly, black text on a white background is the commonest form on computer screens. The idea of black ink is also used to represent the metaphorical eternity of a love formulated and, through this, made everlasting in writing, as in Shakespeare's famous line:

> "And in black ink my love will still shine bright".

So, the power of the colour black has literary, symbolic and ambivalent as well as age-long visual-art repercussions –above all a marker of strength and boundedness.

The colour red

Red is the most visible and eye-catching of all the colours and, as such, has a long history in human culture. In a sense, it is the colour; in several languages, the words for "red" and for "colour" are the same, its precise meaning distinguished only by context (such as the Spanish *colorado*). In books about colour, red regularly comes first, and because its molecules are densely packed, it creates friction and everywhere commands attention.

Red, then, was the first true *colour* – the colour of colours. It was common in prehistoric cave paintings to complement the lines of black to convey the body of some great conquered animal. At first it came from ochre and iron oxide; later, as the popularity of red continued, from additional sources such as cochineal, a vivid scarlet dye made from insects by the Aztecs and others, and the plant-based red dye from the roots of madder, plus, more recently, from chemically based pigments.

As a highly attention-calling colour, red has been used for a multiplicity of purposes – artistic, symbolic, functional, even, judging from the vial of deep red lip-paint found in an Iranian grave from 5,000 years ago, cosmetic. Ancient Egyptians and Mayans coloured their faces red in ceremonies; Roman generals painted their bodies red to celebrate victories, and red was the colour of the Roman god of war (the planet Mars was named for him because of its red colour); it was also the colour associated with the Roman army: its banner was red with gold lettering. The colour went on to be used by mediaeval European rulers as a symbol of majesty and might, with *red* the colour to be flaunted in the clothes and accoutrements of the powerful. Red had a marked religious significance through the Middle Ages: the colour not only of the blood of Christ and the fires of Hell, but of the flamboyant glorifying church, still visible in cardinals robes. In Renaissance art, red colours drew attention to the most important figures in a painting, while in the nineteenth century, proponents of the new movements of socialism or communism used red to stir attention, as in the song "the people's flag is deepest red" and the red flags of the Soviet Union and China.

It is everywhere the colour of blood. This is its fundamental association, built on in myriad ways. In clothes, it says "look at me!" and, as in the army "Red Coats", suggests energy and action. Its healing associations bring this out too: red is good for anaemia and bad circulation (remember the red of blood) and for those with poor libido or energy.

Because it is the colour that brings the strongest and most immediate reaction, it is commonly the colour for urgent warnings; it is the internationally recognised colour of fire engines and stop signs; the idea of "Red for danger" is engrained in us all. It is the elemental colour of blood, fire, and molten iron. Standing out from its surroundings, red comes in more than three quarters of national flags and in countless emblems and adverts, drawing our eyes through its striking and highly visible presence.

It is also, in some contexts, used to signify love and joy. In many Asian countries, it is worn at weddings as the colour of happiness and good fortune. In China and Japan, it was traditionally seen as the colour that could actively fight evil and disease, and the gates of temples were painted red.

It has a dark side too, and red is the colour most frequently associated with hatred, anger – "seeing red" – aggression, and provocation, as in "a red rag to a bull"; sins are described as "scarlet" and criminals as caught "red-handed". It is associated with anger, lust, energy, war, passion, murder, power, and aggression and is the traditional colour of heat, warning, and danger. A red flag on the battlefield or a red flag hoisted by a pirate ship meant there would be no mercy; in the early days of motor cars, a man with a red flag had to walk in front to warn horse-drawn vehicles of the approaching danger; while in football, a player flagrantly breaking the rules is given a red penalty card and sent off. It has overtones of seduction, sex, immorality, lust (as in "the scarlet woman"). In seventeenth-century New England, red was the colour for adultery; prostitutes have, at times, been required to wear red, and a red light signifies a brothel in a "red-light district".

Red in nature has two sides to it too.

> Red toadstools, red ladybirds, red poppies are dangerous to eat but red tomatoes, red strawberries and apples are good. The open mouth of the aggressive monkey is threatening, the red bottom of a sexual receptive female is appealing. The flushed cheeks of a man or woman may indicate anger but they may equally indicate pleasure. The colour red of itself can do more than alert the viewer, preparing him to receive a potentially important message; the content of message can be interpreted only when the context of the redness is defined. (Humphrey 1984: 152)

Perhaps the evolutionary significance of the red has somehow seeped into our subconscious, alerting us whenever we see the colour.

Its wide range of associations and uses at first seems contradictory. But beneath them, all runs the continuing characteristic of red as a colour with active and positive force. There is nothing neutral or apologetic about the true red (as distinct from more muted pink or mauve shades). Above all, it is the strongest of colours.

The colour white

White was the other very early colour used in human art. Many thousands of years back, artists were using white made from calcite or chalk in cave paintings of animals, sometimes as background, to highlight, or to divide space. From that early start, though without the strong force of black or red, white has continued to have an important role in colouring.

Like black, it was, at first, not really a *colour* but, rather, an *absence* of colour, keeping a space between other colours. When it started to be used more deliberately, as paint, it became, as it were, visible to human eyes as a colour and was, thus, able to actively function as a medium of communication and art. True, this was, and is, mostly below the level of explicit consciousness but, as with other colours, that does not mean it is any less powerful.

White is the least visible and least attention-demanding hue – defined, it might seem, by absence. But it is actually, in some ways, the most complex colour of all. Think of a spinning top with wedges of the seven colours of the rainbow on it; when it spins fast, the colours become a single white – a colour that is, therefore, in a way, all the colours, a form of light. It may seem negative, but it makes its presence felt by bringing out the neighbouring colour(s) by its contrast as well as somehow making small spaces seem significant and by its decluttering effect on the whole.

Though it can, in one way, be viewed as negative, it generally has very positive associations. It has, for millennia, been connected with ideas of purity health, beauty, innocence, and peace. In the past, priests and priestesses have worn white, white garments were worn to protect against the plague, a white flag signals an end to fighting, and the commonest colour of a wedding dress is white – a symbol of the bride's purity and innocence. White is the colour of milk, our earliest experience, and one of the four sacred substances in the Talmud; the ancient Greeks saw white as a fundamental colour in a world made of light and darkness; for the Christian church, white garments symbolised purity, sacrifice, and virtue; and the white dove brought peace to a warring and threatened world and regeneration after the flood. A white lamb became the symbol of the sacrifice of Christ; the (mythical) white unicorn is a sign of purity; white is the spiritually imbued colour we imagine for angels and for haloes. and during the transfiguration, it is fitting that Jesus's clothes shone "exceeding white as snow".

Overall, white is imbued with the symbolism of purity, innocence, and lack of sin, often just through unthinking but, nevertheless, richly meaningful tradition, but also, at times, it is consciously chosen: for flags, for jewellery (pearls above all), and in the attire traditionally worn by nurses, the pope, and many pilgrims and religious orders. In pictures, religious leaders, saints, priests, angels, and missionaries are clad in white. White (not red) poppies were worn by members of the twentieth-century Peace Movement, an example of the use of a meaningful colour to convey an idea in a visual, materialised form.

White has, it would seem, fewer negative associations than other colours. On the other hand, white, being non-pushy and opposite to the powerful strength of black, is on the feeble, fainter side of neutrality and innocence, sometimes scarcely *there* at all – just a kind of empty space between black or red lines. It is somehow paradoxical that the purest and simplest of them all can convey an idea of power*lessness* – its presence somehow conveyed by a non-presence.

The colour blue

Blue is most people's favourite colour. It is common in nature – the blue in the sea or the hue of a clear sky. It is something of a surprise, then, that it was apparently not one of the first colours in visual art. In early human history, there were no accessible sources of blue pigment, and painters on cave walls used black, white, and red ochre. Interestingly, these are also, it seems, the earliest colours to be distinguished in languages – first black and white (dark versus light), followed by red, then the other colours. Blue was late.

Blue has a long history, nevertheless, and, in time, derived from multiple sources, has been important in art and decoration since antiquity. For many centuries, the source was the semi-precious stone lapis lazuli, an important source of blue throughout the ancient near east. It was used to produce the intense colour of Egyptian blue in the third millennium BC, famous in jewellery, art objects, and tomb paintings. An azure sky-like blue was developed in China in the eighth century AD and used, among other things, to decorate their delicate blue and white porcelain. It came from cobalt imported from Persia and was a scarce ingredient, even in China. Its availability in Europe was even more limited, as it had to be brought across long trade routes from the East, so it was immensely expensive and was used only for high art such as stained glass windows and religious pictures, unlike now when this lovely colour is as cheaply and easily available as any other colour.

"Prussian blue", a darker hue, was developed in the early eighteenth century and became popular for wallpaper and among French impressionist and Japanese painters such as Hokusai. It became a common colour for military uniforms and, in the later twentieth century, for business suits. Plant-based sources were also drawn on, and for centuries, Europeans wore clothing coloured by a dye from the leaves of the cabbage-like plant *woad*. Later, this was replaced by the finer indigo dye from America, also plant-based. Since the nineteenth century, though still greatly valued, blue has, as with other colours, become cheaper and more easily obtained with the move away from organic and mineral sources to synthetic dyes and pigments.

Blue evokes many reactions and has had an important role worldwide in both art and utility. In political contexts, it conveys the idea of conservatism and authority. It is predominantly associated with calmness and serenity – a calmness that does not, as with green, reside in a process of growing but, rather, in an unproblematic, settled, state of calmness. It is associated with the throat *chakra* (an originally Sanskrit word meaning the point of energy in the body), the site of self-expression and the art of communication. It conveys emotional sensitivity, inspiration, mysticism, and the reaching out of intellectual consciousness into the spiritual. As a "cool" colour, it is thought good for soothing fever, inflammation, and pain.

Connected with this, blue conveys the idea of holiness in church decorations, seen in the virgin Mary's robes in paintings and stained glass windows, and in art, with connotations of spirituality and peace. It has also come to be seen as a colour of royalty and aristocracy (as in "blue blood"). It appears in willow-pattern china, in many flags and uniforms, and in images of the earth as viewed from space as well as in more mundane associations with "blue-collar-workers", and, of course, in the ubiquitous blue jeans of today. Its associations with peace and harmony are reflected in the blue flags of the United Nations.

Like all colours, it can also convey negative vibes. The ancient Greeks saw it as barbarous, while the early Britons used woad to paint their faces to frighten their enemies with their terrifying blue look. Even now, we associate "blue" with being depressed and down, as in "blue Wednesday", "feeling blue", "having the blues", and (the other side of its evocations of infinity and distance) the "blue with cold", and "the blues" are songs of mournfulness and lament.

Overall, however, blue is a clear favourite throughout the world and remains the colour most commonly associated with harmony, knowledge, intelligence, calm, the imagination, spirituality, and infinity.

The colour green

Close to home, the colour green is common in art, clothes, literature, religion, science, politics, and everyday life. It was not one of the prehistoric cave colours but still has a long history. The ancient Egyptians used green earth and malachite, while, later, the Greeks used verdigris. Green pigments were difficult to produce and even harder to fix, so though green has, up to a point, been featured over the centuries – in jewellery, for example, or the grass in paintings – it was possible by advances in producing green pigments.

Even more than other colours, green has outstandingly strong symbolic associations, though, as for other colours, the precise import of this has varied. Mostly, it is a symbol of life, luck, and hope, but also, sometimes, of jealousy, disorder, lack of experience, and even the devil. Not surprisingly, it has been associated with all that is changeable and fleeting: childhood, love, and money and represents new beginnings, growth, and, with it, at times, abundance.

Today, green has mainly positive connections. It is associated with fairies, spirits, and magic, sometimes dangerous but mostly good. Dragons are often seen as green, and green is the colour of the widely found magical and spiritual "green man" images and of Irish leprechauns' clothing. It is the traditional colour of Islam, with its literal meaning of "peace". According to tradition, the robe and banner of Muhammad were green, and those in paradise wear green silk robes and recline on green silk embroidered cushions. Muhammad is quoted as saying that "water, greenery, and a beautiful face" were three universally good things. Al-Khidr, "the Green One", given that name because of his role as a diplomat and negotiator, was an important Koranic figure who was said to have met and travelled with Moses.

On similar lines, green can indicate that it is safe to proceed with something, as in traffic lights or the green tick on a computer screen, and a green light signals that a system is turned on and working as it should; in many video games, green, opposed to red, signifies both health and completed objectives. In contrast to the associations of red with heat and action, and blue with cold and withdrawal, green is the colour of positive neutrality and calm. Due to its connection with "nature" (always imagined as green), it evokes feelings of revival, freshness, vitality, and peace. It aids relaxation and links to environments that are peaceful and nurturing.

Overall, green is felt as soothing, an aid to calmness, concentration, and natural health; a green cross is the internationally recognised sign of a pharmacy. From biblical times, and perhaps before, the phrase "green pastures" communicates a feeling of calm, spiritual fulfilment, and being in the care of a loving shepherd.

In recent years, green has become the inspiring, everywhere understood, symbol of the mission to value nature and save the planet, above all, in the name and symbolism of the "Green Movement". It is the colour of political parties organised around environmentalism, chosen for its association with nature, health, non-violence, social justice, and democracy. Greenpeace, for example, is an environmental organisation that emerged from the anti-nuclear and pro-peace movements in the 1970s and now has branches in many countries. Many cities have a designated garden or park as a "green space", with green trash bins and containers, and aspire to be known as "green cities", close to nature, with green grass as its symbol. In China, green is associated with the east, with sunrise, and with life and growth. Some people have especially close links with green as being expert gardeners with "green fingers" or a "green thumb" – those for whom, like my mother, plants, however apparently carelessly just "dibbled in", always grew.

In earlier centuries, however, and in some contexts still, green has had bad associations. It was associated with jealousy ("green-eyed monster"), the seed that, like a plant, grows unseen beneath the surface. It can also – the other side of youth – suggest inexperience or ignorance, as in "still green" or "a greenhorn" (usually said tolerantly, however). For some, its verdant brightness is too overwhelming, and it is thought to bring bad luck. The serpent that caused the downfall of Adam and Eve in the Garden of Eden was green; in ancient China, prostitutes were called "the family of the green lantern", and a prostitute's family should wear a green headscarf; in Victorian England, green was associated with (despised) homosexuality. Green is often associated with toxicity, poison, and sickness, as in "feeling green" or "green at the gills".

Still, for most of us, green communicates hope and springtime, freshness, and greenness and is seen as conveying the faith that things will improve even after a period of difficulty, like the renewal of flowers and plants after the winter season. This is increased as it has strong associations with natural healing. It is the natural colour of the heart *chakra*, connected to heart beats, blood, breathing, and natural immunity as well as, at a spiritual level, to an individual's life's purpose, emotional stability, and soul. Green helps to restore balance and natural healing, linked to the natural, universal, and non-artificial arts of gentle song and dance. Above all, it tells us of the growing vitality found in nature.

The colour yellow

The appreciation of yellow as a distinct colour goes a ways back. Its first literary mentions are from the Neolithic period: "yellow as honey", or "yellow as ripe wheat". It comes in a variety of shades, ranging from sunshine yellow to mellow golden yellow, saffron, and yellow ochre. From the earliest times, it was seen as the colour of the sun. In ancient Egypt, the bodies of the gods were painted in vivid yellow to resemble gold, "the flesh of the sun"; for Aristotle it was one of the basic colour triad of white, yellow, and red; and, recurrent in myth, yellow was the hue of the golden apples of the Hesperides and the priceless Golden Fleece.

Yellow has been derived from various sources. Yellow pigments from richly ochre clay soils were used as early as 45,000 BC for decorating human bodies and the walls of caves. "Indian yellow", created from feeding cows on mango leaves, was the pigment used by mediaeval painters. The resultant colour was turned to many purposes. It stands for hope and joy and is seen in the lithe power of tigers and yellow-spotted leopards and the jauntiness of plants and flowers such as honeysuckle, dandelions, daffodils, and yellow-eyed daisies, all renowned not only for their bright beauty but also for the poetic metaphors in which they often appear.

A beneficial colour and the colour of sunshine and of sunlight at its bright rising and its zenith, yellow brings a smile to the face and conveys the happiness of the bright light of the summer, shot through with youthfulness, newness, and fresh vigour. Also, the colour of gold, it speaks success and accolades. It is the cheerful clothing of clowns and court jesters, and, notably, is the colour of honey and bees. Impressionist and post-impressionist painters used yellow to suggest light, vibrancy, and life. Among his many striking yellow and orange paintings, there is Gaugin's "the Yellow Christ", while Van Gogh, fascinated by the colour, used a riot of yellows in his fields and flowers. As he wrote in 1888, "the sun dazzles me and goes to my head, a sun, a light that I can only call yellow, sulphur yellow, lemon yellow, golden yellow. How lovely yellow is!". Goethe called it "this joyous colour".

Yellow is hope, seen in the colour of ribbons tied to a tree or doors for a loved one kidnapped or in peril; it is also the colour of honeysuckle, dandelions, and primroses and communicates cheerfulness, warmth, and friendliness, conveying ideas of mental clarity and sharpness because of its youthful and eager energy. Consonant with that, it is the colour of the healing that comes from intellectual inspiration and being cured from nervous exhaustion.

Yellow makes people feel spontaneous and happy, carrying associations with fruits such as pineapple, grapefruits, and golden sweetcorn. A splash of yellow on anything dull or dark can make you feel cheerful and optimistic. Symbolised by the sun, it communicates joy, light, and mental positivity and is spiritually embodied by the solar plexus *chakra* – the seat of power and will.

As the colour of happiness, fresh flowers, the spring and summer, fruit growing on trees, the sun shining down on them with a golden glow, it recalls the yellow bees as they fly from flower to flower to return in their secret ways to work together in relays to produce golden honey, like gathering golden words to create poetry – a poetic "anthology" literally means "a collection of flowers". As in the common saying, "busy bees", yellow honeybees have become a symbol of hard committed work:

No bees no honey
No work no money

Yellow is a great communicator in logos and political slogans. It was used with great success by the young political party, the Liberal Democrats, to suggest freshness and vigour in their striking emblem of an eagerly flying yellow bird. As the third most popular shade, yellow is often used in heraldic designs and in flags, with the yellow cross in the Swedish flag emphasising their tradition of Christianity, and was the imperial colour of China. As the most visible colour from a distance, yellow is often used for street signs and for a visual warning, as in life jackets, police cordoning tape, and hazardous areas. It is a colour that stands out, the colour of the lead cyclist's jersey in the Tour de France (a tradition that began in the 1919 race because the race's sponsor, *L' Auto* newspaper was printed on yellow paper). It works as a *between* colour when yellow-orange ("wait" comes between red for stop and green for go), as the daylight brightness between darkness and light, and the contented happiness between ecstasy and despair.

It is also an ambiguous hue, for yellow, like other colours, can be felt as negative as well as positive. The yellow leaves of autumn can convey the beauties of the fall but also the dryness of past-their-season leaves, soon to fall and die, forgotten, on the ground. The sunlight that we need for our sight can be too intense and harm the body or hurt the eyes. We know the bright health of yellow grapefruit and the gold of mature corn, but it is also the colour of *over*-ripe plants. There is the fear of "the yellow peril" from the east, the invaders, the blonde (yellow-haired) Viking attackers. Even more negative, is the yellow of deceit, betrayal, and cowardice: calling someone "yellow" is to insult them as a coward, while the gold of wealth can equally be seen as the filth of "yellow lucre". Yellow's negative side also comes out in yellow fever, bile, urine, rotting vegetation, and yellow jaundice.

In this vein, mediaeval and Renaissance painters used yellow to convey evil and rejection. There was no need to say in words that Judas was a traitor or to search for him in a picture when he was depicted wearing a yellow robe. It was the agreed code for cowardice, bad characters, and outsiders; executioners were painted dressed in yellow. In the Middle Ages, Jews were sometimes made to wear yellow cloth insignias, probably inspiring the star of David the Nazis forced Jews to wear and of the prominent yellow triangles they had to wear in concentration camps. Lunatic asylums were painted yellow in central European countries, and sex workers wore yellow clothing to draw attention to themselves in the dim light of street lamps.

The negative associations became even more prominent from the fourteenth century, as yellow grew to be the colour of jealousy, envy, dishonour, and treason; from the late Middle Ages, yellow was the colour used for the duplicitous and untrustworthy. Similarly, in the medicine of the period, yellow bile was associated with a violent and unstable, lying temperament. So no longer the hue of sun gods and golden harvest corn, yellow became the colour of deception and outsiders. This negative reputation is still with us, evident in in the yellow flag that warns of possible infection and that is flown by ships from foreign port awaiting clearance; opinion polls report that people generally think of yellow as one of the least popular colours.

Against that though, there is still Van Gogh and his sunflowers.

There are many more colours, and blends of colours than those explored above: ultramarine in the sea, the power and majesty of purple, or the magic pinks of dawn. They seem, at first sight, to be irrelevant to communication but yet, unawares for most of us most of the time, can have powerful, hidden, strong effects. As Picasso had it, "Colours, like features, follow the changes of the emotions". And vice versa too.

Finally, it is, at least in part, the reason that the following short poem.[5] is so evocative. Through the art of the pen, and no doubt, at some point, in vocal presentations too, it communicates using few words.

"When the Violin," by Hafiz

When
The violin
Can forgive the past
It starts singing.
When the violin
Can stop worrying about the future
You will become
Such a drunk laughing nuisance
That God
Will then lean down
And start combing you into
His
Hair.
When the violin can forgive
Every wound caused by
Others
The heart starts
Singing.

Notes

1 For more on the associations of the number seven, see Wikipedia and Bellos 2011, Kohli 2023, Saaty 2016, also general references on numbers, below.
2 Speech and lyrics (variously reproduced and set) at https://www.americanrhetoric.com/speeches/mlkihaveadream.htm/, luther king I have a dream song utube/, song utube luther king, dream/
3 Further on the Number 3 in Dundes 1968, Lease 1919, Leonhardt 2019, Meyer 1906, Olrik 1909, Parsons 1916, Sanders 2011, Tavenner 1916.
4 On numbers, generally, see Bellos 2011, 2014, Cain and Finnegan 2020, Corry 2015, Dundes 1968, Eastaway 2024, Helmenstine 2019, Hogben 1989, Lowie 1925, Seagull 2018, Stewart 2024.
5 "When The Violin" from the Penguin publication, *The Gift* by Daniel Ladinsky, 1999 © with permission. www.danielladinsky.com

6

THE LYRE WITH ITS MUSIC

The resource of music – the voice, the lyre, and the multiplicity of other instruments created and used over countless millennia – is often reckoned as among the most precious tools of human communication and expression. The voice is something we are all endowed with from birth; instruments are mostly played by those with some expertise (there always seem to be some) to the joy of themselves and their hearers.

For humans, as, above all, social animals, the voice, the lyre, the harp, and their fellows are infinitely useful and beautiful tools for realising and enhancing that social life. For music can be found – can be created, that is – everywhere, its tools are something that can be turned to use for just about any occasion. It is played and heard both during gatherings of intense emotion and in the ordinary occasions of everyday life, bringing people together to create the sounds of music or to listen, or both.

The tools of music, thus, make a significant contribution in the life of humans and in our sociality. It is a little surprising, therefore, that music, as such, is not more central in studies of communication. As Sarah Izen and colleagues wisely point out,

> Communication has been studied extensively in the context of speech and language. While speech is tremendously effective at transferring ideas between people, music is another communicative mode that has a unique power to bring people together and transmit a rich tapestry of emotions, through joint music-making and listening in a variety of everyday contexts.
>
> *(Izen et al. 2023: abstract)*

DOI: 10.4324/9781003496007-6

Perhaps its lack of centrality in communication studies – it has been much studied elsewhere – is because music, always, in a way, elusive, is not easily related to language and to the linguistic analyses that have played such a prominent role there. At any rate, whatever the background or the problems, music certainly needs to be near the heart of any work on communication.

Music and humans

There is no known society without music. It was there from the start of history. From the beginning of human beings in this earth – we may be uncertain of the exact date, but we know it was some hundreds of thousands of years ago – we humans were born with the gift of a voice of some kind to be used voluntarily or involuntarily. And at least from Neanderthal times, there were instruments, evidenced by the discovery of a bone flute from that period. There are archaeological finds of other flutes and of percussion instruments from the Palaeolithic Period that stretched from from about 2.5 million years ago till 10,000 BC, and clay drums and shell trumpets from the Neolithic Period of 10,000–c4,500 BC. The civilisations of Mesopotamia, the Mediterranean, India, East Asia, and the Americas all possessed diverse and well-developed assortments of musical instruments in ancient times, suggesting that there had been a long previous development behind this. And for more recent times,

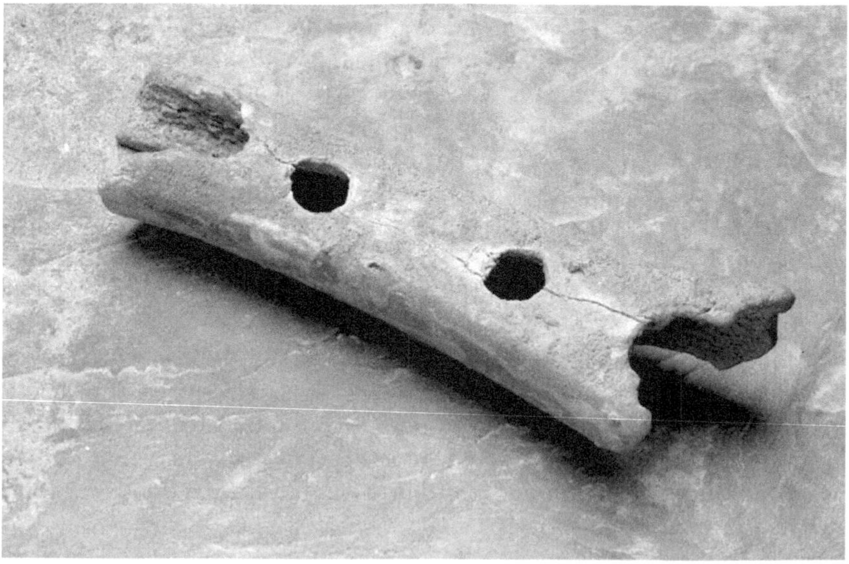

FIGURE 6.1 Neanderthal flute.

there is plenteous evidence of a multiplicity of musical genres from Africa, India, Bali, China, and Europe across the centuries. It seems certain that we can conclude, with Blacking, that music, like language, is a species-specific human trait (Blacking 1974: 7).

So, music dates back to the earliest times of human beings. Its ancient origin is further attested in the human body, for we know from functional MRI scans that the brain has links for the hearing and creating of music; while there may have been detailed changes, the basic functions of the brain, doubtless, continue to function on the same fundamental principles, so we can be sure that the propensity for music is always there, set within the human body.[1]

Music has attracted huge interest and a plethora of myths and cosmologies through the ages. All the great religions connect music in some way with the divine and envisage music as having the ability to affect our emotions, intellect, and psychology and as coming from some place outside this earthly life, perhaps stolen but mostly as a gift to us on earth where, in music, we can listen to the voices of the gods.

The philosophies of all the great traditions are much concerned with the nature and importance of music. In myth, we hear that God created the world from sound and that music played a major role in the beginning of the world, originating in a primordial divine power, as in the nāda-brahman "God-as-sound" of Hinduism. In some, music plays a cosmogonic role in the maintenance of the world, as in the drum-playing and cosmic dance of the Hindu god Śiva Nataraja or stories of gods who "sing" their creations and creatures into existence. Music is also seen as brought into existence through the efforts and discoveries of such human originators as Jubal, Shah Jamshid in Persian/Iranian mythology, the goddess Saraswati in Hinduism, and Ihy jointly with other deities in ancient Egypt. In Chinese myth, the musician Ling Lun invented the bamboo flute by imitating the song of enchanted birds. The common thread in these diverse tales is that music comes somehow from the divine – it is something enchanted, coming from beyond ordinary, earthly life.

Among the Greeks, famed for their rationality, Plato held that music had a direct effect on the soul, while Pythagoras believed that music and harmony is present in the entire universe, as each heavenly body has its own sound, all playing in perfect harmony. He included music in his mathematics department and was the first musical numerologist and acoustician, linking sounds to lengths in string – not so far from our modern concept of vibrations, sound waves, wavelengths, and pitches.

Scientists, philosophers, poets, writers and artists too, of all kinds, from Milton and Keats to Albert Einstein, have paid tribute to music. Among a host of references, we have Shakespeare, "If music be the food of love…", from Shelley, "Music, when soft voices die", Wilfred Owen's shattering, "I know rage music ...", Kurt Vonnegut's "Let this be my epitaph: 'the only proof he needed for the existence of God was music'", and the biblical

> I will sing to the Lord as long as I live
> I will sing praise to my God while I have being.

(Psalm 104)

And since music cannot be conveyed by words alone, let me cite words in a poetic frame for us to hear the music in them, for as the Greeks well knew, poetry and music lie together, the beautiful fruit of the human-divine muses. As in

> Full fathom five thy father lies;
> Of his bones are coral made;
> Those are pearls that were his eyes:
> Nothing of him that doth fade,
> But doth suffer a sea-change
> Into something rich and strange.
> Sea-nymphs hourly ring his knell:
> Ding-dong.
> Hark! now I hear them, – ding-dong, bell.

(William Shakespeare)

And from years back it was a musical instrument that inspired the mediaeval poet Hafiz in his music-infused poem that still sings for us:

> When The violin Can forgive the past
> It starts singing.
> When the violin can stop worrying About the future
> You will become Such a drunk laughing nuisance
> That God Will then lean down And start combing you into His Hair.
> When the violin can forgive Every wound caused by Others
> The heart starts Singing

Here, the pen too takes its place in the praise of music and assists the metaphors of that great resource that is always with us.

It is not only in philosophy or high literature that music is seen as something divine and poetic. For the Aztec, songs were flowers, birds, pictures, and the spirits of dead warriors called back to earth, and in mediaeval Europe, songs were flowers garnered in the bees' gatherings of nectar. In many cultures, music is something that can only be sought away from the common run of life, in contact with the divine. It may come in dreams or trance, or in communion with the spirits or the ancestors or God. Inuit poets sat in meditation awaiting their songs, Plains natives in America sought them as a "vision" in the solitude of the woods, and mine come, unsought, in dreams. In Fiji and other Pacific islands, elsewhere too, poets received their inspired dance-poems through induced trance or in meditative solitude as they waited in deep concentration for the song to be given; sometimes, it was in the enchanted liminal edge between reef and ocean. John Blacking, near to death, said he felt "the eternity of music", and Handel famously spoke of seeing God and the angels while composing the" Hallelujah" chorus – to say nothing of the religious experiences the chorus continues to evoke for its performers and hearers.

Nor is it just in the distant past or high-flown language that music is cherished. I remember a porter in Los Angeles International Airport giving careful consideration to my question of where he thought music came from: "from the soul" he said. And a chance taxi driver, a talented musician as it turned out, described his "real life" as being in the "parallel universe" of music.

Just about everyone today is in some way in touch with music: listening with more or maybe less attention to musical devices at home; overhearing it in the street or in a shop (played there to communicate a feeling of welcome and of marketable goods); playing in a small band of companions, conveying one's loyalty and commitment by turning up with the right instrument and required skill time after time; attending a live concert or some religious or social occasion embellished, as so often (and, doubtless, since the start of human culture) with music; recording a favourite song for a friend, an expression of affection and fellowship; or just piping while shepherding the sheep.

So it is everyday. But at the same time, playing or hearing music is often felt to be something special: from the soul, in the heart, perhaps "lost in music", and to provide the appropriate, necessary, framing for great individual or community occasions. As the neurologist Roland Devere felicitously expresses it

> Among the most significant artistic expressions, music is embedded in the fabric of human culture and identity. We have all been exposed to music in some way, whether by listening to recordings, playing an instrument, attending concerts, or dancing. It provides a unique emotional experience that takes on personal and social meaning in endless respects.
>
> *(Devere 2017)*

Judging by the attention paid to music by scientists, cosmologists, and poets alike, music is of huge significance in human art, communication. and expression. Many have been the commentators who have spoken of music being everywhere. As Elgar put it, music is in the air, it is all around us.

But given this centrality in our life and thought, together with the fact that we all know – more or less – what music is, it is surprisingly difficult to give an account of it. It may be both precious and ubiquitous but that doesn't stop it being notably more elusive than other human communication skills to describe and to winkle out just what is going on when we use its tools to create or to hear its sounds and join in their celebration.

The voice and the instruments of music

Music may be everywhere, its tools always, within the conventions of day and age, open to use. They are multi-functional and can be turned to multiplex purposes. But to work, they, obviously, must be used. It is human hands and human voices that accomplish music on earth.

There are many ways in which humans are able to do this (despite what some high fangled "experts" sometimes try to tell us), for *everyone* is born with the capacity for music. Even infants, it has been discovered, can detect the music they prefer, maybe even before birth. *Everyone* can sing and dance. For instruments and solo singing, it is more selective. Certain people choose, or have the opportunity, to self-teach, learn by copying others, or be taught. Sometimes, this is to elementary degrees of skill, sometimes to the highest level. In return, they share their expertise on the occasions when these skills are enjoyed and needed.

The expected occasions for wielding these tools are innumerable. There are formal concerts, competitions, and talent shows; home dinner parties where the children are expected show off their latest piano pieces; religious services, rituals, and seasonal celebrations; weekly or monthly music events in pubs; celebrations and memorials with colourful marching bands; dances; singing at football matches; teaching in primary schools and specialist music colleges; carol singing at Christmas and the new year – the list goes on. Music in a multitude of diverse forms is all over the place – the pubs, churches, schools, homes, concert halls, hilltops, greens, streets, and garages.

Such occasions, differing only in detail according to local conventions, go a ways back.

The music is used to various purposes. Sometimes, the players are deliberately wielding the musical tools to hand to bring about certain effects; at other times, they may have no particular aim beyond just taking part in a taken for granted and enjoyable part of the culture or of an expected ritual; sometimes, like the examples in the previous chapter, some or all of the participants are not really aware of what is coming across to either themselves or others.

Sometimes, the participants seem to know fully well what they are doing. Music in ritual occasions may be intended specifically to communicate with God (remember Augustine's "he who sings praises twice") or in a similar way to how, among many others, Catholics in America join in the sacredness of charismatic "visionary song" (Marini 2003: 247) and the Native Australian Yolngu use music to communicate both with each other and with the ancestors (Magowan 2007: 105). Music can bring what had been apart close, making communication possible. For the New Guinean Kaluli, singing is interwoven into the associations they feel between "birds, weeping, poetics, and song", and is designed to express and bring about a feeling of sadness. They live in and through a complex sonic world, singing sorrowful songs in night-long ceremonies and filled with the tears that the songs evoke. Thoughtfully composed and deliberately rehearsed, the songs are oriented to making the listeners sad and nostalgic, moving them to tears, consciously deploying musical forms to communicate the desired effects and to organise feelings of sadness and rage. The songs are performed by a dancer

> whose downcast demeanour and paced solitude, moving up and back the centre aisle of the house, creates an image of loneliness and isolation. The act of moving the audience to tears is marked most socially by the instant retribution of burning the back of the dancer, a mark he wears for life ... The way the songs persuaded the audience to tears is what dominates both the aftermath and the remembrances of [the event].
>
> *(Feld 1982: 215–217)*

Other traditions differ. The freelance Limba musician Sayo in northern Sierra Leone used his vocal-instrumental performances to express a deep sense of sadness, misfortune, a lack of ability to control life or destiny. But the listeners to these sorrowful songs did not show sadness. As members of the chorus, they seemed concerned not with the words but with the enjoyment of responding, clapping, and dancing (Ottenberg 1996: 92–93). Their reactions, culturally specific, stand in stark contrast to those of the Kaluli but were no less a real dimension of their musical experience.

Different again is musical lamenting in Caucasian Georgia, where the women "carry out emotion work" for the community. Their laments are not the outcome of spontaneous, irrational, forces, but planned and worked-on artistic performances. The singers' management of their feelings structures the emotional occasion and enables the audience to grieve.

> For the lamenters aesthetical grieving means to keep control over their feelings. They cannot let themselves go. For some of the listeners the process is the other way round. They are inflicted with their pain ... [The occasion] involves the audience in grieving ... coming to terms with the loss.
>
> *(Kotthoff 2001: 192, 25)*

Sometimes, music is deliberately used to help and communicate with others as in music therapy, while in Nigeria Yoruba, players explicitly use band performances to communicate and generate happiness, relaxation, and enjoyment, where the juju music

> rushes over the listener in a continuous stream ... or blows flutteringly, like a flag in a strong wind ... [as] social power, musical sound, poetic rhetoric, and sentiment are woven via performance into whole experiential cloth.
>
> *(Waterman 1990, 187–188)*

Or, again, the ever-ready tool of music can be used, at least in part, as a personal resource. Ottenberg traces how the individual lives of three blind musicians interpenetrated their musical performances (1996), just as Cavicchi (1998) describes individual Springsteen fans intertwining their personal histories with how they experienced his music, absorbing it into the fabric of their lives.

Around the world, rituals marking identity or personal transformation are a key phase in community life. The organisers ensure that music is there, celebrating, communicating, and framing. There are, for example, weddings, funerals, graduation ceremonies, anniversaries, and public holidays; the return home of successful competitors; festivals; and the colours and flamboyance of carnival. All these are typically intershot with music, and those responsible are expected to arrange the appropriate musical tools to make this happen. The music makes a contribution, often regarded as a necessary one, to managing what can be fraught events in human sociality, organized occasions for the (potentially dangerous) expression of possibly over-wrought emotion.

The outcomes and experiences of such events naturally come in an infinite number of variations depending on the purpose and setting. But, whatever the variations, music is commonly expected to be part of the rite, and it is a remarkable feature of human interaction that it so often is.

Of course, there are exceptions, and not everyone necessarily enjoys or approves of the music, but, in general, the deployment of the appropriate vocal and/or instrumental musical devices not only decorates such occasions but has a necessary role in fulfilling them. Whether fully intending or subconsciously expecting it, people deploy the tools of music and the encompassing capacity of sound to marshal a sense of *communitas*, of trance, of transformation from one state to another: in Van Leeuwen's words, "listening is connection, communion" (1999: 197). Shared experience can be dynamically co-created, as people smile at or dance with each other, beat time, move together –realisations of human sociality that recall Schutz's "mutual tuning-in relationship" (1951: 92).

Thus, Georgian lamenters seemed able to overshadow the here and now (which in Sierra Leone could be grim indeed) because their troubles could be publicly expressed through music, and the singing chorus could be happy in a sort of pleasant, timeless musical world.

> The repetitiveness of the instrumental music and song, the steady rhythm, sometimes the repetitive movements of dancers in a circle, and the minimizing of everyday time allowed not only for a sense of momentary social solidarity but also for a special sort of inner individualism ... swinging back and forth between full consciousness and daydreaming.
>
> *(Ottenberg 1996: 192–193)*

It does not do to romanticise. Music is also used to divide, to be aggressive, to mark out boundaries around oneself and against others, and to be a weapon in war. In fact, music, with its emotionally charged communication, is a supremely effective tool to signal hostility. Consider the aggressive racist songs in certain situations or the way that, in the Balkans, epic-singing was heard with pride by Serbs but conveyed terror to their Croat neighbours. In Ireland, listeners of different backgrounds experienced the sounds of Orange flutes and drums in contrasting ways, bound into long historic-mythic associations of protestant Orange platers aggressively and ostentatiously marching at certain times of the year through the domains of their Catholic opponents. Not everyone, even among those involved, interpreted this as a hostile act, and some on either side of the political divide simply enjoyed the colourful display, but it certainly did not communicate peaceful intent. National anthems and songs, such as "Rule Britannia", to some convey a sense, historically rooted, of pride and unity but for others – as emerged in the emotive debate over its inclusion in the London Proms – an unwelcome divisive signal. Music has long been used as a tool of war, signalled by military bands, trumpets, and warrior songs; and suppressing the songs or instruments or anthems of a subdued people has long been understood as sign of a conqueror's forcibly imposed rule. Because it is music, such acts are deeply felt.

Even within a single culture, there can be bitter divisions about music, even more so given the high value generally accorded to music: getting it "right" matters. In the fifth century BC, Plato was already complaining about people going in for new-fangled music, and through the centuries, changes in church music were, at times, strongly opposed by the authorities before the new forms became established, only to be themselves hotly defended against yet newer changes.

Closer to home, it was, at one time, thought inappropriate to consider the chants or drumming of Africa, the songs of Brazil, the sounds of black instrumentalists, or the popular bands of Liverpool as "music" at all. Jazz was, at one time, regarded not just as non-music but as a threat to civilisation itself or, more moderately but equally dismissive, as "nigger jazz bands" making "pointless noises". A BBC executive, speaking in 1933, castigated the "negroid type of music", or, again, the "musically incompetent" habit of "crooning ... the emasculated singing of sickly sentimental stuff".[23] A quarter of a century later, I recall the horror of staff at an elite girls school when their pupils showed an interest in rock – it was forbidden (without success of course), the music staff, predictably, taking the lead. Music that stressed performance rather than printed score was not in favour, the more so that it was often associated with people who could be regarded as outsiders – the marginalised, the so-called-called "primitive", or otherwise despised or non-literate groups. Music is important enough for its definition to be the subject of passionate debate.

To return to the common patterns in which the channel of music is deployed, the prime setting for the tools of music is and, no doubt, always has been in the context of ritual: religious, spiritual, the personal rites of passage of life and death, celebrations of great events and of the display of power, and the turnings of the year. In these, music, above all, can set a ritualising frame around time and space, leading people from the "ordinary" run of things into a liminal place where all things are possible. Like the sounds of an organ as one enters a church, the musical actions signal that this is a time and occasion that is separated by its sonic frame from the ordinary run of things. Such temporal and spatial framing can be fairly light and short lived but can also move to the intensity of trance or possession for some or all of the participants. The capacity to move players or listeners into another, transcendent sphere is a well-known property of music – any music but, above all, when there is rhythm and the beats of a drum.[4]

The natural sounds can be tapped into, as in the Kaluli identifications with birds or the Native Australian's use of "sounds of the natural environment [to] shape modes of communication between people and the ancestral realm" (Magowan 2007: 105).

Healing and comforting through music is an age-old practice, now regularised in the practice of music therapy. Music is officially recognised as a means to communicate deeply with people's minds and emotions. It can reduce heart rate and blood pressure; relieve muscle tension; help people manage pain; trigger hormones to ease depression, anxiety, and agitation; and have a positive impact on people's mental abilities and memory. It is commonly used to help people with dementia for which, remarkably, listening to or engaging in music – including by singing, dancing, or playing instruments – can help such people to communicate their feelings both verbally and non-verbally, delve into their memories, share their personal history, reduce distress, and, overall, to connect with the past by evoking memories, feelings, and emotions that they otherwise find hard to express. They may recall memories when they hear pieces of music that are significant to them, like a favourite song from the past or a lullaby they used to sing to their children. Even individuals from whom it is nearly impossible to elicit any behaviour, let alone something spontaneous, responded spontaneously when hearing music by "smiling, extending hands, tapping feet singing, interacting verbally, touching, hugging and holding hands" (Aldridge 2008: 53).

There is no doubt that music can communicate with people no longer reachable by other means, and it is now widely relied on as a seriously useful tool for constructive communicating with and caring for people with dementia. And if, as it now appears, communicating through music is accepted to be a unique and powerful stimulus for reaffirming personal identity and social connectedness in individuals with dementia, can we not take it that it can have the same role for anyone? And perhaps in the past, and the very beginning, too?

Mind, body, emotion

Before moving on to look at the experiential dimension of music, let me return to the question of "emotion", a topic more fraught than it seems at first sight.[5]

Drawing attention to music's link to emotion might, at first, seem a highly positive characterisation: emotion is something we can all relate to, a valued dimension of life. But at the same time, characterising music as something specifically tied to emotion has also, at times, been understood as a negative, dismissive, comment on music: downgrading it as marginal, secondary, and not to be taken seriously in the way that "properly rational" things are.

There is a background and apparent rationale for this. It is rooted in the long theme-with-variations running through Western thought – the value-laden oppositions between intellect and emotion. Romanticist accounts used these polarities to celebrate the emotional side. More commonly, reason has been set on top, its role to control our lower "animal" nature and lead upward into the scientific, emotion-free enlightenment of human language and writing. It was these cognitive elements, furthermore, that were regularly (if not quite invariably) taken as the fit focus for scholarly analysis.

These ideas have long influenced our models of culture and, with it, of music. Western classical music – the assumed norm – has regularly been assigned to the "rational" side of the equation, connected with the intellectual elements of cultivated human society. Scholars privileged music's cognitive and non-bodily features, highlighting composition, written scores, and the rationality of classic music theory: *these* aspects, not "primeval emotions" were the appropriate subject for analysis.

The communication of emotion was not held to be *irrelevant* in traditional musicology but seen, in judgemental terms, as being bodily and, thus, opposed to the intellect. Insofar as emotion was there, it was something to be controlled and refined by reason. In the traditional and, still in some circles, influential view, music is

> a language of the emotions, through which we directly experience the fundamental urges that move mankind ... A dangerous art ... But under the guidance of the intellect and the enlightened moral sense, it is surely as safe as anything human can be – as safe ... as religion or science.
>
> *(Cooke 1959: 272)*

The study of music. in this view. was to provide an intellectual channel for regulating these primeval urges. This was feasible with "true" music but not with non-notated forms such as jazz, rock, or African drumming, which were long seen as irredeemably "physical", the "mindless" outflow of primal emotion. A throng of twentieth-century "listeners' guides" offered intellectual expositions of the expressiveness in musical works (not in the listeners), focusing on the musical text and teaching listeners "how musical elements fit together". Thus, Leonard Meyer's *Emotion and Meaning in Music* did not delve into ordinary people's experiences or how they used the tools afforded by music to reach out to communicate but the "syntax" of musical works and the judgements of "composers, performers, theoreticians and competent (*sic*) critics" (1956: 197).

This cluster of assumptions is not now the dominant one, but traces remain and tend to spill over from the study of music to that of communicating more generally. The implication is that communication is to do with the transfer (of course, through verbally articulated language) of information and rational knowledge, reflecting the highest and most truly human part of the tripartite view of the soul that we inherited from the Greeks. Things such as emotion, gesturing, or other non-intellectual aspects are, thus, merely "peripheral".

And yet it can be precisely these aspects that, once we focus on how they are actually used, can be crucial in the process of communicating.

Fortunately, by the end of the twentieth century, emotion and experience were becoming matters of interest in many areas, not least music.

The anthropologist John Blacking pointed to experiential processes such as falling in love, ecstasy, or joy in dancing, and his analyses of music (1973, 1987) brought together body and thought, feeling and practice. Vic Turner was, meanwhile, developing the "anthropology of experience" (Turner and Bruner 1986), and the study of emotions and their role in communication was increasingly being taken seriously[6].

Emotions and, with them, shared experiencing turn out, unsurprisingly, not to be settled universal facts of nature but to be differently formulated in different times and places. Like the Kaluli singers or the Georgian lamenters, we have to *learn* how to feel and how to deploy particular emotions in ways and contexts appropriate to our culture and situation. People also learn the vocabulary through which their emotions are more, or less, verbalised. Conceptualisations differ too, ranging from the "hydraulic metaphor", underlying many Western views, to the Sudanic Dinka concept of emotions as forces acting from outside. In Helga Kotthoff's account of musicalised funeral dirges in Caucasian Georgia, "feelings are no longer regarded as something innate and inward, but rather as a culturally interwoven and shaped mode of experience" (2001: 169).

In such analyses, the boundaries between mind and body, cognition and emotion, inner and outer are correspondingly dissolving. Experience is increasingly envisaged not as a mysterious inner state or some unthinking primeval impulse but as something embodied and lived, intertwined with culturally diverse epistemologies. The Enlightenment ideology of language and scholars' preoccupation with cognition and verbalised texts are being undermined and enlarged by a growing appreciation of human life as everywhere intertwined with imagination, with value, with connotation; thought and communication are understood to be intershot with emotional meaning. These perspectives enable analysts of music to bypass the tendentious mind–body polarity and the prescriptive model of music associated with it, to look at the diverse ways that, in practice, people actually experience and make use of music.

Certainly, emotion is involved, as it is in all interaction among social beings as we utilise the various tools of communication at our disposal. Our communicating is less likely to be purely intellectual, as communication is so often envisaged (as if what is involved is "transferring the cognitive content"), than a kind of emotional and experiential shared process. It is not "emotion is transferred", as if it was a thing in its own right, but more a matter of a kind of adverbial twist on how things are shared among the participants: a process imbued with emotionally experienced feelings such as fear, delight, pleading, a sense of the other's aggression or opposition, personal reassurance or awareness of identity, or maybe a mix of these and the similar things that can emerge between people.

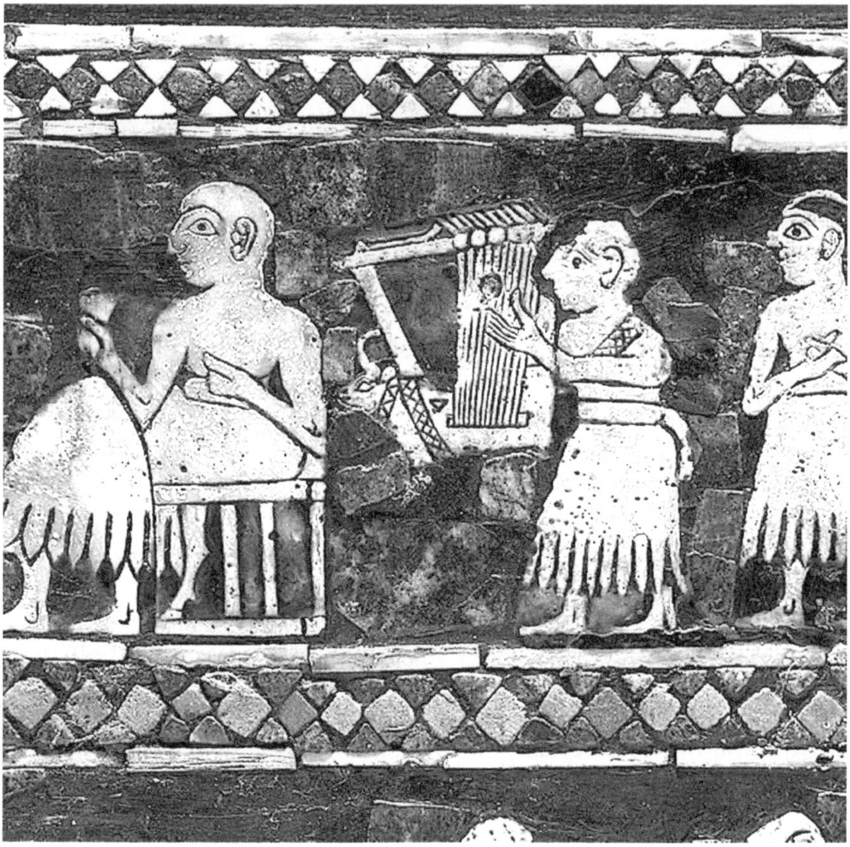

FIGURE 6.2 Ur banquet.

In the voice and instruments of many many kinds, then, humans do, indeed, have, and make good use of, manifold tools for musical communication, a multi-sense experience. As ever, these tend to work together and in multi-modal settings, the voice often together with instruments, both primarily auditory, coordinating with the visible actions of gesture and body movement, sometimes also intensified in dance; and then further with costume, product of the needle, and, where appropriate, of the pen. It can be a rich, and emotional mix.

The experiential dimension of music

Because it has been common to focus on the musical "work" or the "musicians" (meaning the lead players), the other active participants have often been neglected. In fact, they are threefold: the composer(s), the player(s), and the listener(s) who themselves may be players, with in some cases the organisers or commissioners behind the scenes. *All* these categories of participants are likely to enter into, and make a contribution to, the communicating process, especially those present in live performance events, though in differing degrees, depending on the situation and setting.

There is good reason to include *listeners'* experiences, well expressed in Ola Stockfelt's deliberately provocative over-statement, "the listener, and only the listener, is the composer of the music" (1994, 19). They play a crucial role. They too will know the expected conventions and are a key part of the performance. In this context, they too are musicians.

Being a "listener" is not a passive process. Sometimes, this is overt, with active audience participation an expected element of performance. They may join in the singing, either directly as a full chorus (the singing in Limba and others, storytelling being just one example among a myriad others) or through, for example, clapping, cheering, head banging, shouting, dancing, leaping to their feet – or alternatively (because disapproval or rejection aggression is another form of participation, booing, slow clapping, ostentatiously stopping listening, yawning, sneering, actively shouting, or protesting by leaving). Because attendance is likely to be voluntary, or, if not under control, participation is mostly positive. Bruce Springsteen's performances, for instance, were *actively* heard by his hugely enthusiastic fans; his performances were not something to be watched passively, but to take part in. "I'm tired after seeing a Bruce show, I've been on my feet, I've been applauding and I've been yelling and screaming" Cavicchi 1998: 93). Another describes the feeling that one has just been to a religious revival, "Faith and Hope and Joy!", while for yet another:

> It gets you into it physically, because you're dancing, you're moving around, you're waving your arms, you're clapping your hands. You get into it mentally because you know the lyrics or you're listening to them again, maybe you're getting another meaning out of them, a new meaning or an old meaning, whatever. It's just such an energizing experience, and it's a spiritual experience. So, it gets you, mind, body, and soul.
>
> *(Cavicchi 1998: 95)*

In less overt ways too, audiences can actively contribute to the occasion in how and where they behave and position themselves, for example, in the way they hold their bodies, what sounds and sights they produce, how they interact with the performers. The jazz musician John Coltrain brings out the sense of communion, almost as if in some enchanted, shared, out of world place in his comment that

> the audience, in listening, is in an act of participation ... And when you know that somebody is maybe moved the same way you are, it's just like having another member of the group.
>
> *(quoted in Shaw 2001: 27)*

The atmosphere, the vibes, thus, depend on audience as well as performer. Audiences too are contributing musicians and have had to learn the skills to take part. Even in classical music performances audiences need to know the expected bodily behaviour and comportment and the conventions about, for example, when to sit, when to move and not move, and when to applaud – all this, to the participants seeming just "natural" and not needing to be learned, makes up an active and essential contribution to the performance.

Listeners to recorded music too may participate creatively, through the ways in which they personally interpret their own experiences and actively formulate what they hear. This is worth some emphasis, for live performances commonly take the centre, as if listening to audio recordings is somehow merely secondary or deplorable, even "not *real* music".

But recorded musical sound is an intrinsic part of most people's lives today and all over the world too. This kind of listening covers a wide range of possibilities – engaged in for various purposes, with varying degrees of attentiveness, in many different contexts, but it is most certainly one form of musical participating. Sometimes, these listening musical experiences are not so much tied to particular events as something intimately interwoven into the participants' lives. For the fans of Springsteen's music, it interacted with their lives and their personal understandings of particular songs. During the commute, at work, at school, "most fans are still listening, making associations between perceived musical structures, potential messages, and the contexts of their experiences" (Cavicchi 1998: 126). For lovers of classical music, for example, there are the overtones that interact with their own lived experiences, just as for fans of jazz or country music, particular rhythms can acquire deeply felt significance, seeping through their lives. Simon Frith describes this for the associations of pop music:

> There is no way to escape these associations ... We need to understand the lumber-room of musical references we carry about with us, if only to account for the moment that lies at the heart of the pop experience, when, from amidst all those sounds out there, resonating whether we like them or not, one particular combination suddenly, for no apparent reason, takes up residence in our own lives.
>
> *(Frith 1988: 148)*

In Liverpool rock performances, music "creates its own space and time where all kinds of dreams, emotions, and thoughts are possible" (Cohen 1991:191), while in the Limba case, musical experience took the participants beyond the here and now of everyday time with its grim conflicts so that instrumentalists and chorus could be happy in a sort of timeless musical world, experiencing both a sense of social solidarity and of personal release.

It is obviously something more than just that their ears were picking up sounds of melody, rhythm, and harmony, as the basic constituents of music are said to be. Nor is communicating through music necessarily always a matter of elaborate explicit epistemologies or highly charged "inner feelings", which are less covered by generalised terms such as sexuality, pleasure, or desire, to which they are all sometimes reduced. It can also be of quieter resonances. Remember the overtones, for some listeners, of Wagner's music; or the multi-layered clusters of associations, partly personal, partly shared, of a childhood carol, a particular recording with special personal associations (for me, it is Faure's *Requiem* bought on honeymoon), the opening of Beethoven's Fifth Symphony, a national anthem, or a long favourite song. Amusement, happiness, intellectual satisfaction, and excitement or even discomfort or disapproval – in specific contexts, these too are part of people's musical experience, both long term and on specific occasions. The relation of music and trance too brings listeners into touch with music, as it is a kind of dreaming in a dimension that can be experienced by participants as of the eternal and the divine within themselves

It is not so much self-conscious internalised "feelings" – though, in some cultural settings, that is, indeed, articulated as one experienced element – as, more generally, the personal and contextualised *manner* of people's musical engagements: joyfully, fearfully, inattentively, reflectively, proudly; in a spirit of exaltation or energy or irritation; in sorrowful, celebratory, or nostalgic mood; with boredom (that too), with dance, with tranquility. Whether in deeply intense fashion or more light-touch action, the tools of music provide a human resource through which people can enact their lives with inextricably entwined feeling, thought, and imagination. People participate and mutually communicate in music in multifarious ways related to the roles they take, the occasion, or their own personal histories.

Experiential expectations are moulded through specific groups, genres, and contexts. In the English city of Milton Keynes, for example, people's experiences in the contrasting "worlds" of jazz, folk, or classical music were interwoven with differing practices and conceptualisations of performance, composition, and learning. For some, it was light-hearted, a way of showcasing their voice, the compositions, or their instrumental skills. For others, it interpenetrated their lives. For a soloist in the amateur operatic world, there was not the only one to convey how, coming up to a performance, she "ate, slept, and dreamed music". It contributed to her being her, both outside rehearsals and performances and during them. She found a sense of identity being communicated, not verbally articulated but lived.[7]

The same music or occasion can communicate different things to different listeners. Expectations and conceptualisations naturally differ over time and place. Someone who heard Chopin playing the piano, for example, formulated the experience through the otherworldly metaphors that were then current: "I could think of nothing but elves and fairy dances ... [The music] seems to descend from heaven – so pure, and clear, and spiritual" (Kallberg 1996: 52) – terms unlikely to occur to a contemporary listener. Specific genres come to have particular associations at given times or places: some with overtones of nostalgia and loss; others with excitement, dance, or rowdy laughter; others, again, with gaiety, solemnity, exuberance, reverence, humour, trance. Some are conventionally heard with full attention or intense feeling, while in others. the experiences are mingled with other sounds or ebb and flow over time. [8,9,10,11]

Because "emotion" is, of course, not context-free, it has to be seen within the shared web of cognitive and emotional experience. In religion-steeped Byzantine Christianity, for instance, the biblical stories and their associated musical echoes ran through peoples' lives. An example is in a composition by the ninth century composer Kassia. One of her hymns was about the woman who anointed Christ. It would have been sung in a service centred around the call for repentance and the cry for forgiveness in Psalm 40:

> Let my prayer be set before you like incense
> The lifting up of my hands as an evening sacrifice.

The hymn was not just focused on intellectual content, but through its melody, words, and the shared echoing associations, it evoked deep religion-imbued and very positive feelings of guilt and repentance and enabled women to suspend the everyday determinism of gender and social position as they shared in "a universal song of repentance" chanted in an atmosphere of what was experienced as divine emotion and paradise nostalgia. The hymn

> energised the emotion underlying the narrative and unlocked its personal significance for the faithful ... [recreating] within the sacred space of liturgy the experience of personalising religious narrative

> not doctrinal proclamation. ... The sacred melody with its occasional cadential melismas represented the ladder of tears that link to God and the world allowing music to become a medium of transfiguration.

Through the hymn, women could traverse social and cultural restrictions in a shared aesthetic experience, which brought them into the intimacy between God and humanity.

> It was chanted with a unique and florid melody which amplified the salvific significance of the narrative, and heightened the tenderness of the image of the woman repenting at the feet of God. The powerful musicality and linguistic economy [could] disassemble logic and provoke introspection through an emotive performance of the divine drama of salvation.
>
> *(Mellas 2020: 167–168)*

Once again, we see the power of music to, perhaps, uniquely unlock the ties of earth and allow people to be transported to a space outside the restrictive bonds of everyday living, maybe even beyond the experience of normal consciousness. Those who see music as bringing something of the divine are not perhaps not so far out.

A final point: with modern technology, there are now more opportunities than in the past for people to listen to individually chosen pieces at a time and place their own choosing, as digital music can be used for people to fashion flexibly to their own occasions. Tia DeNora explores the example of how "Lucy" uses Schubert's Impromptus to "retreat into" and "soothe" herself, actively putting together memories, musical recordings, furniture, current emotional state, timing, and biographical associations (DeNora 2000, 42–43):

> There is nothing untowardly mysterious about this process ... [where] the sum is greater than its parts: music, plus the ways that [Lucy] attends to it, plus the memories and associations that are brought to it, plus the local circumstances of consumption. Through this alchemical process of pulling together a range of heterogeneous materials, Lucy herself is ... a contributor to the constitution of the music's power over her, its ability to move her from one emotional location to another.
>
> *(DeNora 2000: 42–43)*

Such accounts illuminate how music, as well as more direct and planned communications and outcomes, can also be deliberately used for extending personal experience and individual creativity.

Such analyses of participation are complex and not without controversy, but they are illuminating because they look to people's actual feelings and practices. This is not something that can be deduced from the musical "work" but only through detailed studies of the multiple ways that people actually participate in music.

We are still faced with the near-impossible issue of how to articulate all this in verbal language. How can you really describe in words the feeling when a piece of music you had never really liked suddenly "sends you". Or the moment you feel truly "out of this world" when, on the radio that had been playing pleasantly soothing but not particularly significant music (but not *in-sign*-ificant either), it is suddenly Zipoli's *Elevazione,* or sitting next to someone you love at a performance of Handel's *Messiah*, or the experience of being (*be*-ing) in a choir jointly singing in Bach's incomparable *Mass in B Minor*, or "Up on the Roof", or "Fields of Gold".

Difficult though it can be to capture the variegated experiential dimensions of music, it is worth the attempt. After all, we know that music can be used as a communicative mode with unique power to bring people together, to frame liminal and sacred spaces, and to reach into a person's depth. And if, as now seems to be clearly proven, it can reach past the fading of an individual's normal powers into a depth of memories and a tapestry of emotions and, furthermore, transcend language divisions, then we can scarcely deny that music is in some way a most powerful tool of communication.

Again and again, we encounter the ability of music to take individuals out of current conditions into somewhere moved from this life that is also perhaps, looked at another way, into the far depths of oneself, opening gates closed to our worldly experience – to what is, somehow, "beyond". As Beethoven so percipiently expressed it, "Music can change the world".

Not just the music

Our musical tools, both vocal and instrumental, are capable of a near infinite variety of treatments by players. The modulations and versatility of the musical voice are comparable to, or perhaps even surpass, those for speaking, rich as these prove to be (as sketched out earlier, in Chapter 2). As for the non-vocal instruments, really only expert teachers and practitioners can explain the full potential of each; beyond, that is, the variations that are obvious even to a lay person – the things such as fast/slow, loud/quiet, staccato/legato, and the like, intrinsic to the effective utilising – playing – of these musically endowed instrumental tools.

The current questioning of ethnocentric ideals of "rationality" in music, together with a greater valuing of the emotional/spiritual (not just intellectual) aspects of experiencing, opens a wider vision of the ways people participate in music. It can take in the multi-sensory body alongside the "mind"; as Simon Frith puts it, "music-making is about the mind-in-the-body" (1988: 128). We do not have to accept the old body–mind dichotomies to recognise that sound vibrates and resonates in the bod, and that the experience of music includes its patterned corporeal engagements. This embodied musical experiencing is the more compelling because it is so often multi-sensory. Musical performances are multi-media events, their sound patterns only one of several communication channels, and, as Leppert's *The Sight of Sound* perceptively points out, the "visual-performative" aspects can be as significant for music as for dance or theatre (1993: xxi).

Purposive corporeal actions are regularly one dimension of the whole experiential process. They range from the studiously still body during classical concerts to the dance movements of other musical genres or the bodily reverberations of hearing certain recordings. Music can, in fact, be said to be multi-modal in the same way as spoken language. We now take it that a full account of speech must include some attention to bodily movement: the overlapping dimensions, that is, of gesticulation, kinesics, and body language. It is the same with music making: it is not only operatic stars and flamboyant soloists who gesture (or deliberately *don't* gesture – itself a form of body management) or add drama to the characters by their facial expressions or bodily movements. There are specific conventions, maybe internalised rather than fully conscious, about how to communicate that you are, indeed, a musician and a musician of a particular kind: how you hold and manage your instrument for instance; sit, stand, or jump around; the technique of handling the bow for a string player (think of the contrast between folk fiddling and classical music management of the bow); or perhaps, even for non-leading players, in how you enter, exit, or jointly acknowledge applause.

Such ways of managing the stationing or movements of the body can add to or, alternatively, interfere with the participants' contribution as musicians, even in quite minor supporting roles. Those aware of the local conventions for communicating through music, in some mysteriously learned way, abide, without conscious effort, by the expressions or stances that "fit" the delivery of specific forms of music – cheerful, sad, solemn, dramatic, or whatever – according to the local understanding of this fittingness. In any given occasion, these are a culturally defined appropriate part of the musical communication in a way that, say, a soloist laughing during a pianissimo section by the orchestra or a choir member jumping up and down at some quietly moving point would not. Similar points apply, even to the less prominent participants categorised as the audience, who still have a role to play in the success of a musically enhanced event. They share in the communicative conventions and, to repeat, can be regarded as an essential part of the process as, themselves, a category of musicians.

Then there are accompaniments such as costume, make-up, ornaments or special meaningful accoutrements. Sometimes, of course, music events are informal or spontaneous, so nothing special is expected (though, even then, appearance and demeanour may send well understood, if subconscious, signals), but for a planned event, both audio and visual cues can communicate emotionally weighted messages about the performers and/or the event, which shape the meanings and emotions that are conveyed.

Think, for example, of uniformed brass bands on the march, the black-costumed classical orchestra, or the carefully prepared and exactly matching garments of a troupe of Samoan dance-singers. They all carry meaning, presenting a carefully managed visual appearance that can communicate messages to all involved. All this can, at times, be as significant to the musicians themselves as to the other participants, for example, as a reinforcement and reassurance of their self-identity, both as a respected musician and an accepted member of some valued group. I recall the vivid joy of a middle-aged Fijian library assistant, for example, as he told me with glowing pride of the costume he was to wear as a drummer that weekend in a traditional Fijian dance song. The climax was his description of how liberally he would oil and oil and oil his skin till it shone – just right for the huge honour of being a lead drummer, celebrant in a great, traditional islander occasion.

In situations in which writing or print are a regular part of life, there are also the products of that same familiar tool of the pen, with the opportunity of adding yet further messages in posters, advertisements, and programmes, sometimes further supplemented by newspaper or social media reports. Bands have their meaningful titles, often communicating in prior adverts or in placards and labelled clothing as they play – names such as (in Milton Keynes) "Martial Law", "Under the Carpet" (a comment on politicians), "Ethnik Minority", "Still Romantics", or the deliberately humorous and self-mocking "Entire Population of China", "Kev's Numb Nuts", or "Bottom of the Bill Band" – along with the music, these cause merriment all round; laughter is, as we know, a peculiarly rich and significant form of communicating.

Their lyrics amplify the message(s), for the voice too is, of course, a tool of music, realised in a musical setting as song. This gives yet a further communication opportunity, for though some songs are, in fact, meaningless, in narrow linguistic terms or their words not detectable by the listeners, in others they come across as intelligible and meaning-laden phrases.

With our long school-reinforced faith in the prime role of verbal language for delivering messages, it is tempting to focus the attention on these words. For some genres, some individuals, and some occasions, they

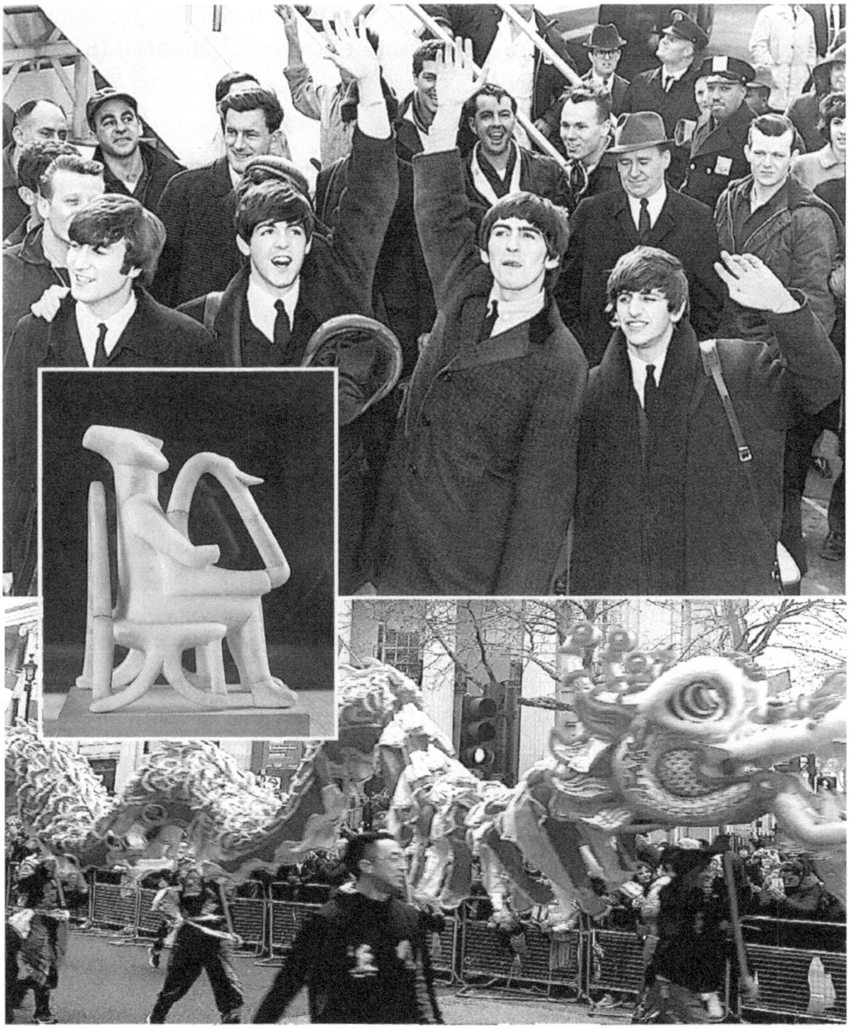

FIGURE 6.3 Musicians.

are, indeed, a significant part of what is intended and/or comes across. But this is not always so, nor are the meanings necessarily agreed. We should not give in too readily to a focus on the linguistic but look as well to performance properties and listeners' multiple interpretations. Cavicchi's study (1998) of Bruce Springsteen's fans, for example, shows how the words of the songs, though resonant for many individuals, did not carry one single message, and seemed less central than the shared expectations of energising religious experience and personal interpretation.

Music is many-sided and centres on *music*, not words. As Plato had it, speaking to us of today as much as to his fifth century BC listeners, "Music gives a soul to the universe, wings to the mind, flight to the imagination, and life to everything".

Music communication

Moving on from these instances, what does music communicate? This seems the obvious, final, question. But it is more elusive than it first appears.

The answer is usually to draw a contrast with language. The conclusion, one frequently drawn, would then be that, while language communicates information and cognitive content, music communicates emotion.

It is not difficult to see the point of that response. But, ultimately, it is hardly satisfactory. This is for two reasons.

First, it implies a stark and (as will be explored in the next chapter) no longer generally accepted or justified contrast with language. It further implies, mistakenly it would seem, that emotion has no place in language.

Second, the question itself is set in misleading terms. It seems to expect some general answer, be it "emotion" or "inspiration" or even something like "God's message to man". But we do not ask what "technology" communicates or "truth" or other generalised abstract notions and expect some straightforward general answer. Why? Because given all the many diverse contexts or aims or participants, there is no general answer. And, in any case, it is not "technology" or whatever that acts and communicates, it is *people.*

The question – an interesting one – for which answers can be sought is: what are the various things that humans, whether with deliberate intent or to a degree without realising but not necessarily against their will, are able to communicate by using the various musical tools at their disposal?

A salient response making a rather similar point was given by painter who, when asked "What lies behind your painting?" replied briskly "the wall", or, more gently and wittily by Bob Dylan who, when asked "What are your songs about?", reportedly smiled, pretended to ponder, and then said with mock seriousness "About half an hour".

The point they were making was that if they had wanted to express a message in verbal spoken words, they would have communicated in words. They did not. They painted a picture and sang a song; they were not going to traduce their art by translating it into some other, inappropriate medium by reducing the song and painting to something else. Why should they when they were communicating using their own chosen form and their own expert tools? It was for the viewers or listeners to experience and pick up for themselves what they found being communicated.

The point is, again, that we need to look to the listeners' as well as the creators' experience and that communicating – sharing – through the tools of what might be called the magic of music-making is seldom a straightforward activity. It is not a matter of sending a message through some kind of hidden code, which, with cleverness, can be "solved". Gene Simmons said it well: "Music is feeling. You cannot try to verbalize it. It really just hits you, or it doesn't.

It must be admitted finally, however, that the precise way music communicating works is still elusive. We can quote the many – very many–attempts to verbalise it, all knowing they have not quite captured the essence. No more than the songs of Bob Dylan or the picture on the wall can it be captured and reduced to verbal articulation. The nineteenth century philologist Max Müller, while pointing to the difficulty of interpreting music, asserted that, nevertheless, it exists:

> Music is the language of the soul, but it defies interpretation. It means something but that something belongs not to this world's sense and logic, but to another world, quite real though beyond all definitions. Is there not in Music and in Music alone something that is not entirely of this earth? ... Here if anywhere we see the golden stairs on which angels descend from heaven and whisper sweet sounds into the ears of those who have ears to hear.
>
> *(Müller n.d.: 43–44)*

But we can at least be sure that a wall is there behind it, that the work was produced by a thinking feeling human being who created it to communicate and express themself; that we know, as in Müller's words, that it is "real"; that we have learned from replicable MRI evidence on the brain, about the way that musical performance reaches into the depth even of people with dementia where music acts as "the fundamental of communication" (Aldridge 2008: 10); and, closest of all, our own personal experience – we know that the performing is, indeed, solidly there, and the communicating is there too.

> [T]he true beauty of music is that it connects people. It carries a message, and we, the musicians, are the messengers.
>
> *(Roy Ayers)*

Notes

1 See Izen et al. 2023, Jeffries et al. 2003, Zentner and Kagan 1998, and further references there.

2 "When The Violin" from the Penguin publication, *The Gift* by Daniel Ladinsky, 1999 © with permission www.danielladinsky.com/

3 Mendl 1927: 48–49, BBC Written Archives (WAC) 7 Dec. 1933, R19/585/1 Entertainment "Jazz" 1933–1946, File 1, BBC R34/281 Policy / Censorship / ... Crooning 1934-1943, BBC WAC.
4 As in the classic account by Rouget 1985.
5 On approaches to emotion and experience, especially in relation to music, see Berger 2007, Cavicchi 1998, DeNora 2000, Feld 1982, 2012, Justin and Sloboda 2011, Magowan 2007, Ottenberg 1996, Turner and Bruner 1986.
6 Crapanzano 1994, Feld 1982, Heelas 1996, Lutz and White 1986, Lutz and Abu-Lughod 1990, Schwartz et al. 1992
7 Further information in Finnegan 1989.
8 Bouwer 2021, Ionescu n.d., Raimondi 2023.
9 For further work on, or relating to, the origins of music and language, see Aitchison 1996, Blacking 1974, Clark and Willernet 1997, Dunbar 1996, Hauser 2001, Hurford 2014, Hurford et al. 1998, Knight et al. 2000, Mithen 2006, Pinker 2015, Tomasello 2008, Wallin et al. 2000.
10 Huang 2017.
11 There is an example of this by a chimpanzee mother when reunited with her baby at https://www.bbc.co.uk/news/av/world-us-canada-63685009/

7

THE START OF MUSIC

The Greek philosopher Aristotle declared: "it is not easy to determine the nature of music or why anyone should have a knowledge of it".

It is true. And though, in a way, we know a lot about the history of the tools of music, it remains as difficult as in the previous chapter to pin down its origin or its true nature. Nor, till very recently, did we have any physical record of earlier human music-making, so talking about its "origin" can only be surmised. In practice, we know near to nothing of the long history of music. Its origins and meaning are hidden to us.

We can say, however, that as far back as we can tell, human beings made music. Oldest of all is the striking wind instrument (appropriately termed "a flute"). It was used 40,000 years ago by a Neanderthal player, presumably to produce music for him/herself and for fellow humans (we can picture it in our mind's eye). It is a fully musical tool fashioned from the thigh bone of a young cave bear, with four pierced holes. Amazingly, it can still be played today, showing that the size and the positioning of the holes could not have been be accidental – they were made with the intention of musical expression and, remarkably, with the full knowledge needed to achieve this.

It suggests – or rather surely proves – that the Neanderthal people were, like us, fully developed, spiritual beings capable of sophisticated artistic expression. Like us, they too were musicians.

From later, but still many thousands of years ago, there are references in ancient texts, such as the ancient Hindu scriptures of the Vedas, in a stunning cuneiform image of a lyre singer-player – a bronze-age Homer – from the fourth millennium BC Mesopotamia, and the depiction of a

DOI: 10.4324/9781003496007-7

singer and lyre player performing for guests at a banquet in Ur (shown in Figure 6.2). The development and widening range and specialisation of instruments presumably continued over the millennia, from Judaic trumpets, Greek lyres, and dancing-singing choruses, drums, player groups, and on to the recent (but not so very recent) spread of full orchestras.

The tools of music – inbuilt, discovered, invented, developed, or whatever (we might guess but do not know) – seem to have been there for the very earliest humans to utilise, a bonding of love and companionship in the far-off beginnings. So too, no doubt, was the artful utilisation of voice with its singing, chanting, speaking, and tones.

From the scattered examples, we do, then, know something about the historical background of human music from a long way back. But what was the *origin* of it all? Why and how did humans take up instrumental and vocal musicking? What first impelled the wish to create physical objects into musical instruments and to spend time (not necessarily a short endeavour) in learning to play them? And then, while all humans may be born with a ready-made voice, why use it for music, not just for speech, for *language*?

Good questions, which I will return to, but first, as a necessary introduction, let me consider the contrast just mentioned between "music" and "language".

Music and language

Music and language look, on the face of it, to be two separate things: speaking is not the same as singing and far less like playing an instrument. Indeed, it was once unquestioned that music and language were not only different but opposite. They were studied by different specialists and under different disciplinary heads; they were located, it was believed, in different parts of the brain, and they were manifested in different ways. Some people, furthermore, who preferred the reading of words, especially in church services, were actively hostile to intrusions of what looked like the opposed medium of music.

But over recent years, the consensus has been changing. Linguists and musicologists have been talking to each other and recognising that, at the very least, there are parallelisms and interactions.

When you consider speaking in all its modulations, it seems that it is not really that distinct from singing. Vocalising too can be melodic and exhibit, even dwell on, musical elements such as rhythm, pitch, and timbre. Instrumental music is arguably different (I will come back to that later), but the modulations of the speaking/singing voice shade into each other and, in some contexts, can be considered, at their root, ultimately the same, on a continuum within a syndrome of, more or less, musicalised vocal communication and expression.

People use the tool of the voice in many different ways: they can vocalise harshly or tenderly, loud or soft, up or down, and – here is the point – in a more or less musical manner, tapping into the potential of melody and rhythm. These can come in a relatively minor way, or they can be the most prominent dimension. In the latter case, we call it "music", otherwise, "speech". In principle, there is no division between the two, or if there is one, it is hard to agree about just where to put it. In a way, it is not a matter at all of a possible distinction between two different things but more something adverbial, as it were, about the manner in which one or more individuals are at some given point using their voice. It is a matter, really, of seeing any distinction more as a comment on how, adverbially, as it were, people are using their voices than any distinction between two different "things".

Linguistic scholars are, in any case, widening the definition of language to include not only gesture and body language but also, the relevant point here, its musicalising features. In this context, it becomes difficult if not impossible to maintain a clear opposition between "music" and "language", even more so given the additional dimensions that are now accepted as part of spoken language that can be seen to pertain equally to what is regarded as "music". In short, it is is now increasingly recognised that "music" and (spoken) "language" are points – shifting and overlapping in different cultures, eras, and social settings – that fall along on a single but also complex, multi-faceted continuum, meeting centrally in the words-and-music-togetherness that we call "song".

We are dealing, in fact, with a broad syndrome – some call it speech–music or musi-language – of human communication and expression, through hand and voice, sound, and, to an extent, vision.

So looking at the work on the origin(s) of "language", for which scholars have had much to say, may also help throw light on the possible origins of music. That, at any rate, is the course I intend to take.

Not, to be frank, that the origin of language is any easy matter either and is far less agreed. It has been endlessly debated, for, as Jakob Grimm wrote in 1851, "the origin of human language is truly secret and marvellous".

"Marvellous" – he is right, and, unsurprisingly, some of the theories interlace with myth, though not necessarily to be discarded for that reason. The wilful snake's Garden of Eden gift of the knowledge of good and evil, which some take to mean language and, if so, must surely have included music, is one insight into the human condition. Next, we hear, came the arrogance of humankind in building the Tower of Babel and the transformation of one, mutually understood language into many (musical divisions as well as spoken, or perhaps music remained as the universally understood language that many claim it to be?). Many years later, thus, followed its reversal in the powerful metaphor of Pentecost – not doing away with the many languages but giving people the power to transcend the differences and understand each other. The myth does not tell us, but we can perhaps surmise that that understanding was through music.

That may be myth, though at the same time, arguably, a story with its own inner truth. Of what followed next, there is historical evidence: the proliferation – an astonishing historical process created through the tools of the voice and, in time, the interlocking pen – of the great branches of language: Indo-European, Niger-Congo, Dravidian, and the rest. In time came the spread of, among others, the great imperial languages of Latin, Arabic, French, and English, followed by the renewed split, still continuing, into multiple younger, kindred, languages (or, rather, a succession of generations of people bringing these languages, with their songs, into being. For a language does not travel and give birth to itself. It is people who speak and, in speaking, create it).

The Babel–Pentecost account is a grand story, brought about, we should again remind ourselves, not by some inexorable spread of language or languages or by "comparative philology", Sanscrit or Indo-European roots but by humans travelling, speaking, communicating, and interacting over the centuries. The results have brought both joy and sadness, enlightenment and oppression, art and the everyday, as the tools of new languages and new cultures were carved out by their human creators.

What was the first language, and how did it start?

I will be returning to the far-back start of music, soon, via language, but, as the Roman scientist-poet Lucretius of *de rerum naturae* so often told us, *per ambages* – in a roundabout way. For now, that the congruence of language and music has been more or less accepted, the extensive work on the origins of language may throw some light on its near twin: music.

Amidst the many speculative and mythic theories, some practical Greek scientists tried a down-to-earth investigation to find out what the first "natural language" was. The Asiatic-Greek "father of history" Herodotus wrote in the early fifth century BC describing a careful experiment. They took a newborn baby and removed it (somehow) from all human contact. After a year, they checked. The baby said something that they thought might be the Egyptian word for bread – so, they concluded, the first and natural language must have been Egyptian.

That Greek experiment was a good try. But neither that, nor the mythological stories, help us very much about the possible ultimate origin of language or, paralleling that, of music.

Mediaeval Islamic scholars, always thoughtful and always early on the issues, were equally, if not more, realistic. They came up with a series of ideas about the nature and origin of language.

- *Naturalist*: There is a natural relation between expressions and the things they signify. Language, thus, emerged from a natural human inclination to imitate the sounds of nature.
- *Conventionalist*: Language is a social convention. The names of things are arbitrary inventions of humans.
- *Revelationist*: Language was gifted to humans by God, and it was, thus, God, not humans, who named everything.
- *Revelationist–Conventionalist*: God revealed to humans a core base of language, enabling humans to communicate with each other, and then humans invented the rest of language.
- *Non-Committal*: The view that conventionalist and revelationist theories are equally plausible.

Though I am not following these ideas up directly, they provide a helpful background to thinking about the origin not only of language but also of music.

How did music start?

The theories are diverse and complex and have long been a matter of debate (it seems that music and its origin matter!).

Currently, the main division is between scholars who hold that music is as essential to successful human existence as language (in this context, assumed to be a different skill). Others believe it had a more limited and specialist background and evolved merely to serve one specific function. Thus, starting from a functionalist standpoint, Darwin thought that music evolved in a similar way to mating calls in the animal kingdom, with women choosing male partners who sang best. Other functional theories were that music emerged because it promoted social cohesion or because it helped children acquire verbal, social, and motor skills. Then there was also the idea that the links between music, religion, and spirituality are innate, starting in the womb and continuing through the mother–infant bond, usefully creating bonds within the family and, ultimately, more widely.

The difficulty of these functionalist theories is that it is hard to fit music into an evolutionary framework in which music is *necessary*. Some suggestions have been that music was developed to assist in coordinating work, helping in long-distance communication, assisting cohesion and cooperation, or enabling communication with the divine. None of this, however, really fitted in with the usual evolutionary imperatives in the literal sense of sustaining life in the way that, say, eating, sleeping, and breathing does. Steven Pinker (2015) built on this difficulty to argue that music, far from having a function for human life at all, is, in fact, something quite trivial and useless and evolved only as an unneeded by-product. It could be argued that these are, in fact, as important conditions as any other for the survival and welfare of human sociality. Thus, it is, indeed, a viewpoint with some support in the conclusion to a recent comprehensive exploration of the origins of music (Wallin et al. 2000).

> However, it was that we came to have music, we found incredible uses for it. In fact, it became part of all our activities and helped us define those activities were. It is hard to imagine who we would be if we did not "know those pieces".
>
> *(Wallin et al. 2000: 483)*

A further, linked division is between continuity and discontinuity theories of language and/or of music. At the moment, the continuity route is more popular. and the theories I am coming to in a moment are basically of that kind. Not all agree. Chomsky, a strong discontinuity proponent, posits a single, sudden change occurring in humans approximately 100,000 years ago, a Great Leap in which a common language faculty developed in a group of humans and then their descendants. For him, this sudden explosion of the acquisition of language was the point at which, he believes, they became properly human:

> Human language appears to be a unique phenomenon, without significant analogue in the animal world ... There is no reason to suppose that the "gaps" are bridgeable. There is no more of a basis for assuming an evolutionary development of "higher" from "lower" stages in this case, than there is for assuming an evolutionary development from breathing to walking.
>
> *(Chomsky 1972: 67, 68)*

There is no final way to settle this, no archaeological find that can suddenly provide the missing link that provides the answer. For many analysts, however, from at least Darwin onward, a continuity approach accords better with the evidence from many aspects of human history as we know it through the ages: little by little and continuity seem to be the themes, not least in our continuity and contiguity with our other primate relatives. We are aware too of the continuity – in all their diverse details – of tools and practices from the far past and back into the worlds of the other primates – why should "language" or "music" be exceptions?

That said, it is worth going back for a look at some of the ideas developing in those fertile centuries, the eighteenth and nineteenth.

A clutch of theories

Many famous theories emerged in this period. The ones of particular relevance here are those started off by the famous German philologist Max Müller. In a fine discussion, also commented on positively by the biologist George Romanes, a keen musician and friend of Darwin. Müller summarised in a humorous but, underneath, perfectly serious way, the various theories about the origin of language around at the time. His opponents gave his theories whimsical nicknames with the aim of teasing their simplicity, the result being that they were for discredited for some time. But in the light of modern thinking, and, in many quarters, the return to Darwin and the idea of continuity rather than sudden dramatic (and, it must be said, unexplained) change, they are very much worth returning to. They pertain to language but, in view of the now widely accepted congruence between the two, they could equally well be considered in relation to music. Indeed, some of them would seem to be more easily applied to music than language.

So here are Müller suggested theories, followed in the list by a few others in a similar vein:

- Bowwow
- Poohpooh
- Dingdong
- Yo ye ho
- Tralala
- Themthem
- Lo lo

An interesting facet of all these theories is that, while each proposes an idea about how language (or, for us, music) first started to emerge and why, they are only convincing if accompanied by an assumption of continuity – of the continuous development by human agents of these early elementary exclamations or mimicries or whatever into the complex arts we know today.

Bowwow

First, there is the origin theory that Müller neatly named the *bowwow*, *quack quack*, or *cuckoo* theory. This had also been espoused by some early Greek writers and, later, unsurprisingly, by Herder. The key idea was that human language originated in *the imitation of sounds uttered by other animals*. Müller elaborates:

> This theory was very popular among the philosophers of the eighteenth century, and, as it is still held today by many distinguished scholars and philosophers, we must examine it more carefully. It is supposed then that man, being as yet mute, heard the voices of birds and dogs and cows, the thunder of the clouds, the roaring of the sea, the rustling of the forest, the murmurs of the brook, and the whisper of the breeze. He tried to imitate these sounds, and finding his mimicking cries useful as signs of the objects from which they proceeded, he followed up the idea and elaborated language.
>
> *(Müller 1862: 359-360)*

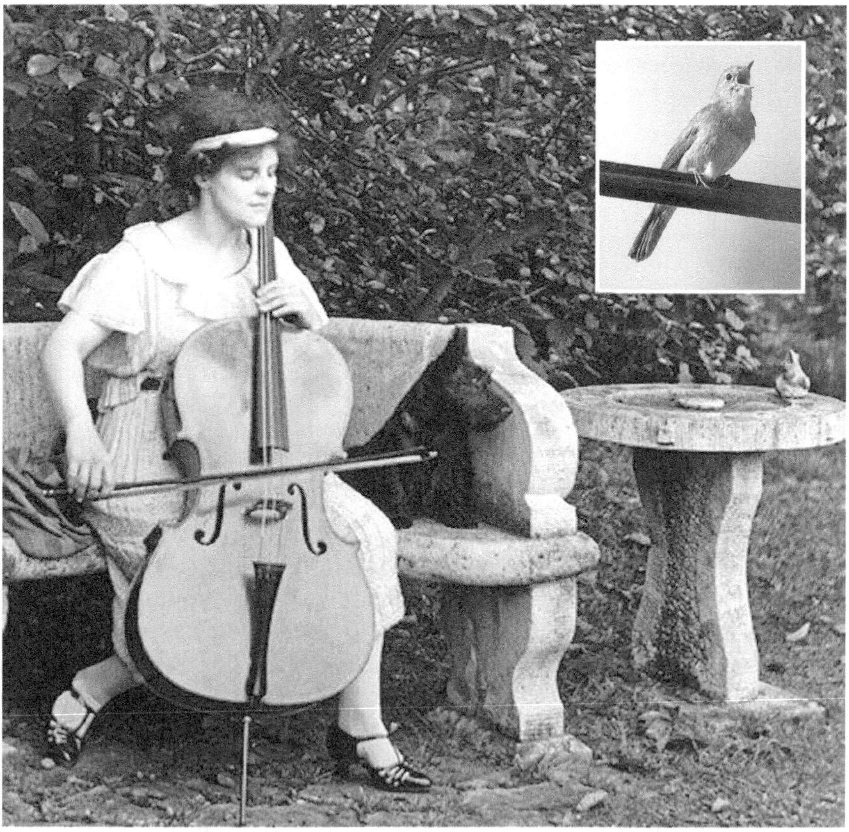

FIGURE 7.1 Bird and cellist.

There is much to be said for this theory. Mimicry is a known human propensity, and children enjoy copying the sound of animals even before they have learned to speak human language. Someone I know is famous for being able to speak "horse language"; her first word occurred when, under the age of 1, she copied the neighing sound of a horse every time she heard one come along the street outside her door, to both celebrate its presence and tell her parents that a horse was there. It was not long before she learned to speak fluent human language (English), but she has never lost her ability in mutual communicating with horses.

Mimicry of animal sounds is very evident in the context of music. Many compositions have copied and beautifully repeated the sounds made by animals, in particular, by birds. Respighi used actual, recorded, music by birds in one of his works, and many famous compositions were inspired by, and endeavoured to mimic, the sounds of birds. Among many there is Beethoven's *Pastoral Symphony*, Handel's *The Cuckoo and the Nightingale*, and, arguably best of them all, Vivaldi's astoundingly vivid birdsong imitations in *The Seasons*. There are also striking and well documented, cases of duetting between bird and human musician which, truly amazing, indicate the congruence between human, and bird-produced music – a strong point in favour of this theory.

Birds and their songs, then, though not the only proposed source, are central to this theory, supported, among other things, by the experiences of the New Guinea Kaluli people; they felt themselves to be birds and to be singing and weeping in the way that birds so melodiously do (Feld 1982).

With all this background, it is not hard to be convinced that there is at least an element of truth in the *bowbow* theory.

Poohpooh

Second is the poohpooh theory, also known as the *interjectionist* theory. The idea here is that language started with non-deliberate, near-reflex, exclamations of, for example, fear, joy, surprise, horror, sadness, and the like. The utterance is essentially emotional and non-intellectual without any referential content.

It is an influential theory, that, again, goes back to the Greeks. The fifth century philosopher-scientists Democritus (the one who coined the word atom: "it can't be cut") and his followers reckoned that human speech came from sounds and cries of an emotional nature – their own or maybe copied from animals. The theory gained further currency through the philosopher Epicurus and the Roman scientist-poet Lucretius.

This too accords well, possibly even better, with our everyday experience. Think, for instance, of exclamations like *oh, ouch, wow, phew, gosh, no*! Being near-automatic, such exclamations would have had no semantic content in the present sense of that word, though they might have acquired meaning through context and, almost certainly, supported, if only subconsciously, by accompanying gestures. It is not hard to see how, over the generations, such exclamations could have developed into longer forms like *oh dear, wonderful, impossible! how awful! sorry,* and *so then* and then on to more complex phrases and sentences such as:

So what did you do next?
I'm so sorry for your loss.
That must have been awful for you.
Sorry, please forgive me.

Again, musical connections come readily to mind. Mourning songs, greeting and farewelling music, and ritual songs can well be seen to have developed from the initial exclamations – a good example of continuity.

Dingdong

This theory arises from the belief that all things have a natural vibrating resonance and that this is echoed somehow by human beings, coming out in the form of vocal speech and song.

This basic idea gets strong support from musicians, such as with Helen Keller, who, blind and deaf, depended on vibrations to "hear" (and it seems accurately and in detail) a radio performance of Beethoven's Fifth Symphony, and, more recently, the profoundly deaf Evelyn Glennie, lead solo percussionist in the world, who uses the vibration of her body and of the things around her to tune her instruments to the appropriate pitch and identify those of others. She is profoundly aware of the depth of rhythm and beats and vibration in human beings that also run through all the world.[32]

This theory accords well with musical processes. If those without hearing in the normal sense of the word can still, in these ways, feel music, there must be be some kind of vibration sense as a musical receptor or creator located deep in the human body. And if now, why not way back then? And maybe, in those days, they were more active in the absence of the clamorous interruptions of today.

That vibration, furthermore, goes closely with rhythm is, perhaps, something of the same thing. From what we know of musical and human history, rhythm has been basic to music from long ago, perhaps predating melody or at least forming an essential component underneath it. And as Evelyn Glennie points out, rhythm is everywhere.

> Clock ticks, heartbeats, the spurts of the blood as it moves round the body sap as it rises in the springtime trees, clangs of iron on iron in Handel's fine blacksmith's, plants thrusting through the earth. Our breathing too, the very stuff of life. The tread as we walk. Oscillations of our swinging arms. And they say that when we hear a piece of music, our hearts listen and turn to beat in time, as most certainly our breathing does.
>
> *(Glennie 2019: 23–24)*

It is noticeable too – and an additional argument in favour of this theory – that the idea of an inbuilt rhythmic propensity is supported both by research on rhythm in primates and other animals[33] and by observations of pre-speaking toddlers' interest in percussion and rhythmic movement. And perhaps, rhythm is, subconsciously, in all of us. In my case, for instance, I was startled to find that my first novel, which I had naturally

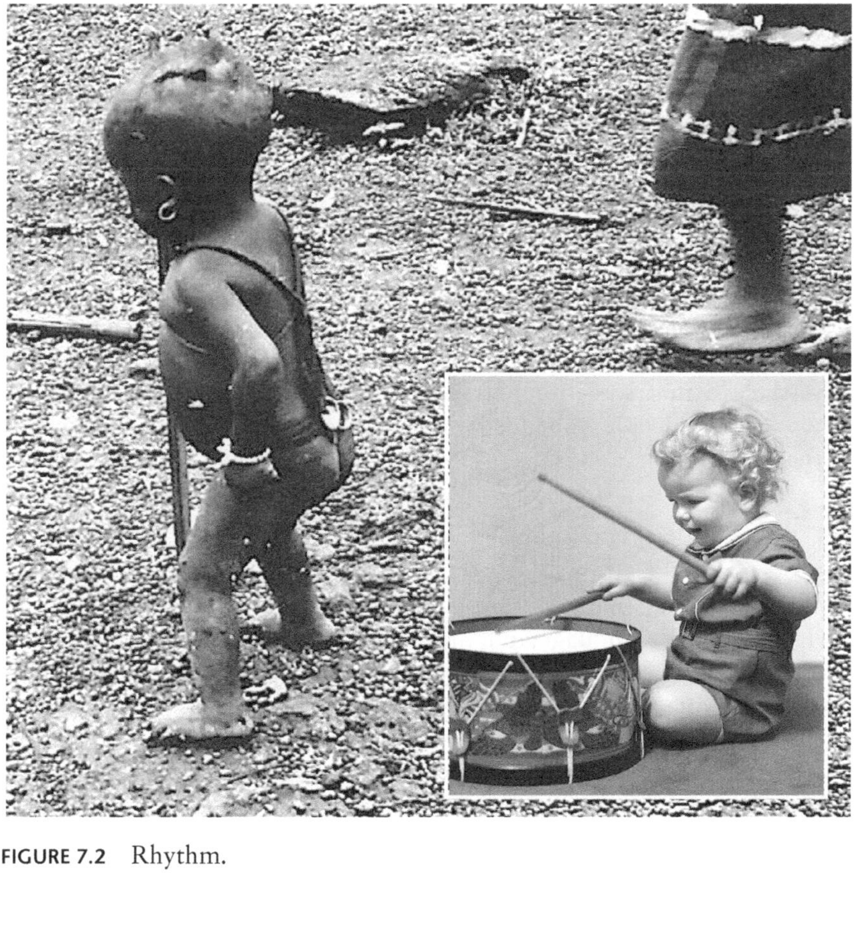

FIGURE 7.2 Rhythm.

assumed was in "prose", turned out, when read aloud, to be wholly rhythmic and in the beat of Shakespeare's blank verse. Perhaps that kind of rhythm is somehow embedded in all humans, in Shakespeare too, from millennia ago, from the start.

This is, again, an attractive approach in both individual developmental terms and evolutionary context, arguably applying better, as it happens, to music than to the speaking voice ("language").

In addition, the idea that vibration runs through *everything*, not just in "living creatures", fits well with the view in some of the new science writers that, in a way, everything, even the sea, has a kind of consciousness. Consciousness might, in this context, be interpreted as the kind of encompassing vibrating awareness of movement and life, which, not just in music but in all things, sustains the world and its creatures of every kind.

And then, an addendum – crickets.

What have crickets to do with music? Possibly, a lot. For here is an amazing thing. A Native American musician, Jim Wilson, made two recordings in his backyard of crickets squeaking. He then slowed it right down to accord with the human rather than cricket life span. The result is remarkable. It sounds just like a chorus of human voices – major scale, melody, and bass ostinato-like rhythms. It seems unbelievable and though Wilson and others attest that nothing was changed or added except for the slowing down, critics hold that it must be a hoax, pointing out, furthermore, that no one has been able to replicate it.

Everyone can listen and make up their own minds whether it is, in some sense, "God's chorus", as it has been called, or a manipulation, whether deliberate or accidental. The consensus now seems to be that putting the two recordings together did indeed unintentionally alter the sound but, nevertheless, that something striking was there, an indication arguably that vibration, deeply embedded in the natural world, may lie, instinctual, at the root of human music.

Yo ye ho

We come back to a more work-a-day level with yo heave ho.

This envisages language and, arguably before that, music, as emerging from collective rhythmic labour in the form of work songs. Synchronising muscular effort works better to music than to spoken words, far less silence, and there is no need for semantic content.

To support this are the multiple examples of music being used to organise group movement into a rhythmic and enjoyable activity. It can be for a band of men hoeing in rice or women weeding in upland Sierra Leone to the beat of a drumming, dancing, lead singer (as being prepared for in Figure 2.3). Without the exact timing of a musical beat, a group threshing grain would be in danger from each others' sticks. Rhythm helps when rowing a boat or keeping galley crews to time, coordinating instrumental groups, or managing a column of marching men.

The ubiquity of such occasions in, it seems, every culture and period of human existence, makes this an appealing theory. An additional attraction is that it brings in movement, fitting well with the increasing awareness of the importance of body language and gesture in song, speech, and musical performance. It also accords well with how children gradually build up their vocabulary and their mastery (a physical as well as a mental thing) of rhythm, movement, song, and, with it, verbal language. In a preschool situation – I have often seen it – children are encouraged to sing the well-known rhythmic verse

> Row row the boat
> Gently down the stream
> Merrily merrily merrily merrily
> Life is but a dream.

While still toddlers, they have no idea whatsoever of the meaning of the words or, probably, even that there are such things as words or meanings. But they enjoy music and respond vocally as well as through movement to the melody and the rhythm, helped by their teachers' gestures. They sing enthusiastically and in good rhythm something that sounded like

> oh oh oh i oh,
> etchee ee ee ee
> Eh eh, eh eh,eh eh o
> Eye i uh i eeeeeeee

The teacher understandably found this perfectly satisfying and knew that the children, as they grew, would begin to pronounce the sounds as words and get an inkling of their meaning. As, indeed, they did.

Work songs – jointly sung, rhythmic words for repetitive labour – seem likely to have been an inevitable, functional part of early human life and labour, as now too. It makes for a plausible explanation of at least some of the roots of language–music.

Tata

According to this theory, humans made the earliest words by mimicking or accompanying manual gestures with their tongues, thus making them audible. That makes sense: you mutter or groan when you lift up a heavy load and give an involuntary but audible sigh of relief when you put it down – not something with referential meaning, just a near-automatic vocalisation. Another example is the soothing (more melodic) noises made, again, almost automatically by a healer to a patient or, more especially, a mother as she lifts her baby – sounds that go two ways, especially between parent and child, as both recipient and speaker/hummer/singer understand and can repeat the sounds. As the baby grows and develops both physically and mentally, the idea is that it goes beyond mere copying to elaborating and experimenting with the sounds. Speaking and music-making gradually develop from this.

The theory is the more attractive in that meaningful sounds and gestures appropriate to the situation are well evidenced among other primates.

Tra la la

These theories have it that language–music began from playfulness and artistry, developing into trills, musical ornaments, decorations, and repetitions with (initially) semantically meaningless nonsense words.

This fits with common experience. We use plenty of what are called "words" that, in practice, have little or no sense in literal terms but that we like to *tralala* with in songs. Nobody knows what, if anything, is the referential meaning of *Hallelujah*, far less the constant *tra la la* and *fa la la* in madrigals and folk songs, or *duh duh de duh duh*, *hey nonny no*, *dilly do down*, or Santa Claus's *ho ho ho*.

This has the attraction that it rests on an implied link between communication and art, rightly going beyond the narrowly referential, cognitive, prosaic, and non-musical view of language. Furthermore, theory gains further credence if we hark back to the *bowwow* theory. For whether humans had actual inbuilt music making ability, they might have had the *potential* to respond to and mimic what they heard. The two theories come together and, together, are the more appealing, Once again, we are brought back to birds singing and to the Islamic theory of the naturalist origin of language.

It is, perhaps, a little hard to see how such nonsense terms grew into more complex *language* in the sense of spoken grammatically and syntactically linked sentences – they seem sufficient to themselves and complete in their settings. But as a theory about the possible roots of music, it makes good sense. Such sounds are quite likely to be both rhythmic and melodic, feeding into the idea that music must have been inbuilt into humans from the start, arguably having this in common with their primate relatives.

This approach receives strong, evidenced backing from research into gibbon singing. In his introduction to his report on this, Thomas Geissmann summarises his highly pertinent conclusion.

> Gibbons (Hylobates spp.) produce loud and long song bouts that are mostly exhibited by mated pairs. Typically mates combine their partly sex-specific repertoire in relatively rigid, precisely timed, vocal interactions to produce well patterned duets. A cross-species comparison reveals that singing behaviour evolved several times independently in the order of primates. Most likely loud calls were the substrate from which singing involved in each line. Structural and behavioural similarities suggest that of all vocalizations produced by nonhuman primates, loud calls of Old World monkeys and apes are the most likely candidates for models of a precursor of human singing and, thus, human music.
>
> *(Geissmann 2001)*

Me-me

For this theory, we might turn our minds to slogans – a modern concept but one that, in essence, surely goes back to the beginning, as in: "look at me!", "see what *I* have!". In the constant jingles that come in ads on radio, social media, and the like, the actual words are often indistinguishable, but we know what they are *really* saying. "It's me. It's us, look here, boast boast I'm the best".

It is not a far step to see this turn into a family song or group anthem or a football or war song. The communicating is again "Me me" or "Us us", a sonic mark of pride with the potential for expanding the cry into verbalised language and gesture – an additional means to focus a vehement look at *me-me*!

As with ads, it seems a small step to transform easily into song.

Lulla

This connects the possible origin of language–music with the fact that, in the early years of human development, hominid mothers, no longer covered with fur for infants to cling to, had to put them down when they were, necessarily in their way of life, foraging for food but, at the same time, needed to reassure the babes that they had not been forgotten. So, mothers developed a kind of "motherese" communicating, calling, humming, and singing from a short distance away.

When together too, mother-to-small-child vocalisations tend to be soothing and gently rhythmic in nature – rocking the baby – a style that recurs in lullabies throughout the world. They are generally characterised by long vowels and, where there are consonants, they are gentle and often nasalised. Lullabies could readily develop into meaningful verbalised vocal interaction that the growing children can pick up, with, it is easy to surmise, the further potential of widening out into communication with other members of the family and eventually more widely.

It is an appealing theory based on real-life experience and observation, all the more attractive as it puts sung music near the start of human expressive and communicative action, making sense in terms of what we know about mother–baby interaction generally. Lullabies are so universal and, at the same time, in a way, so necessary that this from lullabies and mother-with-child origin is highly attractive as one among the doubtless multiple roots of language.

Them-them

Let me, near finally, come to a theory that many, perhaps most, ethnomusicologists together with social scientists – Muslim conventionalist scholars too – would probably take for granted without the need to argue or would, at the least, find fitted well with their general perspective. With something in common with the *yo ye ho* theory, this is the view that music has an essentially social origin – something, in fact, that many scholars today would take as given, even if just how to interpret and apply this is not so clear.

As was evident in the previous chapter, music making plays a key, arguably essential, part in the rituals of life, death, war, hunting, and the like as well as of marking the seasons of the year, most or all of which are likely to have been a part even of the earliest way of life. It is not too hard to see how songs, even if, at first, without much or any referential meaning, could have been developed, guided by the conventions of the local group, into more verbalised chants and then into spoken poetry and speech.

This view is the more persuasive in seeming so true to life. We can well picture early musicians being encouraged to play and compose music for certain occasions following local patterns of what was expected and the consequent development of accepted sung and speech genres. These kinds of performances, in keeping with local obligations and conventions, are a constant facet of social life and one we know well.

Although, of course, music is carried on in a social setting and a great deal of work has been carried out that illustrates this, is this really an explanation of how language–music originated in the first place? It could equally be argued that a social setting or function could be the result rather than the cause of human musical practices.

Lo-lo

Here finally is another speculative theory – the *lo-lo* approach. It has something in common with the poohpooh interjection theory; indeed, it could be regarded as a subset of it but with the notable difference that it lays a special emphasis on awe and wonder, with some such underlying meaning as in "Lo and behold"; "Lo here is something wonderful – *music*"; "Lo, here comes music from above, lo it is divine". These or similar interjections are the kind of exclamation especially likely to occur in religious and ritual contexts or while attending an exhilarating musical or spoken performance of some kind.

So, people pray, as they have done for centuries, for millennia perhaps, in words such as "Oh, Great Wonder of Wonders I adore you, I beg you, I pray you" or the beautiful Islamic "there is One God and Muhammad is his Prophet" and its longer version" I bear witness that there is no God but Allah and Muhammad is the Messenger of Allah", or the succinct but full of meaning "salaam". Or, think of celebration songs just for fun, but suffused with the wonder of joy and company or of delight over a new baby or rites-of-passage ceremonies. Nursery rhymes too, full of emotion, wonder, music, have no need to linger over referential words.

This, again, connects language–music – not just its roots, but its continuing enactment – with enchantment and ritual and, associated with that, with trance, possession, and dance.

This brings us back, finally, to the persistent idea, in just about all cosmologies including the Muslim revelationist theories, that music must have a God-given, divine origin, accessed in dream, spirit possession, and the liminal space of meditation. Here, music is the beginning of creation outside of time and place.

From this perspective music and its tools can be perceived as a very special human mode of expression and communication – or better put, it can be seen as transcending normal human communication – going beyond the Tower of Babel, to hark back to the earlier myth. In many cultures, music comes in trance, in ecstasy, communing with the ancestral spirits. In fact, it is common throughout the world for music to be somehow received by its composers in some kind of possessed state, as a medium, from an oracle in a dream. Homer, we remember, began both his epics with an invocation to a goddess to sing her song.

It would scarcely be easy to produce any evidence for all or any of this if it were to be taken literally rather than as some kind of metaphorical commentary. But, perhaps, in one sense, the Pythagorean were not so far off when they thought of music as of supra human origin, beyond the normal tools of human communication and expression.

And so –

All these theories have something to be said for them. They all offer something about the way we think of music, connecting, therefore, with what we surmise about its possible origins. All attractive in one way or another, but, to me, the most compelling are the *tra la la* combined with the *bowwow* ideas. In addition to the highly cogent primate research, we have good evidence from archaeologists and zoologists that birds, no doubt, singing from the start, were flying the earth millions of years before humans, and humans are very imitative creatures (another of our given tools one might say). It is fully credible that, with our inbuilt primate potential, not just rhythm but melody, harmony, and counterpoint were copied, and beautifully so, from the singing – communicative as well as expressive – of our companions. This certainly receives some support from the linguistic authority Jean Aitchison's apt comment that human language "has more in common with birdsong than with the calls of other primates" (1996: blurb).[34]

Darwin's composite conclusion about the origin of music is as good as any:

> I cannot doubt that language owes its origin to the imitation and modification, aided by signs and gestures, of various natural sounds, the voices of other animals, and man's own instinctive cries.
>
> *(Darwin 1871, 1:56)*

So. though none of these suggestions is conclusive or best taken on its own, each and all of them give us some insight into the background of language and of music, something which – another speculation but quite a common assumption – could well have proceeded or at least underlain communicating through spoken words, the more so if we emphasise *ding-dong* and the imitation of birds.

But, that is precisely the trouble. We *may* have reached some deeper understanding of the nature of, and conditions for, music-making. Once it had got going, its continuity and development makes sense. But this doesn't tell us how it first started. Its actual continuing enactments or the conditions for its performance are not the same as its origin.

Furthermore, though it is in the nature of humans that we want to know the causes for things, and it is not wrong to seek them, all these suggestions end up as speculative, not evidenced. True, there are shreds of evidence – principally archaeological, physiological, and biological – with some more convincing than others in the light of modern behaviour. But there is no sure evidence for any of them.

The one point worth emphasising, however, is that humans themselves did not start from a blank slate. It is near certain that it was not humans at all that began music. They were, and are, primates. As such, they began with already inbuilt tools and potentials: an interest in rhythm and, with it, no doubt, dance; probably also exclamatory vocalisations, a facility in gesture, and very likely mimicry.

It would be no surprise, therefore, if we human primates followed up and developed the potentials that we came with. Amidst our awareness of the continuities of human history, we do well to recall a further continuity – that with other animals, above all with our relatives the other primates. This is the foundation from which we come.

Apart from that not unimportant point, we will have to rest content with what these speculations about the origin(s) of music can tell us: they do not, they *cannot*, in the end, answer questions about the hows and whens of its first beginnings. But they have told us something. To end on a positive note, we may not have – perhaps never will – reach a conclusion about who, how, or when. But we do have some pretty credible ideas of *why*.[35]

And the further questions ...

We are left with two further questions.

First, is it true, as many strongly believe or, without any particular evidence, wish to believe, that music came before language – or, put in better terms, that people uttered musically vocalised sounds before those with referential meaning – that, in short, as held by some of the continuity proponents, language evolved from the human capacity for song.

There is no direct evidence. But there are some slight indications that might support the idea that singing or other musical sounding may have been a part of human action before prose (as it were), and was there from the first, before spoken language.

Not all agree. Stephen Pinker (2015), in particular, holds that music is merely an unimportant offshoot from language. But there is a general tendency to see musicalised sounds as having come first. Rousseau's view, still powerful, was that music, with its emotional appeal, was the start of language; Darwin saw music as taking the form of love songs before humans could speak articulate language; and, coming to more recent scholars, the anthropologist Robin Dunbar (1996) and others suggest a very ancient origin for music, long predating the evolution of vocalised referential speaking. In support of this, it seems established that even very young children are aware of, and able to follow up on and imitate, melody and rhythm well before being able to manage "language" in the sense of referential meaningful words.

Second, this could be said to be an ultimately fruitless question, and for more than one reason.

First, it presumes a distinction between two things – music and speech – a distinction that, as we have seen, is rightly in question. And second, at this distance in time, we have no way of telling. Certainly the pictograms for "harp" and for "musician" are among the earliest known examples of writing, and we know that instrumental music goes a ways back in the form of flutes (something it is tempting and, perhaps, correct to see as a kind of extension of the voice, amplifying the regular c sounds of breath into melody and further rhythm). From finds of drums and other instruments, we know that instrumental music-making goes a long way back. There are no comparable traces of the voice, but sounds do not leave fossils for archaeologists to find so that is no evidence one way or another.

But it does seem that primates have musical rhythm similar to humans. This is reinforced by MRI results that suggest that awareness of music is built into human bodies, giving further credence to the view that music is something natural, not newly imported but a tool from the very start of human experience and expression. It seems that capacity for music must be built into the structure of the brain.[36]

For more recent times, linguists and historians have found poetry (musicalised speech) coming earlier than prose, and study after study by ethnomusicologists, anthropologists, and others have found singing and music generally a prominent and valued element in the local value system. This fits too with some of the origin theories: a mother holding and soothing a baby even in the earliest days would surely have a bit of a croon or a hum to her voice,[37] mimicking birdsong would involve melody and rhythm, and the natural rhythm of our bodies and the likelihood that involuntary exclamations might well have had a musical tone rather than a shout. After all, it is said that it is physiologically easier and more natural for people to sing rather than speak, continuing even when people have lost the capacity to talk. As a group of American researchers put it, concluding from an analysis of indications like these that music came first, "language is better thought of as a special type of music. The music developed first and provides the foundation – from an evolutionary and a developmental standpoint – for language acquisition" (Moore 2012).

What of instruments?

The second and, for present day musicians, more pertinent question is that speculations about the origins and early history of music have, without making this explicit, mostly focused on vocal music, as if this was the whole of music.

So what about instruments? It is not self-evident that they must have come from the same roots as the musical products of the voice, even though the two now go closely and sweetly together.

The evidence about great apes' awareness of rhythm is relevant. They clap – and clapping, after all, is a form of percussion. As John Blacking once pointed out, it is more important as a percussive instrument in Africa even than drums. They also rhythmically strike their chests. Macaque monkeys do this in a rhythmic way to show social dominance, suggesting an evolutionary origin to percussion as part of social communication. Other primates, including gorillas, make drumming sounds by chest beating or hand clapping.

Early hominids are likely, therefore, to have done the same. It is not too far a stretch to imagine the gesture of tapping or beating the breast could have, at times, been similarly enacted on the branch of a tree or a stone and that stone, in time, be lifted as a tool to bang rhythmically and with a satisfyingly louder noise on another stone – not such a great leap as, after all, chimpanzees, fellow primates, know about using percussive stones to crack nuts. Then, in time, we might speculate the attraction of creating sound by using something as a instrument might have grown over the generations (or perhaps quite soon given that the potential was already there to be adapted) taken over by increasing numbers of fellow humans. The idea of a drum as a percussive instrument is actually not complex and one of the oldest of human instruments – its basic design has not changed over thousands of years.

Given the gibbon example mentioned earlier (from Geissmann 2001), melody might or might not have been something newer for human primates. But, ever imitative beings, they had the birds to copy, the wind's changing tunes through the trees, the twang of fibre or gut, the ping of a bow string, and then there were the pleasingly changing tones from a blown trumpet shell that some might have experimented with. That flutes were constructed from the earliest times, we know from the happy find of a Neanderthal player's flute (let us, again, imagine the player and the playing – an individual, perhaps, of genius and inspiration).

In time – remember we are thinking of thousands of years and many generations when anything could happen not excluding the occurrence, from time to time, of players of unusual talent – there could have eventuated the rudiments of a lyre or its fellows, and of wind instruments. And once, with the rudiments, human intelligence must surely have gone on from there.

In this view, the roots of the instruments or music are to be found not in the vocalisation but in body movement and gesture – from hand not voice. If so, their union under one concept followed only many thousands of years later.

This again is speculative. There is no hard evidence, but it is not impossible and does fit with what facts we have and with the recurrent theme of continuity in the lives of humans and of other animals. And it is, after all, satisfying, even at times illuminating to speculate, perhaps throwing some light on present uses of the voice and instruments.

But they are just speculations, not evidenced history. For the moment, we must rest content with celebrating what we have in the human uses of the voice and in the instruments of music.[1]

For music, above all, can remind us of how much, as humans, we really do share.

> As many myths about the origins of music tell us what is important about the sounds of these voices is that they move us to elation, to pride, to calm, to action, to tears, to new understanding. What is important about these sounds is they change us, that they tell us who we are, and give our lives some purpose.
>
> *(Wallin et al. 2000: 483)*

Note

1 Further on the priority of music or language respectively, and related questions, Blacking 1995, Brown 2017, Levitin 2008, Levman 1992, Mithen 2006, Pinker 2015 ; on children and music Buren 2021, Provasi 2003.

8

THE MYSTERIOUS WORLD OF INTERCOMMUNICATING

There is a further form of communication: communication achieved not through using (for the most part, at least) any of the tools treated so far or building on the regular sensory resources of humans or other animals. It is the mysterious intercommunicating exhibited during swarming or flocking by some animals, and by humans too, and the extrasensory communicating in states of what has been called "alternative" consciousness, such as dreaming, extrasensory contact, and trance.

At first sight, these will all seem to be startlingly different kinds of communicating from those that usually appear in communication books. Maybe they are not "real" communication at all? They are not brought about by the use of the generally recognised human communication tools (except that music sometimes has a role), nor do they seem susceptible to the usual forms of analysis of human action.

Nevertheless, this kind of communicating clearly does, at times, take place and seemingly has a significant and, perhaps, once we look, not uncommon place in human communicating. Certainly, it should, as far as is practicable, find some place in any serious study of communication.

Swarms and swarming

"Swarming" is the collective behaviour of decentralized, self-organized systems, natural or artificial. These systems are typically made up of a number of individual agents interacting locally with each other and with their environment. There is no centralised control but local and, perhaps, to a degree, random interactions between the agents leads to an unusual

DOI: 10.4324/9781003496007-8

communication process to the emergence of intelligent overall behaviour, unknown to the individual agents.

A description like this makes it seem impossible. But actually, we are probably all familiar with the swarming process. We know it from seeing or hearing about bees and other insects swarming, birds flocking, fish schooling, and, in a partly parallel way, individual robots, self-directed, coordinating their actions with others.

Not all animals swarm, and it is a just one phase of their lives rather than a perpetual condition. But many do. It occurs with creatures as outwardly different as ants, bees, birds, and fishes and even, surprisingly, among *non*-social, solitary animals such as lobsters, cockroaches, and moths. It may mean going in a line rather than a spread-out group but still with self-directed agents acting together in coordination, still a case of swarming. It has the advantages for the animals that engage in it of flexibility, robustness, decentralised control, and self-organisation, with similar benefits in the otherwise different-looking situation of the battlefield.

How does it work? It seems impossible that hundreds or thousands of birds (to focus on that example) can fly together in a huge flock that wheels and turns at absolutely the same moment, totally coordinated – a

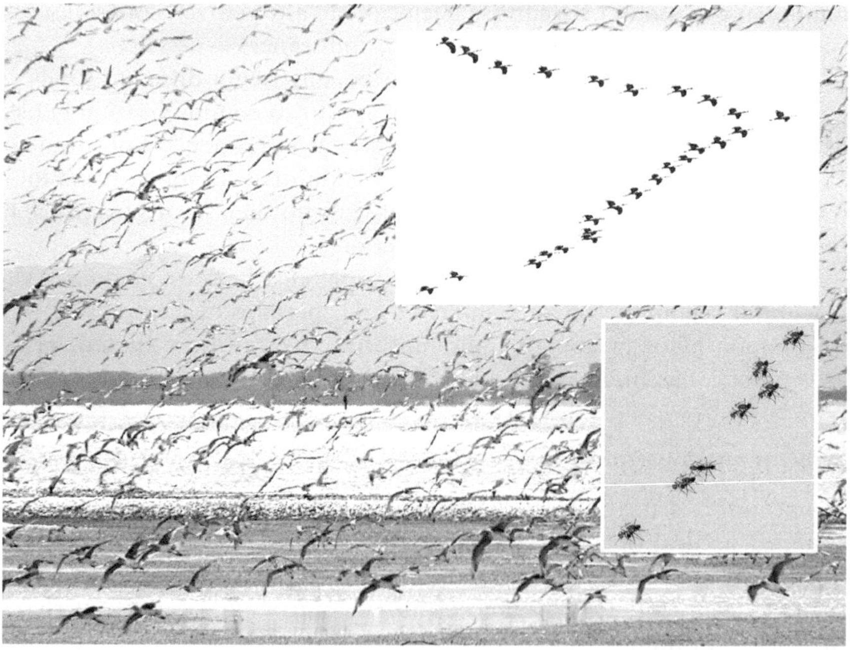

FIGURE 8.1 Many in one.

kind of single organisation made up of thousands, sometimes tens of thousands, of individual birds.

One explanation used to be that they were kept together from a signal from a leader in front or that, having seen or heard a companion turn, a bird then followed suit. But it is now realised that the turns are too rapid and too coordinated to result from the sending and receipt of individual messages or from waiting for a signal. And even in wedge-shaped flights, like those of migrating geese, in which we can see that one is in front, there is, in fact, no leader.

How then? What *does* happen, we now know, is that each bird coordinates its position in relation to the seven birds directly surrounding it, no matter how close or how far away they are. The many, still individuals, have become one organism and act as such – coordinating, self-directed, leaderless: a swarm.

Birds, as I say, are only one example, a familiar one. What is even more remarkable is that the behaviour of plants too can be interpreted as a species of swarm behaviour, if in a different way from that of freely moving animals. The individual roots grow in patterns that are more common than could happen by chance, indicating the presence of communication between them. Robots too, to researchers' amazement, have been found exhibiting swarm intelligence.

We may not know how it works, but some kind of communication is clearly in play.

"Flocking" in human communicating

This kind of intercommunication happens among humans too.

It is particularly salient among musicians. Think, for example, of the, in one way mysterious but in another natural – and necessary – communicating in joint music-making. Choir singers know it well. Each singer must keep coordinated with the rest without either anticipating others' actions or being late and dragging others back – not, one would think, an easy task when sometimes a hundred singers or more must keep totally together. And yet, in an any way good group, it happens.

Yes, there is a conductor in front, and yes, it is good that this conductor sets the tempo just before the start. The singers internalise this. But, if either at the start or during the singing, a singer waits for the conductor's signal (as the audience no doubt assumes) and then follows it, however carefully – they are late. The same all the way through. Each singer is just one item in a whole (so too is the conductor) and coordinates their breathing, their voice with those of others – a self-directed and, in that sense, leaderless element in a single organism.

Sarah Izen, well understanding joint music-making, explains it in more detail.

> Another key component of communication between performers takes the form of joint action. Although conversational speech does involve turn-taking and mirroring of body movements (e.g., gestures, head nods), the degree of interpersonal bodily coordination involved in a musical interaction is typically much more precisely temporally aligned, can have a large impact on the interpretation of a piece, and is often required for the interaction to run smoothly.
>
> For example, musicians must breathe together to align note onsets, and coordinate head, arm and even leg movements to maintain a steady tempo. If this bodily system of the ensemble becomes misaligned, it can have disastrous effects on the musical outcome, potentially requiring the players to start over. Beyond large-scale, visible bodily coordination, players also must precisely coordinate intonation by making micro-adjustments to embouchure and strings, which involves listening and matching at multiple levels ...
>
> Broadly, communication is a requirement for coordination, which is particularly relevant for joint music-making among all types of human interactions. Although incidental synchrony could theoretically occur in the absence of communication (e.g., if two people played at the same time by individually following the beat of a conductor without seeing or hearing each other), this would not represent musical coordination or communication between players. Lacking the in-the-moment, interpersonal adaptation that makes every performance unique, this would almost certainly yield a less naturalistic, less cohesive, less beautiful result.
>
> *(Izen 2023)*

Musical coordination happens. And it sometimes, near-unbelievably, allows improvisation in a large group without the need for prior plans or leaders. A recent study noted how a group of 16 musicians were able to act as one, together, while performing free improvisation – creating highly complex and unprecedented music without a previously agreed plan or a conductor.

> They achieved significant levels of coordination, both at the level of their musical actions (i.e., their individual decisions to play or to stop playing) and at the level of their directional intentions (i.e., their intentions to change or to support the music produced by the group) ... [through] decentralized and unscripted forms of collective behaviour.
>
> *(Goupil et al. 2020)*

Similarly, players of two violins, viola, and cello in a quartet kept in communication through being mutually attuned empathetically. This enabled them to produce wholly spontaneous musical variations during performance; it was "empathetic creativity".

It is not just in music. Another example is a certain form of coordinated farm action, again observed among the Sierra Leonean Limba speakers in the 1960s. As upland rice farmers, one phase in the agricultural year was always the extremely heavy work of hoeing the ground for the rice seed. This was undertaken by a group of young men and boys working side by side together in a long horizontal line. In front stood two drummers, while the line of workers progressed with amazing rapidity up the hill together to the rhythm of the drums. It was not the sound of the drums, pleasurable and rhythmic though that certainly was, that kept them together and enabled them to keep going for hours in what was seriously exhausting work. It was the coordinated bodily movement in the line as they rhythmically and uniformly hoed in the seed. It was, as it were, a shared near-tactile experience, felt through their bodies as they marked the rhythm in coordination – communion you could call it – with their fellows.

Nor of course is this somatic dimension confined to far away or long ago. It is a known feature of military marching, of a ballet troupe, and of some martial arts and dances. The executants somehow internalise the beat and coordinate – co-feel – their movements with others.

So, humans too, at times, engage, usually unthinkingly, in swarm or flocking activity. At a simple level, it has been observed that it is common for people walking side by side, or even a small group of people who know each other, to quite unconsciously fall into keeping step with each other. At other times, it may be planned and deliberate as in a rowing team, a column marching together, an experienced sports team routinely coordinating their movements in the field by somehow sensing (without consciously working out or "knowing ") where their teammates are and how they will move next without the need to look round for them. It is the same in a practised team of synchronised divers or swimmers, in dancing, military exercises, ritual processes, and other group activities that require the kind of intercommunication that allows immediate and exact coordination in both space and time.

There are also many unplanned swarming events. Think of a large crowd enthusiastically – mob-wise it is sometimes said – taken beyond themselves; a clapping and cheering gathering of tens of thousands at a political or religious event; a panic-stricken crowd rushing from danger; a group of girls living together unknowingly coordinating their menstrual times; an audience standing up "as one" to cheer at the end of a music performance. The individuals may be many and certainly not unconscious nor directed by a leader, but swayed by some kind of joint emotion, "beside themselves" with joy or uplift or, alternatively, with hate or terror. They may be in the kind of joint communication with others that could, again, be described acting as a kind of single multi-item intercommunicating organism.

Or, again, there are the willed group events that might eventuate not so much in physical action as in some kind of group experience: a deeply moved audience hearing a talented musical performance; people in a religious service; congregants in a "gathered" meeting in the silence of a

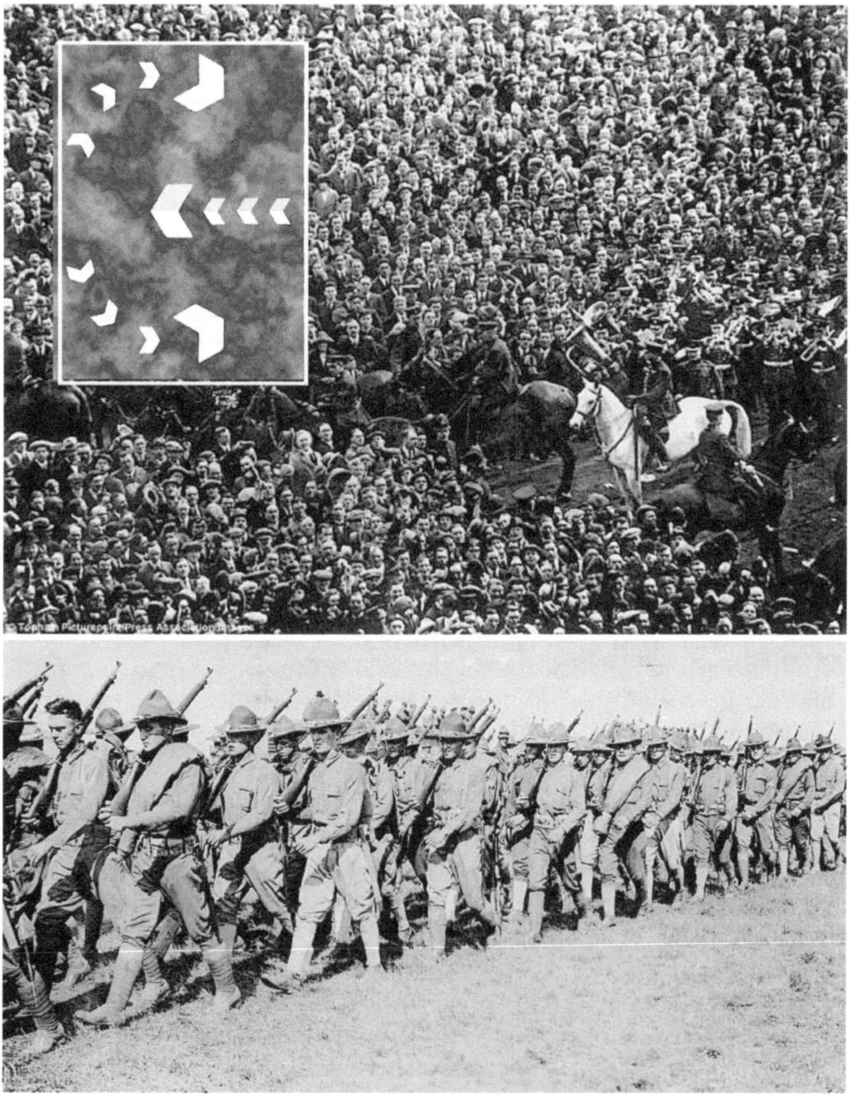

FIGURE 8.2 Human swarming.

Quaker meeting for worship (even sometimes, it seems, if only via Zoom); the feeling of attunement among Buddhist chanters; concentrating watchers at a close, tense football match; or hushed listeners to an inspired speaker – all these could be seen to be essentially the same as the flocking of birds.

It may at first sight seem inappropriate to call this swarming because, as in the examples above, physical movement may not come into it. But it is at least analogous to birds flocking or fish schooling, exhibiting the same basic characteristics: a number of individuals, leaderless, gathered into something working as some kind of single unit.

Some examples of swarming have had a negative press, described in such terms as for example, "a mindless mob", "mass emotion", "group hysteria". Such descriptions have a point in drawing attention to the apparent loss of individual humanity and sense of responsibility (especially castigated, of course, when the music or speech or religious occasion conflicts with the commentators' tastes or values). Such judgemental assessments, however, whether justified or not, in any particular case, do not really undermine the conclusion that there are cases of communicating, albeit of the still somewhat puzzling kind, that we can refer to, for short, as the intercommunication of swarming.

Recent approaches have been more positive, turning instead to the concept of a welcomed "mass" or "global" mind. This builds on the idea that many people working together in a coordinated way and building on the wisdom of a group can produce wiser results than a series of separate individuals, however talented. Similarly, the military advantages of swarming tactics, demonstrated over centuries, have been convincingly laid out in a recent book by Sean Edwards (2000). Much research is needed and will, doubtless, be undertaken to follow up such leads.

This kind of flocking-like intercommunication – sometimes referred to as "herd mentality" – is not, then, so very uncommon in human communicating. It happens from time to time, that is, not as a permanent form of human action, for though it is consonant with human sociality, it is not a necessary or continuing condition. It is now a subject of intense study. All armies of any worth, for example, today spend immense amounts of money on research into swarming, sometimes under the label of telepathy or robotics.

All these cases, in short, even if at first sight unusual, have been summed up under the head of "superorganisms of mutual intercommunication": one in many and many in one.[1]

Lessons from robots

A related point of interest is that work on this type of intercommunication now goes along with a surge in the field of *robotics* – one that inevitably brings a new perspective into the understanding of communication. This studies the coordination of systems composed of a large number of robots in which collective behaviour emerges from local interaction among teammates and between the robots and the environment.[2]

The robots can be autonomous, as, for example, probes and self-driving vacuums and cars; in other words, they are acting without recourse to human control. Industrial robot arms on assembly lines inside factories are also autonomous but in a more limited way, as their autonomy is restricted by being in a highly structured environment, so they are unable to locomote. Overlapping with the study of swarming, the field of robotics and, in turn, of artificial intelligence, this has opened up fresh approaches to sensory perception and experience that may, in time, lead to new perspectives on communicating.

There is still so much that we do not yet understand about human communicating. One of the areas with possibly the greatest potential at the moment relates to the topics – complex and variegated as they are – that have been considered in this section. They are still a puzzle. But it looks as if the field of robotics may have much to reveal on the nature of communicating. And, as the famous missionary hymn (another great communicator) had it, "Westward look, the land is bright".

Tools of the unconscious–conscious

No one would say that those men marching or those singers in a choir are not conscious, that they are *un*-conscious. Nor do we think of a painter fiercely concentrating on completing his picture as not conscious. But their consciousness is not of the same kind as when someone intentionally takes thought and then lifts up a pen or a brush or a lyre to communicate or speaks deliberately with vocally enunciated words. Rather, we could say that they are in a state of what has been called "alternative consciousness".

The painter example is not necessarily something strange or unusual. It is a familiar experience to be fully focused, even for just a few minutes, on, say, putting the final touches to a dish for the family meal, completing a marathon, or devoting oneself single-mindedly to finishing some given task (like, say, this book). Such consciousness can be viewed as not necessarily ethereal or unearthly, but just a common, though not permanent, phase of human living. For all that, this is a side of communication that we are mostly not aware of – or rather, we are not aware of at a surface level. But there it is, working away deeper down.

So a consideration of communicating needs to go on from swarming to a more general account of what happens when we are in a state of alternative consciousness. However strange it may look at first sight, this is another area, it emerges, for human expression and, in a wide sense, communication.

There are many forms of this type of consciousness, such as dreaming, the experience of communicating with and from the dead, non-local communicating, and, overlapping to an extent with dreaming, the state of being in some sense out of usual time and space. It has been called various names: by Teilhard de Chardin "the noosphere"; in my own work "there"; elsewhere "transformation" or "state of reason"; in religious contexts "ecstasy", "spirit possession", or just "heaven", "nirvana", "*sagga*" or "paradise".

It does not have to be "out of this world" in a literal sense; it can also, as I say, be being in a state of intense concentration. It can also be looking, alone, at the beauty of the night sky or the sea or the rays of the setting sun, being deeply moved by a poem or a piece of music, or feeling the vibes of a sacred place or of a spot of overwhelming natural beauty such as the magical Altar Stones Nature Reserve that inspired the verse

> You see fairies dancing around you,
> you hear the spirit voices chattering away
> and feel the memories of ancients under your feet.
> One day, a little bit of us will be there too.
>
> *(John Hunt)*

There is now a growing interest in alternative consciousness among scientists in, that is, the ways that in dream or trance or music we can somehow access a different, deeper, layer of knowing – of how when we dream, we can be "carried away", be open to communication from "the beyond", be somehow in touch with the dead, or be inspired to create some work of visual or sonic art, "in-spired", that is, through our breathing, our in-*spir*-ation, our *spirit*, our breath, which is another name for our soul. Many feel – though seldom speak of it – that, at times, they have some kind of contact (and not by earthly means) with others far away, with the supernatural, God, or fate, by whatever name; what else is "praying", "meditating", or yoga?

Something is going on behind the ordinary and the everyday. There are hidden layers within us not to be found through the common resources of the human senses or to be directly achieved through the tools, fine though they are, of the voice, the pen, and the lyre (though the lyre and its allies often have a part in the play). It is not only the poets and the seers who live in the fire of inspiration and of being somehow "beyond" themselves. It is not just the people of far away or long ago that have experience of the "sixth sense "or "extrasensory" perception – a common enough concept to have acquired its own acronym of ESP yet still little incorporated into the study of communication.

Here, then, are some examples of the communicating of the unconscious.

First, there is the many-sided subject of dreams, a topic that has long fascinated human beings and has drawn numerous studies through the ages.[3]

Classical and mediaeval authors took dreams seriously. For them, dreams were not misleading and mistaken bad-sleep visions but more just another kind of reality, in a different mode of experience. With the twentieth-century turn to more materialist science, the subject seemingly lost something of its academic appeal to scholars with the exception of the enormously influential and mind-opening but, from some viewpoints, questionable perspectives on dreams by Freud and Jung. But by now, with the opening up of new science perspectives, the subject is receiving more academic attention (the popular interest never wanes) and is widely studied by such disciplines as psychology, anthropology, neuroscience, and cultural history.

There are many accounts that suggest that dreams come from deep within the self, communicating things that are, in some sense, already there if we will but recognise them. If this seems to deny human intelligence and free will, it is worth recalling that, in some sense, dreams and oracles themselves do not lie: it is the dreamer who can misinterpret. The often quoted example of this occurred in the early fifth century BC when the Emperor of Persia was planning to invade Greece. Being careful, he went first to the famous Greek oracle in Delphi. The answer came: "If you invade, you will destroy a great empire". Encouraged that that meant he would succeed in conquering Greece, he invaded. The result? The prophecy was fulfilled – his own, the great *Persian* empire, was destroyed.

Dreams, or at any rate dream-like consciousness, have long been known to have a role in artistic creation. Few of those educated in a Western tradition will fail to recall Coleridge's *Kubla Khan* and the ever-cursed "man from Porlock" who interrupted and spoiled poet's dream-memory of the poem. Not so many know that Montezuma was led by dreams and divination, and writers from saints and scholars in the Middle Ages to Mark Twain, in more recent times, have been inspired by communications in dreams. Einstein too, it seems, and perhaps Newton and Descartes, not to speak of the pre-Socratic philosopher-scientists, were influenced by dreams as much as by this-world science. In political life too. It was what he experienced in his dreams that guided Churchill's war policies. The same was true of Joan of Arc and Abraham Lincoln.

Dreams can also, it seems, communicate knowledge about far away or yet to happen events. Or, perhaps better put, some people (maybe, potentially, all) have the ability to tap into the alternative consciousness that we term dreams or trance to receive or send these communications.

Dreams can be prophetic, something much built on in the oracles and auguries that have flourished in many cultures and eras, and while there have always been doubts about their validity, there have also been many clearly evidenced examples. One striking example told to me by a friend was that when her father was 9 or 10, he one night had a dream that the Titanic liner had been hit by an iceberg and sunk. In the morning, he told his father who laughed and said "the Titanic will never sink, it cannot". But, unknown to them, it had been that very night that the sinking had happened.

What can be the explanation of such experiences? Can dreams really tell us of what is to come and somehow[4] pull in knowledge and inspiration from beyond? An appealing theory is that what we call the future is somehow already there, it is just that we have not yet reached it. From time to time, the veil is a little drawn aside, and we are allowed the opportunity, already in principle there for everyone, to catch a glimpse of what we call the future. And for dream-led military or other policy and new inventions, some would say that this is a matter of things already known surfacing either in sleep or in that liminal inbetween state that, akin to dream, is neither awake or asleep but something of both – states when we somehow let go of the bonds of conscious thinking and, freed from them, are open in a special way to communication from our subconscious, thus becoming aware of and reaching conclusions about things that, on some level, we already know but have not yet recognised or put together. Certainly, that has often been my own experience.

Dreams in this perspective are not, as in other views, seen as beings of some kind coming from outside us, whether dead loved ones, currently distant friends, or heavenly spirits, but emerge from within ourselves, able, in some way, to reveal deeper truths than we are ordinarily aware of but are somewhere there, waiting to be uncovered. They exist in that below-conscious-consciousness communicating of dreaming.

The dying, it seems, have many dreams: predicting, threatening, consoling, posing problems that demand solution, and summing up their lives. This comes out especially in the by-now extensive investigations of dreams among those approaching death, that deeply emotive period. Thus, a chaplain in a hospice reported that some patients suffered terrifying guilt-drenched dreams but that after they had, in some way, resolved the issues, they received, instead, fortifying dream messages, foretelling the welcome tunnel through which they would pass on the way to heaven. Often, as they neared death, they dreamed of preparing to set out on a journey – putting on or taking off shoes or a hat, the approach of a train, a ship – sure signs that their last voyage was approaching.

Those who work in hospitals and hospices are the confidants of these dreamers. "Hiroshi", for example, just 28 years old had been diagnosed with terminal lung cancer. He knew that he was dying. He was desperate, terrified that his Japanese ancestors were angry with him for becoming a Christian, thus abandoning their religion. But a week before he died, he told his carers that he had a marvellous dream, "so real that it must have happened":

> The doorbell rings, and I answer it. There stand my aged grandparents, very short, neatly dressed, bowing and smiling. They slip off their shoes in the traditional way, enter the room, and hold forth two very large bouquets of pinkish orchids. I bow deeply and smile in return at their happy faces. I accept the bouquets, and that was the end of the dream.
> *(Bulkley and Bulkeley 2005: 74)*

Sometimes the dreams came in the form of music, as in the lovely negro-spiritual:

> Swing low sweet chariot
> Coming for to carry me home.

A communication coming in the strongest of forms, attested by both music and dream. It would be hard to deny that, in such dreaming, there was something of communication from beyond, opening doors that, in normal consciousness, are kept firmly closed.

Unearthly communication

It is striking how many accounts there are of earthly visitations from the dying on their way to another world, something I have myself experienced. One, unexpected, was from my dying mother (in the shape of a tortoiseshell butterfly, her favourite and also the symbol of the soul) and one from my oldest friend, visiting me in farewell (but not goodbye for ever) on her way to heaven. A third was as I felt to be closely accompanying, in a way to *be*, a dear scholar and musician friend as he walked through the woods he loved with, on either side the strains, of Bach's *Air on a G String*, true foretaste of heaven. And a father I know, as he was about to draw his last breath, reached out to his beloved daughter to be with him. She was many miles away in physical distance – but she knew and was fully "there" with him as he moved on.

After many years on earth, a dying person may not wish to relinquish their life without some sign, perhaps some urgent practical message, to a loved one or at least a mark of farewell.

A homemaker in Florida, in one well-evidenced report, told of how she was lying on the sofa one day when she suddenly – not in a dream – saw her father. His presence was clearly there, smiling at her.

> "It's all right, honey. It's beautiful over here! I'm really happy, so don't you worry". Then he laughed and added, "Now I don't have to pay for all that furniture your mom and sister bought". Of course, I didn't know what he meant.
>
> Almost simultaneously, the phone was ringing. I could hear my husband in the background saying, "Oh, my gosh!". He learned that my father had just died from a heart attack. My father was only 53 and had been in excellent health.
>
> After that, we got a letter saying my mother and sister had gone out and bought house full of furniture just before my father died. But my father's insurance paid for all of it! That was verification for me that my experience was real.
>
> *(Ellen in Guggenheim and Guggenheim 1995: 247)*

Or again there was the message from a dying, perhaps by then dead, colleague heard by his friend at home. Early one morning, she was pinched awake to see him standing by her bed. "I'm sorry Clare. I didn't make it". He added, "Goodbye", as if forever. Then he just vanished. She sat up wondering what it was all about. Then the early morning news on her clock radio announced that his seaplane had gone down the day before. He didn't make it ashore and had drowned.

Though some tales can be discounted, many are credible accounts in both the past and the fully attested and witnessed present. Sometimes, it is not so much an intimation during the dying transition or in a dream, but what is felt as a direct message from a loved now-in-heaven soul bringing comfort or information for the survivor(s). Such accounts of messages from the dead are legion and have been so throughout history.

And then there is other communicating to, with, and from the dead. It is scarcely strange that people of all religions and none wish to keep in contact with loved ones now in another place. They may commune somehow with the ones they love and endeavour – many would say with some success – to remain in communication with them: through prayer – whatever exactly that is – in church services, through hymns, through silence, music, dance, meditation, spirit possession, or, as is not uncommon, trance.

It can come in dreams too. I recall one night before I went to sleep, urgently asking – I didn't think of it as prayer but just an urgent request, a *demand* – that my parents, long dead, would somehow contact me. I relaxed and, forgetting, drifted off to sleep.

That night, my father (my mother too, but that is another story) came to me in dream to tell me a side of his nature that I had not realised during his life. He communicated this in the form of a piece of music, Handel's stirring *The Harmonious Blacksmith*. He used it to intimate to me that he was not just the man of intellect and principle that I knew and revered, but, like the blacksmith, also a fully physical man of strength and rhythm. That communication forever turned around my view of my father and my relationship with him.

Another kind of communicating in this strange area is when certain individuals return from death. It happens; I have met and questioned some of them – one a stern upright German professor. These returnees from death or, as many of them put it, from heaven, can bring information about how their loved ones are now faring and what it is like in heaven.

This, no doubt, sounds impossible, fantastic. But it is well attested through the ages and from at least the time of Plato, who spoke from his own knowledge and apparently was himself convinced of it. The subject, controversial or not, is obviously one of profound concern to humanity and always has been. Return from death appears in humanity's greatest tales, illustrated in Joseph Campbell's *The Hero with a Thousand Faces*, and deep, it seems, in the psyche of our humanity, inspired who knows from where? There was the Welsh Powys visiting and returning from Anwin, the underworld, the tales in the Mabinogion, the evergreen Greek stories of Persephone's return and of Alcestis brought back from Hades by the burlesque hero Heracles, of Odysseus, and Orpheus, and kings such as Arthur returning after death to check the state of their earthly kingdoms. We can recall too the iconic Christian tale of a resurrection. The return-from-death narrative, it seems, is a seminal myth known throughout the world and forever.

But it is more than "just" a myth if by that term we imply a delusion, a misconception, even a fabrication. There are plentiful first-hand, credible accounts of the experience of dying and returning, usually with reluctance, to exist for a while again on this earth. It seems that there are thousands, indeed millions, of people worldwide with stories to tell, communicating what they had of themselves seen, heard, and felt. As a result, there are multitudes of death-and-return reports and seemingly have been since the beginning of time.

Interpretations of this that are incompatible with the ruling physicalist and reductionist stance are often ruled out of account. Indeed, even mentioning it is impossible in certain circles so that it is often only at the end of their careers, after retirement, that scientists come out with what they have been doing and complement the official accounts by first-hand human tales of contact with the dead and their experience of, as Annamaria Hemingway (2008) has it, "the eternal continuum of consciousness".

There is, by now, a large and scholarly literature on the subject of people returning from the dead. One of the most detailed is the striking account by the previously highly sceptical neurologist Eben Alexander in his book called, significantly, *Proof of Heaven*. There are many similar examples of "trans-earthly voyagers, people who had glimpsed beyond the veil and returned to tell about it. Today they number in the millions" (Alexander 2012: 133). It has long been a common theme in literature and mythology, as, it seems, it is deep in the psyche of human beings.

That ties in with the related subjects of inspiration, trance, and music. There are many cases of this. Less often recalled than Coleridge's, there are countless poems and pieces of music created in some mode of trance by their composers. There is a sense in which creativity, today a topic of such interest, is often the fruit of some other plane of existence than the ordinary workaday world that we know. Siberian epic poets were endowed with a mysterious gift bestowed on the person of the singer by a prophetic call from beyond, a lone sailor was tranced in the ether's "Song's End" before his death, and Paul and others experienced their enchanted (as it were) Damascene moments of revelation in a vision from somewhere beyond this world's ways on the road to a revolutionary turn in their lives. Denise Saul, London poet and fiction writer, finds her poems arrive from somewhere beyond her, ready-made in their appropriate genres, rhythms, and sonic assonances.

So I am not alone in finding my poems and novels, with their sonic, unusual words and rhythms arrive from somewhere outside me, without, it seemed, conscious thought or planning but, again, in that trance-like liminal state between sleeping and waking. It was my poems that were the most surprising. Poems, as we know, are complicated, many-layered compositions, complex with sonic echoes, assonance, end rhymes, verse and line construction, meaning, and final climactic words. How could something so subtle and complicated just suddenly be communicated as a whole, ready-made, just there! They were complete with rhyme, sonic echoing, and even, sometimes, an unexpected twist in the tail. And yet, it happened, unexpected, unsought – not just once and not just to me.

In an earlier chapter, I used the example of my reading from a chapter of John's Gospel about Christ casting out a devil to illustrate how the histrionic devices of the voice and body are not just things of far away or long ago. I return to this now to describe a later, surprising, aftermath. It arrived again, fully formed, in that indescribable magic space that is neither sleep nor waking, yet both – liminal. Or perhaps it had somehow been there ever since the time when the words glowed in the reading; of before.

It was indeed a poem. It stood ready-made in my mind, waiting for me – a message of assurance and consolation, and as it unscrolled, I learned that *I* was the evil spirit speaking, in part redeemed, speaking to Christ of that golden moment when they met. This was its last verse.

....I am the evil spirit,
the one that shrieked and fled.

> You gave to me to recognise,
> the first,
> the very first,
> the first
> to see
> to see and say
> that, yes, you were
> you truly were
> the Son of God.

The dreamlike strike of trance sometimes, it seems, just arrives. But it can be induced too. Humans have developed ways of laying themselves open to this: through drugs, prayer, self-abnegation, solitude, physical exhaustion, the rhythms of music, withdrawal from normal life, spirit possession, religious rituals, and more. Searching for divine wisdom in ancient Greece was commonly undertaken by going deep into underground caves, a major setting for prophecy-giving and mystery initiations. It was in the dark of these caves that sages, seers, and initiates sought for the hidden truth experienced as revelation or vision.

> The cave environment creates conditions which force the human mind to deviate from its normal waking state and to enter altered states of consciousness, in many cases leading to the sensation of ineffable revelation of ultimate reality. Altered states of consciousness often occur in people exposed to sensory deprivation. As a result, various mediators between gods and mortals practice prolonged isolation in caves and other closed spaces in their quest of ecstatic illumination. The ... multiple cave experiences of the Greeks are culturally patterned responses to the states determined by the neurology of the human brain.

Yulia Ustinova explains further:

> The Greeks perceived mental experiences of exceptional intensity as resulting from divine intervention. They believed that to share in the immortals' knowledge, one had to liberate the soul from the burden of the mortal body by attaining an altered state of consciousness, that is, by merging with a superhuman being or through possession by a deity. These states were often attained by inspired mediums, impresarios of the gods – prophets, poets, and sages – who descended into caves or underground chambers. ... the darkness of the caves provided conditions vital for their activities.
>
> *(Ustinova 2009: blurb)*

Music often comes in too, like the dreams (dreams – we never, it seems, get away from that mode of consciousness) that inspired Brahms and Mozart – but then, how could the origin of such heavenly beauty be purely mundane? There was also the baroque violin virtuoso Tartini. His near unplayable "Devil's Trills", so the story goes, originated in a pact with the devil who came in a dream to play them to Tartini overnight – and hard enough they were, a movement full of trills and double stoppings that, forgetting the rest, he still remembered when he awoke. Until Yehudi Menuhin, it is said, Tartini alone could play it, using his six fingered devil-endowed left hand.

Music can be treated, rightly, as a crucial if puzzling element in this entrancement and altered consciousness. We can remember Albert Einstein who, when asked about the origin of his theory of relativity – the start of modern science – is said to have replied:

> The theory of relativity occurred to me by intuition, and music is the driving force behind that intuition. My parents had me study the violin from the time I was six. My new discovery is the result of musical perception. ... I often think in music. I live my daydreams in music. ... Imagination is more important than knowledge.
>
> *(Root-Bernstein 2010)*

Although not much included in studies of communication and of consciousness, music is right in there. It is related to dream-revelation, healing, psychic energy, the emotions, our sense of structure and rhythm – outcome of the deepest and most enduring, as it seems, of the human senses, touch-audition. Like dreaming, meditation, and the experience-and-return from death, music enables the re-creation of mind and supports the enhanced and altered states of consciousness we term entrancement. Chanting too is accepted as carrying deep meaning, widely utilised in healing, meditation, hypnosis, and shamanic trancing.

And who, one might ask, can picture any kind of heaven without its trumpets and its choirs of angels? Music, it turns out, is both obviously and, to many, unexpectedly crucial for the study of communication.

There is much still to be investigated and understood, but even thus far it becomes clear that music is central if we wish to delineate and integrate new approaches to, and dimensions of, the unconscious–conscious.

That leads on to consciousness itself – something closely linked to the study of communication. This, it scarcely needs saying, is a deeply complex and controversial subject which, like the rest of us, no doubt, I am far from understanding. But it is worthy of note that it has become a keen object of study, building on but challenging the insights that have formed our awareness since the time of Plato and, doubtless, before: after all, the pre-Socratics had much to say on this, not least on the fluidity of not stepping in the same river twice, a notion that has returned.

So now we see in science and spiritual thinking, working for the moment together, an opening up to new ways of appreciating the nature of consciousness. The confidence of the twentieth-century science seemed to suggest all was already known and understood, forever fixed in a materialist and conquerable universe. Much was, indeed, known, and the fruits of the scientific endeavours of those years are much with us and to our benefit. But gradually, first since Freud and Jung and their (variegated) views of the unconscious – unseen, unheard, un-experimentally proven – then, more decisively, with quantum and chaos theory, brain scans, advances in neurology and MRI, new worlds are being revealed, comparable only to the new worlds uncovered, revolutionarily, by the findings of telescope and microscope. Then too there is the theory of relativity and the elision or conflation of the concepts of time and space. The neurologist Eben Alexander is right to point out that:

> The modern study of consciousness includes the tremendous evidence for the reality of non-local consciousness, such as telepathy (sensing others thoughts and emotions), precognition (knowing the future), remote viewing or extra-sensory perception, psychokinesis (the manipulation of physical matter by the mind), and even past-life memories in children indicative of reincarnation. But the tip of the spear in demonstrating mind and consciousness independent of the physical brain remains firmly in the realm of near-death experiences and related studies.
>
> *(Alexander 2020)*

The universe has changed – that is, humans' understanding of it has changed.

As a series of research works have suggested, consciousness runs through all things – animals (little surprise there), plants, the sea, and the earth. The emphasis on psychedelic drugs in the 1960s has been superseded by an interest in the study of the nervous system, including the relationship between drum rhythms, brain waves, and shamanic states of trance or ecstasy based on the experience of soul flight. This merges into the study of altered states of consciousness and the light this throws on the study and nature of communicating.

Across the globe

This brings us to telepathy, that difficult term better expressed as shared minds – *koinonia*, or communion, a word, fittingly from the Greek – with appropriate theological as well as philosophical connotations. Here, researchers speak of communication as a species of somehow "shared experience irrespective of time and space", again a new view of consciousness that has attracted much interest, both popular and hard-headed academic. Answers have turned into questions and visions into journeys of exploration. We no longer know just what consciousness is, but we do know we need to try to understand telepathy in the sense of communicating at a distance without reliance on the normal sensory resources.

Many people, of course, do not believe this is possible or, at any rate, when asked in public affirm this position. Nor in some moods do I think it could happen on this earth (in "heaven" or "beyond time and space", yes, but not here). I too, like my readers no doubt, am a scientist, and everything I have been taught since I was a child seems to point the other way.

And yet there is now serious scientific interest in such topics. We seem to have reached a new, or perhaps ancient, hidden, mode of consciousness – knowledge shared in our communicating that is now being re-discovered.

This apparent mode of consciousness has now become a topic that, complex and in a way hidden though it is, can, in principle, be investigated like any other. Our own – often quite ordinary – experience attests it too. We know when someone, unseen by us, is looking at us across the room or reading our newspaper over our shoulder in the underground. It doesn't surprise us or even, until we start thinking about it, seem strange – and yet, how can it be possible in our normal scheme of things? Animals know when their owners are coming home or are in danger. Hunting herds, whether of animals or birds, keep in touch, somehow, non-verbally and effectively. Should we rule out that potential skill for us humans, that supposedly superior species, and say that it must be "impossible"?

Twins, we accept, are different – a bit mysterious, "special" (but why? They are human just like the rest of us). We recognise, almost as a matter of course, that they can communicate in ways we do not understand – not necessarily deliberately, or it seems not, but emotionally, spiritually, intensely. Somehow. I have seldom met a twin who denies this, and I always ask. Small babies too, it seems, pre-speech. Is it that twins are together in the womb (what could be closer, more intertwined?), in death and even perhaps in life, bound together as one being?

And today – even psychotherapists seem to admit the possibility of this – we accept some continuing deep connection between living and dead – different, but continuingly reaffirmed in many people's experience and sometimes, in times of crisis, by a recourse to prayer. Have we not all known of at least one such enduring, mutually loving relationship – between mother and dead child, born or unborn; husband and wife; passionate lovers? So why do we exclude it between the living?

What is involved, it seems (if, that is, we can temporarily suspend disbelief), is that two intimately linked souls do not so much send and receive messages at a distance (tele -) as find themselves merged, the thoughts and feelings of the one interpenetrating the other – less email message than being together on the cloud. It is *koinonia* again, that classic Greek word for sharing and fellowship, rather than discrete communications. In our unconscious consciousness, we somehow know deeply but without, on the surface, knowing that we know and that we communicate.

These topics remain strange and puzzling, something out of the ordinary that it is hard to analyse by our usual resources or describe in terms of the functions of voice, pen, and lyre. And yet, from another viewpoint, they are, in many ways, quite ordinary in that many, perhaps most, people have, from time to time, some personal contacts with one or more of these topics.

At any rate, it is clear that here is an area full of communication: communication that comes to us through dreams (or perhaps from deep in ourselves, our subconscious); communication to and from the dead; messages brought by those returning from death, or heaven, or whatever it should be called; non-local communicating with those distant from us in time and space; and communication to and from oneself in a state of trance.

Minds at work

It need not be trance-like. For at a more ordinary level, how can we explain the way discoveries and inventions so often come simultaneously to more than one person? It is not only usual but expected that a Nobel prize has to be awarded to two or even three people who have, separately, made the same discovery. It is almost routine. And, in fact, it seems that the occurrence of multiple discoveries, often simultaneous, has become accepted as the usual pattern in science. Remember, for example, the multiple, often near simultaneous, discoveries of oxygen, the planet Neptune, calculus, and concurrent advances in the area of medicine.[5]

It is astonishing really. Explanations have been offered, such as that it is in accordance with the spirit of the age or the prevailing or emerging paradigm, that it is serendipity, telepathy, the "right time", that it is needed, or even the collective unconscious.

For the present time, it is not so very hard to account for it, given the existence of widely shared data, online journals, the international interaction of scientists, and the probability of many people simultaneously working on the same issues. But in the past? Think of the telephone, steamships, the discovery of oxygen, Uranus, calculus, evolution, magnetism – all discovered independently at least twice. Marconi is celebrated for the discovery and implementation of radio, but we now know that Tesla was also right there with it, and scores of amateur experimenters (my grandfather among them) were apparently already working on it too.

In the further back ages, we are fairly sure that some things were discovered just the once – that individual genius at work again – for example, printing, the stirrup, gunpowder, and the bow and arrow, and that these, then, over generations, spread from being transmitted from person to person, group to group.

Others, it seems, were truly independently discovered or invented at different parts of the globe – agriculture, the wheel, fish lures, the blowpipe, metal smelting, a range of musical instruments, inscription implements, pyramids, beer, some foodstuffs that are now taken for granted, pictographic writing systems, and mathematics and the systems for representing numbers. Amazingly, more than 100 such mathematical systems have been devised and used over the past 5,500 years, including glyphs able to represent any conceivable number, as well as, starting even further back, the tally marks of perhaps more than 40,000 years ago. Further back still, we can imagine, perhaps, multiple discoveries of the use and control of fire.

We can never, of course, be certain of what happened those many thousands of years ago, but that there could well have been simultaneous discoveries like these seems not at all improbable given the other things we know.

And what about what is often seen as the beginning of it all – the purposeful making of flint tools that marked the Palaeolithic Old Stone Age? We know that non-sapiens hominids had discovered and practised this, so it is no surprise that our ancestors did too and developed the practice into further more elaborate tools.

And it seems too that, as primates, there was some inbuilt readiness for this judging by the recent account of a bonobo chimpanzee creating flint implements to assist in getting at hidden food; it is true that he was captive and had had some initial training, but he went on from there to develop his own tools, suggesting that there was, indeed, a primate propensity. There is more, for it seems that some clever chimp had already been at work, as wild chimpanzees create physical devices for acquiring drinking water and make habitual use of tools in the contexts of comfort, play, self-directed behaviour, and communication.

And it seems, further, that, using direct percussion, chimpanzees were observed to use:

> a variety of flint tool types than hitherto reported, and used them task-specifically to break wooden logs or to dig underground for food retrieval. For log breaking, small flakes were rotated drill-like or used

> as scrapers, whereas thick cortical flakes were used as axes or wedges, leaving consistent wear patterns along the glued slits, the weakest areas of the log. For digging underground, a variety of modified stone tools, as well as unmodified flint nodules, were used as shovels. Such tool production and utilization competencies reported here in Pan indicate that present-day Pan [chimpanzee] exhibits Homo-like technological competencies.
>
> *(Roffman 2012)*

This recent research means that we can now be assured that – continuity again – our sapiens ancestors were better set up at the start than we used to imagine.[6]

The cave painter's art

Cave paintings are often seen as the true start of our ancestors' ascent to, eventually perhaps, the stars. People have long puzzled for an explanation of the amazing similarity of these paintings, found in continents right across the world, even in the Americas and the far ocean-girt lands of the south seas.

It is a puzzle and a mystery. For how could these striking likenesses have come to pass?

There are possible explanations. The most obvious one is that humans, like great apes, always had the potential for such art and that confronted these huge beasts, and when armed with available pigments and an empty wall – voila!

The propensity for drawing is, indeed, credible and proven. But from what we have seen of great ape painting, as shown so stunningly in Desmond Morris's account (1962), early humans might, as primates, have had a *potential* interest in colour and lyrical design, but one not likely to be activated until, like Desmond Morris's Congolese ape friend, they were offered paper and pencil. Besides, there is no trace of great apes, unlike humans, showing any interest in representational, far less figurative art. And when there are so many *different* subjects that could have been chosen and so many ways they could have been depicted, why are cave paintings so often in the style they are? We are still left with a mystery.

There is another more specific and more credible hypothesis – one, furthermore, with some indirect supporting evidence. This builds on the fact, now more widely recognised, that, even in the most ancient of worlds, there was more trade and travel than once imagined. That would, though slow, have allowed the spread of artistic ideas. It would not have been a Marco Polo journeying across the breadth of Eurasia, just one person travelling to a nearby settlement and sharing their ideas, then that individual or, more likely, another paying a visit to the next settlement or taking a spouse from there, then another to another, and then another. Just a few miles each time. There were tens of thousands of years for the process to have happened, little by little by little, aided by the human capacity, even the urge, for imitation.

We can readily imagine that, through the millennia, this could, indeed, have taken place. In fact, we know it did – are there not maps detailing the spread – the travelling, that is – of *homo sapiens* from Africa across that continent and into Eurasia and across the globe. We know it happened because here we all are.

And if this sounds impossible, recall that it was not just one generation but generation after generation, with thousands upon thousands of years for it to come about. It was no miracle, just the continuing of history.

But against it is difficult to see how the specific cave painting arts were, in fact, transmitted in this way, as there was no photography then; and would the ephemeral shaping of gesture be sufficient to convey what was involved – the lines, the shapes, the subjects, the colouring – or be describable in words or, better but even so scarcely sufficient, gestures? Besides, it feels slightly unlikely that it would have been the artists, however part-time, who would have opted to travel – they would surely have been fully occupied in getting on with the long task of working on their paintings. Or, supposing that they did, would they have wished to settle long enough with another group to complete and demonstrate a full painting? It is not impossible but seems unlikely, especially as, for it to be effective, it would have to have happened multiple times.

It seems impossible. Unless, somehow, subliminally from one mind to another … ?

In the light of the human way of habitual multiple discoveries and of the workings of the unconscious–conscious described a little while back, that possibility unavoidably floats into mind. Now that there is a greater readiness to consider non-sensory communication, however extraordinary this might seem for traditional science, new ways of looking at the cave art resemblances, even Jung's once suspect concept of the collective unconscious, begin to open up. If twins can communicate extrasensorily both nearby and at a distance, if swarming individuals can be in contact without overt means of communication, and if a group of dogs or San hunters in deserts of South Africa know, without a leader, signal, or verbal language, how to coordinate so as to best surround their prey – if all that is accepted, as it surely now must be, might we not consider the possibility of this kind of intercommunicating working among others? And those others to include our own ancestors?

Listen to the words of the American scientist Howard Bloom

> A worldwide neocortex – complete with whales – is not a gift of the silicon age. It is a phase in the ongoing evolution of a networked global brain which has existed for more than 3 billion years. This planetary mind is neither uniquely human nor a product of technology. Nor is it a result of reincarnation, or an outgrowth of telepathy. It is a product of evolution and biology.
>
> *(Bloom 2000: 1)*

I know little about the 3 billion years, and would myself emphasise rather human intelligence and initiative, reaching out again and again and yet again to create using our human-managed tools. But, in other ways, that statement, I believe, is exact. For "from the beginning we have been yanked together by the tug of sociality" (Bloom 2000: 1).

Homo sapiens, therefore, had a good start, with, we cannot but think, something of a substrate – something below, that is, of what we now think of as the "normal" above-the-level consciousness. Could there have been something like a thousand minds in one, one consciousness somehow influencing another – in-*fluen*-cing, *flow*-ing into those of others (language can hide such wisdom)? And why not originating from a chimpanzee – the idea of tool creation had to start somewhere? And why not, again, multiply? After all the concept of continuous creation always seems more realistic than one big, sudden bang out of nowhere.[7]

And if non-sensory communicating is possible across short distances, what is to stop it working equally over longer distances, even those that separate, in both time and space, the peoples of Eurasia, America, and Australia. Precisely because this kind of subconscious dream-like communicating is defined as non-sensory, non-bodily, it might well also be non-distance-sensitive.[8]

This leads to a wonder of whether the world of humans (or, perhaps, of all living creatures) was once united in a kind of distant, telepathic intercommunication web. Or, going further, whether at some deep unawares level, this might be so of our present world too.

Notes

1 Despite the problems, moves are going on toward unravelling the process(es) by which such intercommunicating takes place, coupled with growing interest in sociality, robotics, swarm studies, and artificial intelligence. See for example Sussman 2004; on swarming see Bloom 2000, Edwards 2000 (from a military history angle), Fisher 2009, Kagan and Ben-Gal 2015, Marabito 2024, Nedjah and Mourelle 2006, Suroweicki 2004 and https://en.wikipedia.org/wiki/Swarm_behaviour/.

2 There is a huge amount of literature on dreams; see, among much else, Basso 1974, Bulkeley et al. 2009, Edgar 2009, Finnegan 2017, Lohmann 2003, Moss 2010, Tedlock 1977, Zangrilli 2012.

3 "Somehow": I see that this is a word I use rather frequently, to my embarrassment, as it doesn't sound very scientific. But it does, at least, indicate my awareness that, throughout the book (not just in this chapter), I am dealing with that mysterious, elusive, thing called human nature – impossible to capture but a topic deserving our best effort.

4 See e.g., Merton 1961, Do Vale 2005.

5 For recent accounts of primates creating stone tools, see Malein 2012, Metin 2020, Pashcheveskaya 2024, Roffman 2012, and https://www.youtube.com/watch?v=j0jqJUF1nOs/, https://www.youtube.com/watch?v=FA3LN4vqtlM/, https://youtu.be/8ndlW3LsHLY?si=C8k0kngdd9EG-Ylg/; also, though not about tool-making, but is relevant as a demonstration – somewhat amusingly – the actuality of primate intelligence.

6 Pollick and de Waal 2007, Prieure et al. 2019, Tomasello and Call 2019.

7 On the hand, see also Alpenfels 1955, Anon n.d.(b), Bulwer 1644, Goldin Meadow 2003, Herz 1960/2008, also the references on gesture, below.

8 Further on gesture: Bulwer 1644, Byrne et al. 2017, DeJorio 1832/2000, First Words Project 2019, Kendon 2004, McNeill 2005, 2012, 2015, 2017, Morris 1977/2002 (also the summary and references in Finnegan 2023 Chapter 6, which there is no need to repeat here).

9

THE HAND OF HISTORY

Let me now return from these elusive realms to the tools and actions of the face, the body, and – we arrive there at last – the hand. Darwin summarised it so succinctly:

> Man could not have attained his present dominant position in the world without the use of his hands, which are so admirably adapted to the act of obedience of his will.
>
> *(Darwin 1871:52)*

The hand

So now at last, we come to the hand, the site of manipulation (*man* – the hand). But it has quietly underlain the discussion of human living from Chapter 3 onward, a necessary condition for our tool usage, and – Darwin's comment was justified – our greatest gift.

Our hands are so much a part of us, seemingly just a handy (*sic*) appendage to our bodies, that we seldom think directly about them. But they have been a focus of interest from cave days (hands were among the first subjects to figure in cave paintings) as for thinkers a ways back. In the fifth century BC (but, no doubt, in others before that too), Socrates commented that if we hadn't a voice or a tongue, and wanted to say something, "would we not try to make signs by moving our hands, head, and the rest of our body, just as dumb people do at present?" (Plato, *Cratylus*).

DOI: 10.4324/9781003496007-9

Some hundreds of years later, the seventeenth-century physician John Bulwer followed this up by penning a perceptive tome on the hand, complete with detailed diagrams of its full-of-meaning signs. The hand, he writes:

> speaks all languages, and as a universal character of Reason is generally understood and known by all Nations, among the formal differences of their Tongue. And being the only speech that is natural to Man, it may well be called the Tongue and General language of Human Nature, which, without teaching, men in all regions of the habitable world doe at the first sight most easily understand.
>
> *(Bulwer 1644)*

In the eloquent language and spelling of his day, words still pertinent for our own times, he expands further in his *Chirologia* or *The Natural Language of the Hand.*

> In all the declarative conceits of Gesture, whereby the Body, in-grafted by Nature, can emphatically vent and communicate a thought, and in the propriety of its utterance express the silent cogitations of the minde, the Hand, that busiest instrument, is most talkative, whose language is as easily perceived and understood, as if Man had another mouth or fountaine of discourse in his Hand. So proper and apt to make signes and work great matters is the Hand of Man …
>
> God commands him natural gestures which had thence the force of miraculous signification, and to these signes God attributes a voice. For he saith If they will not hearken to the voice of the first, they will believe the voice of the latter signes; and as there is in the supernatural, so there is a signifying voyce in the naturall signes of the Hand...
>
> For the Hand being the Substitute and Vicegerent of he Tongue, in a full and majestique way of expression, the signifying faculties of the soule, and the inward discourse of Reason; and as another Tongue, which we may justly call the Spokesman of the Body, it Speakes for all the members thereof, denoting their Suffrages, and including their Votes.
>
> So that whatever thought can be delivered, or made inwardly felt by the united motions and connative endeavours of all the other members, the same may be as evidently exhibited by the sole discoursing gestures of the Hand.
>
> *(Bulwer 1644)*

This viewpoint is not adopted by everyone. For many, the conviction is that verbal language is the key feature of human beings, its possession almost the definition of humankind. This presupposition comes, for example – only one of many similar cases right back to, and beyond, Müller's gentler formulation (1862: 13) quoted earlier) – in the somewhat presumptuous subtitle of Guy Deutscher's 2006 book on language as "mankind's greatest invention". His summary, in extreme, but not unparalleled terms, is that:

> The advent of language is what makes us human. Compared to language all other inventions pale in significance, since everything we have ever achieved depends on language and originates from it. Without language, we could never have embarked on our ascent so unparalleled over all other animals, and even over nature itself.
>
> *(Deutscher 2006: 2)*

Darwin's view is different. Verbal language does, indeed, play a significant part, but it is, ultimately, the hand that makes possible our distinctive human existence. Where would we be without it? It is the basis and setting that enables our full use of the tools of humanity and our enjoyment of their products – they are all around us.

This is in several senses.

First, though it is right to stress our continuity with other animals, there is one thing that is, in large part, unique to human creatures. Alone among mammals, the established habit of humans is to stand and walk upright, bipedal – on two legs. Unlike with the four-footed gait of other animals, our heads are high for looking wider and for communicating with straight looking; and, that great tool, the front limbs are free to use for their many purposes. We may not run as fast as four legged creatures, but we are *habilis*: we have our hands.

There is a long background to this. In Colin McGinn's perceptive *Prehension*, he points out in words worth pondering for more reasons than one:

> We became what we are today because we were driven down from the trees and forced to adapt to a new and hostile world. If life in the trees had remained hospitable ... our hands would not have been transformed into the prehensile prodigies they are today ... What looked like a catastrophe turned out to result, in the fullness of time, in an unprecedented species success, largely because of what the hands became under the new selective pressure. We snatched victory from the jaws of defeat ... The hands played a pivotal role in this reversal of fortune. They allowed us to claw our way back after a shocking and perilous deracination.
>
> The abilities of the hand are not all acquired, however. There must surely be a strong innate component. Hand competence is essential to

human survival and hence is best not left to chance. The human infant develops the basic grips and skills without instruction so that an innate program must be controlling the proceedings.

(McGinn 2015; 20, 23)

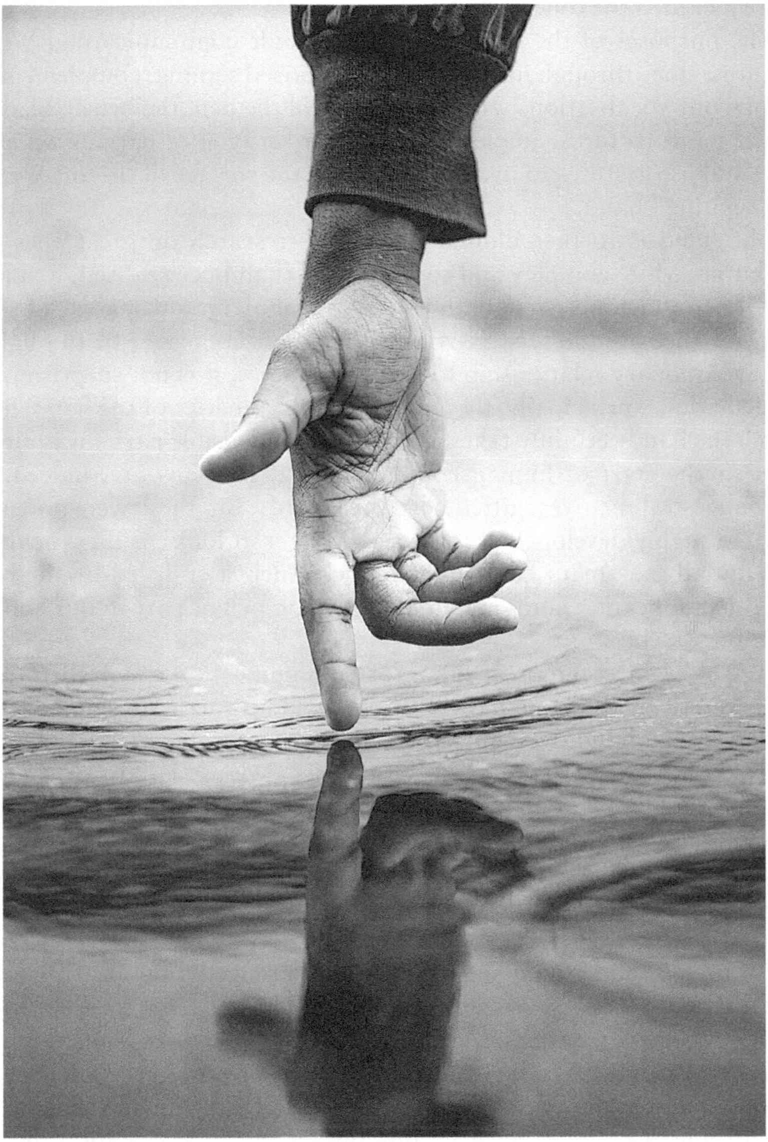

FIGURE 9.1 The hand.

Think of what we humans owe to the hand in the many products that surround us and have done so in their many forms through untold ages. There is no need to recite them, as they are the manifold arts and artefacts and constructions around us, the fit and necessary concomitants, one might say, of human life as it is lived on earth today. What are they but the products of human hands? Some come from the direct work of hands – "handmade", "traditionally crafted" – but all have, at some point, in their history needed the touch of a hand.

The purposes of the hand, crucially, include communicating. We can gesture a story through informal or systematised signing; complement and deepen our vocalisations with gesture; wield the pen, the brush, blade, or finger; paint pictures; employ the hand for scribing or carving on a surface; and use gestures to inscribe shapes on the surface of the air. We have the "signing" hand.

The hand is further illuminated by the research on great apes' gesticulating. More complex and sophisticated than once realised, it appears that it is, in fact, a system with its own vocabulary and syntax, of something of the same nature as vocalised human language. In the light of our evolutionary relationship to these great apes, it is not surprising that gesticulation – principally, though not wholly a matter of the hand, but in which the hand certainly takes a prominent and visible part – was already there at the start of human communicating. Humans are, indeed, like their ancestral relatives, gifted with vocal cords. But these were not, at the start, as highly developed as they became later. It looks as if gesticulating was initially the main communicating channel. It still, led by the hand, plays a significant, signifying, and highly competent part in our communication system.

Gesture is a common medium of communication everywhere today and, doubtless, all through the past. We hold up a hand to signify stop or no entry; raise hands to signify surrender or salute; and stretch out a hand of friendship or of enmity or of self-defence. We use hands for clapping, blessing, holding in companionship and love, in worship, obeisance or religious attention, in reaching out desperately for help, waving to attract attention, or holding out to curse. It is still important enough to have its own set of up-to-the-minute emoji signs. Figure 9.3 shows are just some of them.

We use our hands to shake in greeting or farewell, pray, seal a bargain, measure, tell fortunes, count on the fingers, invite, repel, play an instrument, and amplify or contradict what the lips are saying. The hands communicate emotion, status, and movement in meeting acquaintances, in speeches, and in dance. Part of good manners requires us to shake hands in the right way, keep them by our side or not as convention dictates, holding them in the way expected, folded or open, stretched or relaxed.

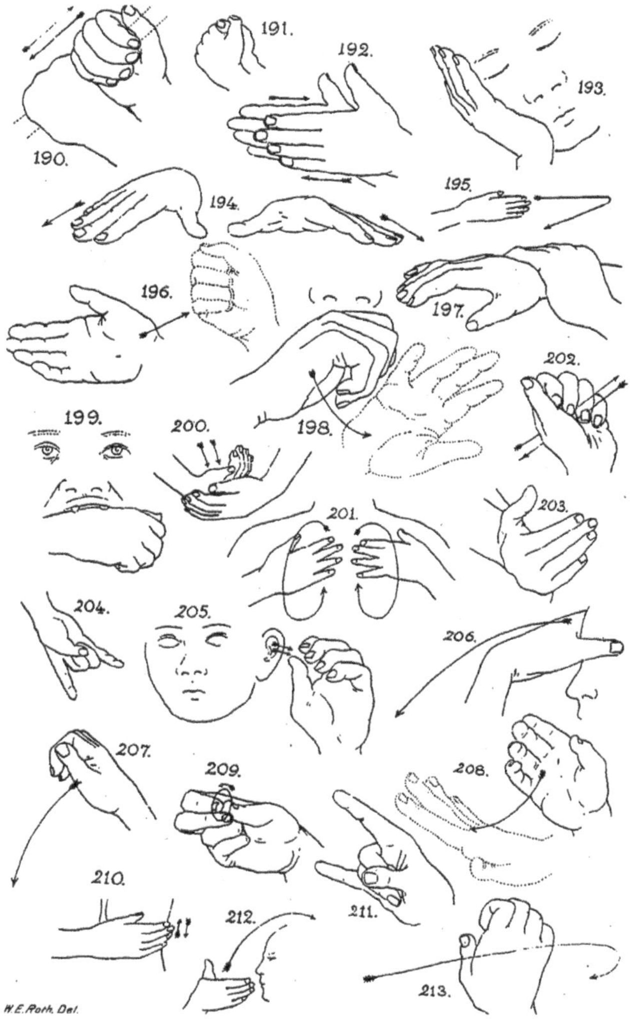

FIGURE 9.2 Native Australian.

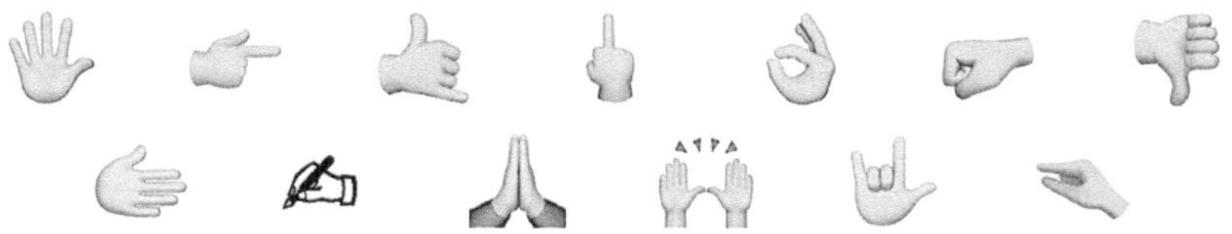

FIGURE 9.3 Emoji symbols.

Comporting the hands not in accord with local etiquette conveys rudeness or, at best, lack of care: in English meals, hands stay in your lap when not being actively used, while in French meals, they rest on the table top. Such management of the hands is a not insignificant part of our non-verbal communication system.

The hand also plays a crucial part in rituals. It is the hands that signify "salaam" and make the sign of the cross in religious services. The transmission of Buddhist teaching is conveyed by joining the tips of the thumb and the index finger together, and in Hinduism and Buddhism, a *mudra* ("seal") is a symbolic gesture of the hand or fingers: each *mudra* has a specific meaning, with a central role in Hindu and Buddhist iconography. Hands often have deep religious significance (as, for Christians, their piercing in the crucifixion or their role in ceremonial blessing or anointing) and are the subject of a famous and moving picture by Albrecht Dürer. The hand is used in touching a sacred object to signify commitment in making a promise or swearing, patting a child's head to convey approval, chucking under a girl's chin for whatever that means, and the laying on of hands in healing. It is the hand that is put on your heart to show sincerity and used by a leader to hold up when advancing in battle, part visible sign, part a loyalty-inducing symbol of inspiration and authority. There are the communicating hands of actors, gymnasts, circus entertainers, dressage riders, and dancers. There is the symbolic "hand

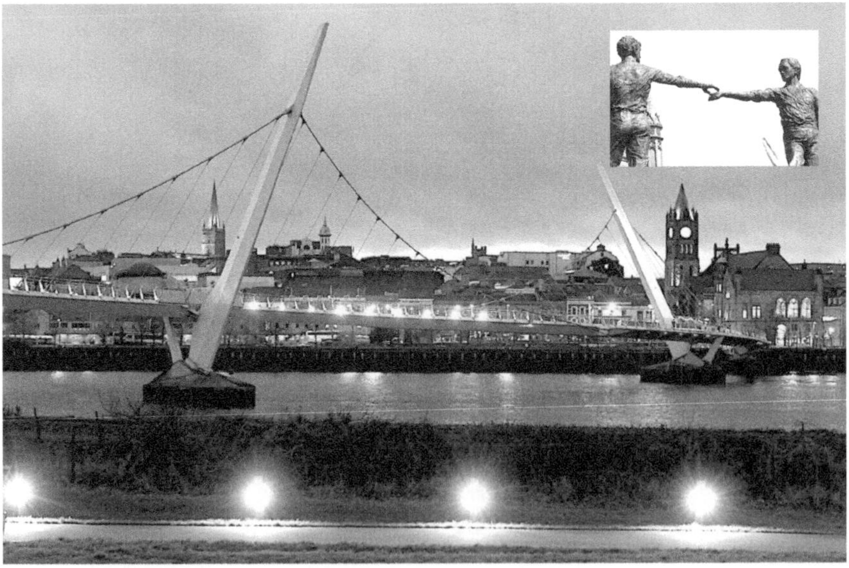

FIGURE 9.4 Peace bridge.

of fate", "offering a hand in marriage", "the hand of God". The joining of hands in a wedding signifies union, and the near touching of hands in the statue near Derry's peace bridge in Northern Ireland communicates a message of hope and reconciliation.

There are other aspects of body language in which hands have a secondary role. We communicate, in part, by the way we walk, the way we move our bodies (have you noticed the special way the leader, the chief surgeon, the officer walks as s/he comes in to take charge of things?), the way we shake or nod our heads, greet our friends, smile – remember Mother Theresa's "Peace begins with a smile", for a smile, accompanied by acquiescent hands confirming sincerity, almost necessarily evokes a smile in response; and so on around the world. Our upright posture, meanwhile, enables a mutually clear view of each others' faces and hands.

It is with the hands that in the most direct and immediate sense, humans engage in creative manipulation – *man-ipulation.* Our hands work with our other tools to manufacture new objects, and from them, yet further tools to use in further manipulation. Around us are the fruits of our hands: tables and chairs, manuscripts, scrolls, carvings, paintings, buildings, bound books – all there, for good or bad (for a hand can extend either welcome or a fist, create a cannon as well as a lyre), created by the work of human hands, of man-the-maker.

It is the hand, again, that guides the pen and its allies in the mark-creating of writing – inscribing, engraving, drawing, painting, carving – a fine tool for creating the print for publicly circulated announcements and for the secret communicating of the Masonic handshake. In the early years when Christians were persecuted, necessitating that they operate in secret, to gesture the shape of a fish (signifying the Greek word for fish, made up of the initial letters of the phrase "Jesus Christ, son of God, saviour") was to communicate their Christian adherence. The hand has no verbal language, for it speaks across, transcends, language difference and can communicate internationally.

It is largely through the hand, too, that humans engage with the wealth of nature around them. They cut down trees for wood to build houses and mosques and cathedrals; they make ships for the sea and bridges to travel over; manage water for cisterns or machines; mine rock and earth for minerals; breed silk worms for silk; dig out red ochre for painting; create and wield weapons for war or the hunt; manipulate wood fibre into paper; and more.

Darwin has it right:

> Man alone has become bipedal; and we can I think partly see how he has come to assume his erect attitude which seems one of the most conspicuous differences between him and his nearest allies. Man could not

> have obtained his present dominant position in the world without the use of his hands, which are so admirably adapted to act in obedience to his will. ... The hand supplies all instruments and by correspondence with the intellect gives him universal dominion. But the hands and arms could hardly have become perfect enough to have manufactured weapons, or to have hurled stones and spears with a true aim as long as they were habitually used for locomotion and for supporting the whole weight of the body.
>
> *(Darwin 1871: 84)*

The hand, then, has manifold functions, both utilitarian and symbolic, in human communicating and for both amicable and hostile interaction, all aspects of the notably social nature of human beings.

Homo faber et sapiens: a hand-skilled, communicating, connecting, animal

We humans are, indeed, distinctive in our palette of communicative skills and resources: predominantly audio-visual but with some use of other senses.[1]

We are distinctive in two other ways too. First, though some animals use external marks to communicate through time, humans have developed these to a degree and in a way that, so far as we know, and despite the great apes' impressive gesticulating systems, no other creatures have so far done. It is not just in writing systems, for all that we tend to think of them first, but also in organised systems such as deaf signing, numbering systems, artistic and pictorial narration, and, up to a point parallel with some other animals, gestures and body language.

The second distinctive feature is the human development of spoken language, an extensive, multi-faceted, and constantly developing resource. It not a case, as some assume, of "the acquisition of language" as the great turning point and definition of becoming "truly human" – that would be to ignore the other human communicative skills and their continuities. Nevertheless, verbal language. with its complex realisation in speech and its transforming of utterances into what can be labelled as literature, both oral and written, are notable features of human life worldwide that are not to be ignored. Add to this, and overlapping with it, the amazing existence of human music – is it part of the same sonic syndrome as speech?

So humans do, indeed, have their distinctive talents and achievements. But consider also the continuity between the communicating resources of humans and other animals. This is one of the most striking things found in this study and my earlier exploration: there is no clear-cut single line of division between humans and other animals. This too accords with

Darwin's vision of continuity – not so much the genetic evolutionary continuity between humans and other animals, but of nature, resources, and action. It is a continuity consonant with the evidence in this book. And as the master historian Arnold Toynbee put it, linking past, present and, maybe future:

> When a hominid chipped a stone with the intention of making it into a more serviceable tool, this historic act, performed perhaps 2 million years ago, made it certain that one day some species of some genus of the hominid family of primate mammals would not merely affect and modify the biosphere but would hold the biosphere at its mercy.
>
> *(Toynbee 1978: 183–184)*

So what were humans doing during that long long period since the first inspired chip on a flint? What came about in that blank (to us) period when, for tens of thousands of years without writing, humans had, some would say, not yet acquired the rational, investigative science-type mentality that goes, it is supposed, with having learned to read and write.

From what we know from a groundbreaking paper (Whiten et al. 1999) about the cultures of our close relatives the chimpanzees and how a useful new habit could be invented by a single animal – as we know happened with the Japanese monkey "Imo" (Matsuzawa 2015) – then passed on from one generation to another, we would expect humans too to have created new patterns of behaviour. And then, if these proved useful, for them to be communicated among and beyond the group where they were first developed. So, indeed, it must have transpired, as members of homo sapiens mutually communicated and shared their developing tools. From the start (if that is the correct word) 300,000 years ago, humans activated and worked through successive "ages of human history".

It is hard for us, now, to take in the immense length of human history. Knowing something of the way it developed through successive "ages" helps to bring some perspective on the timescale and context on what was happening. So here are some dates to give a rough idea of the time involved. They are only approximate – the best we can do for now – and constantly being revised. Many of the innovations seem to have started in Eurasia and then spread, so the dates of the "ages" varied in different areas of the world. Whatever the details, the time span is immense.

It begins with the "Stone Age" two to three million years ago.

- Stone Age 2,000,000–3,000,000 BC to about 7,000
- Copper Age about 7,500–3,000 BC
- Bronze Age 3300–1200 BC
- Iron Age 1,200–100 BC

Consider for a moment – the timescale is staggering. So are the discoveries. What must it have involved to get iron smelting going, a huge step on from the pre-Iron Age practice started thousands of years earlier in the cold-metal use of meteoric iron. For someone to surmise that that black stuff in rocks could be of use; dig it out; prepare it for smelting; build, stack, and blow the fire; develop the tools, including the anvil and hammer; and, maybe hardest of all, have the intention and know-how to produce the desired wrought iron objects.

Small wonder that the original meaning of *faber* of *homo faber*, that we usually translate as craftsman, was smith. And that the most common name in England is, likewise, Smith, reflecting a mighty near-miraculous far-back craft.

It is true that back then, coming out of the Copper and Bronze Age, there were people who already knew something of metals from working with copper and tin and making the alloy that was bronze – but how had they discovered that, and how many thousands of years had it taken?

So, for stone, copper, bronze, and iron, let alone the developments that came later, could it really have happened, even with those thousands of years, even with the forever human tools of voice, pen, and lyre?

Anyhow it, somehow, did! I imagine there must have been many flashes of genius (the "Imos" and other innovators) but also the many many men and women who continued the chipping away, literally and metaphorically, progressing just that little bit further each time. It wasn't history or evolution or the next coming age that accomplished it – it was the succession of individuals called (say) John and Mary, Jean and Marie, Ali and Fatima, Karanke and Mma, Joseph and Mary, the Native American Chardin and Chetan, or the Chinese Dawi and Luda, and all those others, their identities and names perhaps at first signed rather than spoken. It was the adventurous little boy experimenting with his environment, the ageing grandmother passing on her wisdom.

It was a combination of all these things and more and over more years than we can imagine. Even if we recite the dates and the ages, it is only too easy when thinking pre-history to lose a sense of the immensity of time. We should remind ourselves that the length of human life, as of now, is merely three score years and ten. Multiplying that up to the span of human existence in earth is near-unimaginable but is another way to help to put things in a little proportion.

But whatever the details, it is an incredible story. And yes, as I have to keep saying, it somehow happened.

Nor did it stop there. If we add a little more detail, it emerges that the inventions, necessarily communicated if they were to be adopted, were astonishing. A quick (incomplete) list would include the following.

- 3.3 million years ago: The first tools (stone-flaked cutting and hammering tools)
- 1 million years ago: Fire and, in time, cooking; cave painting, trade, hunting bands; petroglyph carving
- 20,000–15,000 years ago: Neolithic revolution
  - Move from foraging to agriculture
  - Domestication of animals
  - Larger settlements
  - Pottery and brick making
  - Woven clothes
  - The wheel
- c 3200 BC: Pictographic writing (Mesopotamia, then Eurasia more widely; later independently developed in Mesoamerica)
- c 1200 BC: Phonographic writing (Middle East, then, in time, worldwide)
- 700 AD: Printing (China)
- 1500 AD: Native American sign languages
- 1817: American Sign Language
- 1876: Telephone
- 1895: Radio
- 1971: Email
- 1983: Internet
- 2001: Wikipedi

And so on to the present. The recent technologies are staggering. But are they more staggering or impressive than those that, beginning from little, humans invented and developed some thousands of years ago? Many of them were in those blank times we know so little about but yet were occupied by living people, working with human intelligence to carry out and improve their lives. The process, sometimes fast, sometimes slow, at many times, perhaps, stagnant or, as happened to the vibrant Bronze Age civilisations, devastated by natural as well as human disasters, must have been marked above all by continuity with the past. One person communicated an innovation within their group, then they and their contacts passed it on further. The new practices were no doubt further spread, little by little through the known human world.

Surely, then, it was, indeed, human will and intelligence that was there at the start: the intelligence of consciousness or the consciousness of intelligence (some may prefer the label of "God", under whatever name) and the will to use the tools of humankind. But how and in what form it first began to manifest itself in human and other animals and how it gradually evolved, we can only guess.

At any rate, here we are. And, with the hand, these three still remain: the voice, the pen, and the lyre. But, throughout those age-long years, the greatest of these has been the human will.

A question

All those years, it must have been gradual. What started it all going?

In a way, that is hardly a significant question, and, in any case, we have no way of finding the answers. What is interesting and open to investigation is how we are using our tools now and to what purpose. Why try to probe into something for which, when all said and done, all we can do is speculate? But being human and curious – not so bad a characteristic for social animals, for all that it has, before now, led us into some sad ways – we would like to know more about our early history.

The obvious first place to look might be, once again, to the work of the pen: to writing in the broad sense used here that includes drawing and painting. The inscription or engraving of a surface – writing broadly conceived – seems to have been there from, or at least very near, start.

It is true that humans developed writing, in the narrow sense, very late in the history of humankind's development. As we know, humans have been on this earth for thousands of years – the date keeps being pushed back further and further and, no doubt, has still a ways to go. It is scarcely extraordinary that, as social animals, they wished, from the start, to communicate and express themselves. What seems to have come about is that they continued and adapted the tool that, as primates, came first and naturally to them: their hands – hands to make gestured signs, and hands to draw on the handiest surfaces near them.

Recall first the marking out of shapes on a surface, then the more simplified abstract marks, which came in continuous lines of development from those first black charcoaled lines, exemplifying the continuum among our multiple pictorial-graphic forms of visual communication. Edward Tufte rightly points out that using the tool of pen "to envision information – and what bright and splendid visions can result – is to work at the intersection of image, word, number, art" (Tufte 1990: 9). Images enter into alphabetic scripts, visual icons mix in with "written words". And where exactly should we draw the line between, say, Mayan pictorial histories and mediaeval stained-glass narratives, wall pictures, or calligraphic manuscripts of a saint's exploits or a sinner's doom? Picture and other forms of inscription surely always interacted and drew from each other.

The boundaries between "writing" and "non-writing" are, thus, blurred and rightly so. What emerges is the overlap between pictures, images, graphics, and scripts. As Roy Harris points out:

> From a technical point of view, writing is an extension of drawing, or more generally of graphic art, if we subsume under that term the whole gamut of forms of colouring, carving, incision and impression of surfaces which writing employs. … Writing was originally merely a term designating the process of scoring or outlining a shape on a surface of some kind. … Ancient Egyptian had one word meaning both "writing" and "drawing". Similarly, the Greek verb γράφέίν ("to write") originally meant in Homer "engrave, scratch, scrape". … Writing stands at the basis of the picture just as much as the picture stands at the basis of writing.
>
> *(Harris 1986:26, 29, 156)*

In these abounding graphic–pictorial systems, humans have been deploying a wonderfully versatile tool of communication, capable of being turned to the multifarious purposes of human interaction. In its manifold forms, writing is in constant use throughout the world – though not by everyone and not equally everywhere, for like other media they are embedded in human social institutions.

And then, looking back to the voice – can we fully separate it from gestures and the work of the hand as "the Substitute and Vicegerent of the Tongue, in a full and majestique way of expression, the signifying faculties of the soule, and the inward discourse of Reason" (Bulwer 1644).

So humans have these complementary and, in some ways, overlapping works of the pen and the voice. But, as between these two major human tools, we, again, come back – to return after this digression to the earliest days – to the question of which came first? That is, indeed, a debate.

The standard view is that speaking, or, more grandly, "orality" must have begun things. The voice seems self-evidently more "natural", simpler, and internally set, an inextricable part of ourselves. It is also, as seems to be implied by the common Western order of schooling, a tool easier and more natural to engage with than writing.

But is this necessarily so? We noted in earlier chapters what complex and sophisticated arts are needed for vocalised communicating. Even if we ignore the immense amount of physical coordination needed between multiple muscles and multiple parts of the brain, think, for example, of the modulations, kinesics, dynamics, and vocal variations, together with all the proxemic and other learned cultural conventions associated with speaking. Are we justified in assuming the sophisticated art of speaking was developed before and separately from the use of the fixed visible marks of drawing/writing/inscribing?

It is true that, in many formal educational systems today, writing, in the narrow sense, doesn't come in until children are, say, 4 or 5 years old or even later. This makes it look as if it must be the more difficult art, therefore, coming later both now and in human evolution. But, remembering the complexities of human vocalisation, perhaps the opposite is true. Children, after all, have already spent several years in the intensive imbibing at an age immensely attuned to rapid and eager learning, of those difficult, sophisticated, arts of vocalisation. And it seems that, as soon as they can handle (hand-le) the necessary tools and have access to them, small children are ready, indeed eager, to draw and paint and do it with, already, some skill – seemingly an inbuilt propensity. So too, it seems, are gestures, as infants can use these to communicate well before they can talk and even the youngest babies seem interested in trying to mimic adults' gestures and facial expressions. And now, in the form of baby signing, infants are able from a few months old to learn to communicate through signs and accomplish this with success long before they are able to do so through speaking.

There is also the question of value. Many people, imbued with the powerful ideas attached in some contexts to "paper qualifications", written laws, and the "religions of the book", might rate writing over speaking and, for this reason, assume (but does this follow?) that writing must have come later in our human "upward" journey. But in classical antiquity, writing was rated a low-skilled task; in Rome, it was to be carried out by slaves while their masters engaged in the higher, oratorical, arts. Plato, in his dialogue *Phaedrus*, reckoned that writing, unlike speaking, only gave you "external marks" which, however often you looked at them, always just told you the same. So, in the worlds of Greece and Rome, writing was far from being at the pinnacle of communication, as it was a plebeian and lowly medium fit only for those not equipped for the higher, noble art of elegant speaking.

We may disagree, as we think of the riches achieved through the pen and the brush and the blade. But certainly, such assessments are reminders that we not too quickly take for granted the view that writing, especially alphabetic writing, is the goal toward which, shaking off the outdated shades of merely oral communicating, human civilisation has rightly moved. Nor should we take it for granted, it seems, that the pen as the tool of writing, in the modern sense of that word, was the step that took us out of some ancient, undifferentiated mire of orality, which was where we, at the start, were embedded.

The signing hand

But were we embedded in orality? We constantly come back not to the voice or to "orality" but to the signing hand. For Darwin, as for many others, it was, again, the hand that was the human's most useful, most necessary tool, "so admirably adapted to the act of obedience of his will".

And what does the hand do? Many things, but, most obviously, communicating. It is there, and essential, for the signalling of gestures. Humans use their hands to make signs and signals, to draw shapes, picture-like, in the air to convey their meaning to those who look: gestures that the hand uses to shape meaning, as visible to watchers as writing on a white page; gestures that the hand inscribes for watchers on the surface of the air. It is a resource, it seems, of the greatest significance in human history – "significance", "*sign*-fying, sign-making, signalling" – a derivation full of meaning.[2]

Gesture is everywhere. It is not just an accompaniment to speech or in some way secondary to "language proper" (merely "paralinguistic") but an intrinsic part of spoken language. Gesture is central too, obviously, to sign language systems of which there have been so many through history: Native American, Native Australian, and, of course, the expert Italian gesturing. There are also the official sign languages of American Sign Language (ASL), British Sign Language (BSL), and the rest, used by deaf and non-speaking individuals, as well as a host of other systems developed independently across the globe such as, for example, the 23 sign languages in Africa described by Kamei (2004). A signer using a sign language today stands next to a speaker on many public occasions, drawing their meanings in shapes to communicate their import to observers whether through a television screen or some other imagined surface – a process that is essentially a dynamic form of pictographic-like writing.

These gestured visual signs can, equally, be printed in books and drawn on any kind of a surface, a form of inscribed written marks akin to drawing and painting. The signs, now drawn in two-dimensional mode are, thus, again, notably similar to some forms of pictographic writing – standardised shapes in two-dimensional form. In Chinese Sign Language, which has been developing since the late 1950s, the signs are based on Chinese written characters, bringing out yet further the parallelism, indeed, the essential identity of writing and signed gestures.

Writing and gesturing, in short, can be regarded as belonging to the same broad syndrome: that concerned with communicating by making shapes on some physical or imaginary surface to visually convey meaning to others.

That was our system at our start, our nature and inheritance as primates. They must have been experts in gesturing, in air writing. But more was to follow. Looking back from now, we know it had to. It was perhaps not so much the standardisation of the related art of pictures to convey meaning that was the real innovation (it seems that, up to a point, the gesticulating was already doing that). It was finding ways both to make these accepted shapes permanent and, eventually, unlike a cave wall, to be inscribed on something *portable* so as to be transported in enduring form to distant times and places.

If ever there was a revolution in communication, this was it: portability in enduring form.

We do not know what bright individual started it, but there it was, the turn-around – not the standardisation and simplification of the shapes, though that was essential, but the amazing, innovative wish and need to devise a means to transport them.

We return, then, as so often, to the work of the hand: the tool that could create both the gesture and, with the hand, the inscribing tool. It must have one of the first ways of communicating, expressing, celebrating, greeting, and storytelling.

Or perhaps, indeed, the very first. It is significant, given our close evolutionary relationship to the great apes, to recall the gesturing research that has recently seen such an explosion of interest. To re-emphasise this, it has become clear, from recent evidence not just speculation, that ape gesticulation is a fully fledged sophisticated system. As with human conversations, there are pauses to allow turn taking, and a range of their gestures, bypassing verbal language, are to an extent intelligible not only between different species of apes but also between them and humans. Vocalisation also had a place, but it appears that gesturing was the predominant channel of communication and in a manner sufficient for their communication needs.

I cannot stress enough that, given this background, it would seem to follow that it would be this form of communication that the earliest humans, like other primates, would, those many years ago, naturally find themselves predominantly using. For why, given all that we now know, would gesturing not have been right there among even earliest hominids?

And then what? For though gesture is still with us, with a much more significant role in our communication that is usually recognised, it could not be claimed that it now takes pride of place. If gesticulating was so effective, how did vocalised sounds come to be useful, then needful, then predominating?

We should recall those tens and hundreds of thousands of years rolling by. In the process, we imagine other innovations to have come about. For communication too, might there not, from time to time, have been a man or woman or child of genius – another "Imo" – who started off the next small step that little by little passed down the generations, mother to child and more, so that the innovation spread and, through human contact, became established over the years. And then, again, over the many years, the next innovation.

Might have been? *Must* have been, because look what we have now. So why and how, however gradual, did the change come about?

It may seem then more puzzling in that gesture has many advantages over speech. It is easily learned and widely understood. Strangers of different tongues can use it as a medium in which to make themselves everywhere understood. As diurnal creatures and, we imagine, living in close-knit bands, a communication system of signs was obviously a fine evolutionary adaptation.

But it has disadvantages too. It is no good in the dark or for those with poor sight, if there are obstacles in the way, or if the potential communicators are distant from each other. The gestures must be visible, and the communicator must have their hands free from other tasks. The recipient must be looking and paying attention.

But even if gesticulation is not a perfect mode of communication, why might early humans have hit on vocalising?

It might have been something like this. Like many great apes, humans must surely have lived, initially, in relatively small groups, visible to each other, active in the day and within easy reach for mutual, gestured interaction. But gradually some division of labour must have started, no doubt accompanied over those many years by challenges, even perhaps utter disasters, from changes in climate or environment. Even if we imagine – unlikely – that everyone around added their own paint stroke to those archer and animal figures rather than several experts handling the brush, holding the lamp, fetching the water, and preparing food and acclaim, we know that the red ochre for painters was not always available on the spot. Collecting it would have needed travel, trade. The same for the carefully wrought ornaments that archaeologists have discovered (might we imagine that then too a man might search for beautiful jewellery for a loved one?).

All this would presumably have meant, for some, travel from home while presumably wishing to keep in touch with their friends back in the settlement while away, like calling back from some point near enough for the voice to carry or announcing their return but too far for gesturing to be seen. Mothers going off to find food and other goods needed to keep in touch with their children; except when they were too far away, this would work better through sound than through sight. Working at night or in the dark of the caves, when gestures would not be easily visible, would have its own challenges. In these conditions, when the sight of gestures – essential if they were to be used for communicating – was impeded by distance or darkness, some other form of communication was needed. It is scarcely surprising that sound, which can go around obstacles and conquer distance and dark, came into its own.

It was not a matter, it could not be, of "switching" into something that, whatever its benefits, was not in any way already there to be adapted and built on. Adam Kendon, world expert on gesture, makes the point clearly that:

> advantages cannot serve to answer the question of why speech was selected. Evolution does not work in terms of possible but

> as-yet-unrealized advantages. It works only by gradual modifications of existing systems selected for their greater effectiveness for current functions. This can and does result in changes, allowing the modified system to be capable of new functions, which may then be selected for.
> *(Kendon 2017: 6)*

In this case, vocalisation was already present, if only, so far, in a relatively minor way. As with the variety built in evolution, it was there to be tapped into and developed. Having complementary, co-existing modes, each suited to its own special conditions, was the real advantage, the true basis for evolutionary adaptation.

This adds strength to the already attractive position of writers such as Adam Kendon and David McNeil that gesture and voice developed alongside each other, rather than, as some had assumed, the voice driving out gesture (which it clearly didn't). The two methods sit comfortably together. It seems, furthermore, that the two are located in the same general area of the brain, yet another argument for envisaging them working together rather than separately in the communicating system.

There is still a puzzle. We can accept that there were advantages in a greater use of the voice and that developing adaptations of the vocal cords were happening, to be passed on both through human contact and through the inheritance of acquired, fitter, characteristics. But how did humans manage to move from a main reliance on the gesticulating and inscribing hand into a greater reliance on vocalising?

We can only speculate, but it is worth looking back to the theories advanced for the origin of language/music (Chapter 7). There are clues there, the more convincing if taken together. It is relatively easy to imagine interjections, *ding-dong* musicalising, lullabies, and imitation of the calls of vocalising monkeys and the music of birds, all playing a part and gradually, unwittingly, becoming not only useful but felt to be useful and fitting both for their usefulness in communicating and (why not?) for enjoyment and – maybe Darwin was at least partially right for all the mocking of his idea – for love songs.

No doubt, vocalisation gradually became more useful and prominent, not necessarily because of any beauty felt to be attached it (though why might there not have been individual seers and poets then too to make their mark and develop the riches of the voice?) but just because it was needed for the basic joint activities of life among the social animals that humans are. Once started, it is not difficult to imagine its greater use going along with further development, then – for such is evolution – this increased the use of the vocal chords, making them receptive for being more adapted still. And as generation after generation, over thousands of years, these human characteristics were passed on for vocalising to be the more relied on. The voice has, after all, proved a good tool for humans.

We can only guess how this happened and all this is, of course, speculation. There is no way we can be sure. But the above seems to fit best with what we know of the nature of evolutionary and transhistorical processes and with what comparative evidence we have. At any rate now, tens of thousands of years later, it has come to be that the voice and its products and experiences are among the prime glories of human intercourse, communication, and art.

What came first?

There is no need to linger, for the answer I have to this question will be clear from what I have already said. Despite previous assumptions, it has to be not the voice but the work of the hand.

And by this, I mean what the hand achieves in all the senses delineated in this study and all that that implies, not just the movements of the hand itself, in its actions of gesturing to an observer on the spot, but also the inscribed, fixed, enduring gestures. These are both the hand's drawing of shapes on the surface of the air – where, indeed, gestures normally happen – and its inscription of those same shapes on some handy surface like a cave wall. The inscribed shapes, perhaps, began with delineations of the hands themselves, then different shapes and petroglyphs and their curtailed equivalents, and, in time, pictographs on a variety of surfaces. And then, if you want to have a fixed enduring communication – unlike with gestures, as you cannot take a cave wall with you – you have to grasp (literally – the hand again) the idea of something portable. And then, in time, again – there were thousands of years for this – or perhaps going alongside, there was the differentiated, but closely related, art of figurative drawing and painting; and then, maybe this time easier, that too developing the option of being transportable.[3]

This is not to say, absolutely not, that vocalised meaningful sounds were absent even in those earliest years. In the beginning, it is still true, was the voice. It is present among other primates, so it would surely be there among human primates too. And to reach the voice's present state as a tool of a sophisticated and complex spoken language, it must surely have been developing not, as some theories have it, directly from gesture but alongside it: in humans that is, for with other great apes, gesticulation has remained paramount.[4]

But it was not the voice that, in the past, started as the main communication channel. It was gesture, communicated both in full physical and dynamic form, and, in time, in gradually evolving shapes, frozen in time and space, fixed and two-dimensional marked on a surface or a portable tablet: a form of writing,

In short, my answer to the question of what form of communication first predominated is that it was communication through making visual marks – a communicating activity with two sides to it: one, that of making free-standing evanescent marks or shapes on the surface of the air, mainly with the hands, in the actions known as gesturing; and two, making comparable shapes in the more or less permanent form of marks on a physical surface – inscribing or engraving in the activity we call writing – writing, that is, in the broad sense (inscribing) that includes drawing, painting, engraving, and similar, achieved by one or other of the many forms of the pen.

It is a tentative conclusion, open to the finding of more evidence, But, it is one to which, at the moment, I cannot see an alternative.

It is a conclusion, I admit, that goes against my own long assumption that spoken – oral – forms significantly preceded the development of writing. It was an assumption I shared with a large number of other scholars, one buttressed, furthermore, by a long held mythical charter about, in particular, the history of the West. But, thinking further about it and looking more closely at what evidence we have, I have changed my mind. I now think that that account was mistaken and that, in general terms, writing, intertwined with gesture and considered, as here, from a broad transhistorical, perspective, goes back to the beginning. The voice was there too, and the two – pen and voice – continued and still continue, to intertwine and cooperate. But at the start, it was the signing work of the hand that predominated.

Notes

1 Discussed in Finnegan 2023.
2 Armstrong and Wilcox 2007, Beattie 2016, Corballis 2002, McGinn 2015, McNeill 2005.
3 Griffiths-Lynch et al. 2013, Gill 2023, Kendon 2017, McPherson 2023.
4 On theories of the gesture origin of speech, see especially Corballis 1999, Griffiths-Lynch 2013, Kendon 2017.

10

"ONLY CONNECT ..."[1]

In the history of our resources and our tools, connected and working with each other, we can perhaps glimpse something of what we are and how, with, no doubt, many byways and turnings, we have arrived where, for good or ill, we now are.

We do not know the detail, but do know that we are fully connected with our inheritances from the past, gathered from the wisdom and ingenuity of the many individuals and generations that have gone before us. In one way or another, we human beings are a part of that continuity. With our inheritance from the past, we make use of our interconnected mortal tools of the voice, pen, brush, lyre, and, basic to all of these, our hands – the key tool of creative human creatures, of the rightly named *homo faber*.

But also, we have to remember that the tools do not work in isolation: voice interacts with gesture and with pen, script interacts with speech and brush, the voice with gestures of the hand and gait and body movement, vocalisation with writing, human life intertwined with the products of the hands, verbal speaking overlapping into the musical expressions that move and transport us (not just through music but through music above all) into some kind of transformative dimension beyond ourselves as if out of time, even perhaps of space.

Music is a very special example of this. Like its close twin, spoken language, from which it is never fully separate, is noticeably multi-modal and connected with other channels. In live performance, it has a notably visual side, well exploited, now, in video. Its auditory side overlaps into touch, and its gestural and body movement, manifested in rhythm, merges into dance. And then, through the many different systems for representing

DOI: 10.4324/9781003496007-10

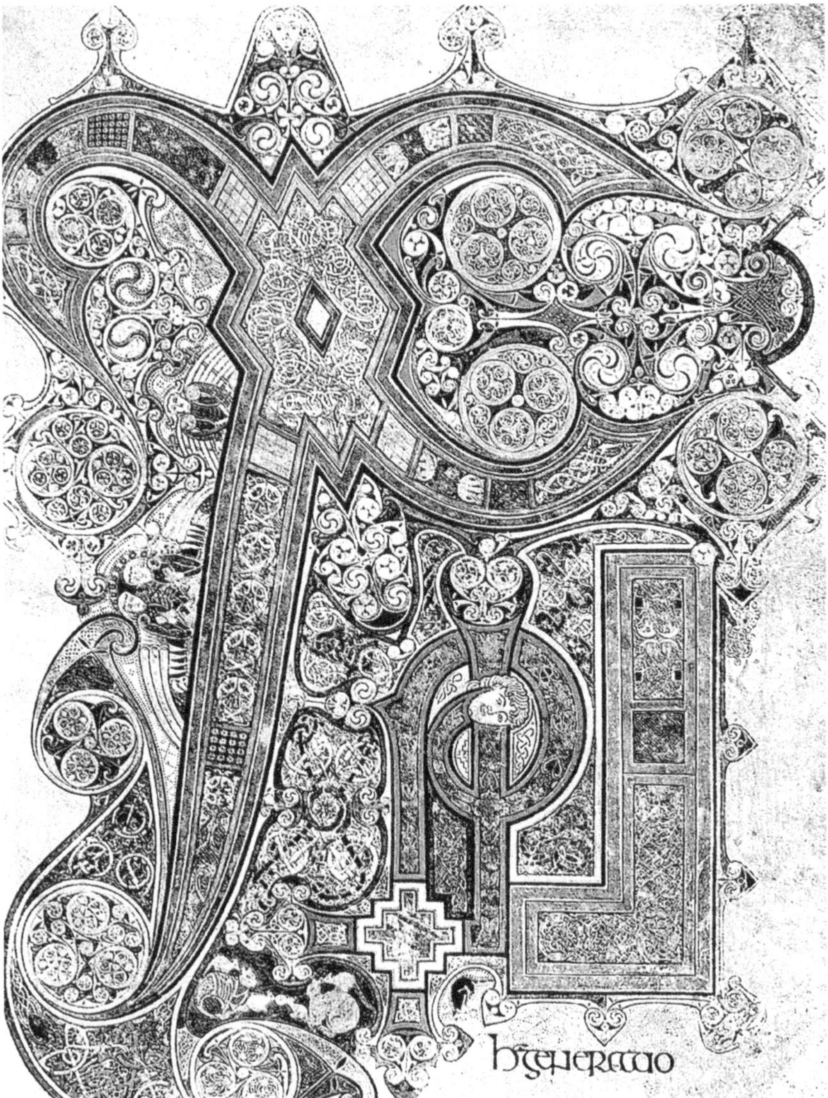

FIGURE 10.1 Kells initial.

music in visual mode, it works with the pen and brush. Our arts link and support each other, building on the tools we humans have developed (or, in another story, been given). "Every song" as Dick Dale put it poetically, "is like a painting".

All our tools connect. And in that, we are fortunate, for they not only complement each other, but if one falters or fails, others can come to the rescue, not perhaps to fill the whole gap but enough. We are fortunate too that, as audio-visual creatures, we have two main channels that connect us: the rich auditory resource of the voice and the visual dimension activated, above all, through our hands together with its servants, the pen, the lyre, and its created artefacts. And beyond the audio-visual, beyond our, as it were, earthly resources, we have the communicating tools of the subconscious–conscious.

And beyond that, again, social animals that we are, we do, we must, interconnect.

When we consider the vast span of the earth and of the population on it, we know this interconnecting can only be relative. We are dimly aware of the global network that, in some ways, connects us now. It is a question whether in the past thousands of years there might not have been a parallel, invisible network as humans travelled the globe across the land masses of Eurasia, then across ocean tracts to America, then further to the far islands of the south seas.

There is another continuity too, an obvious one – much mentioned, though, perhaps, not equally often remembered: our continuity with other animals. Distinctive we may be, in some respects, but we also share so much with others. There are overlapping senses, movement, life on earth, and, it must be, shared consciousness, mayhap in part subconscious, both between ourselves and with other animals. How else do companion animals know when their humans are coming or hunters intuit which direction their prey is taking? What but through our common consciousness?

We should remind ourselves, like Darwin, of the continuities between living species, of the parallels between the resources of human as compared to other animals. Looking to this, is consonant with the broadly pragmatist approach underlying this book – one that looks to the actions of human agents within the continuity of nature with culture, taking it that humans act in their communicating essentially as animals do, merely in different ways and in a partially different dimension.

What next for human communicating?

Who can tell?

Many things will no doubt stay the same – our interpersonal interacting, our social nature, gesturing, and use of colour and the human voice. Our basic communicative tools – voice, pen, lyre, and hand – are still, in one form or another, key to our communicating and, hence, our sociality. But when we think of the amazing changes in communication practices over the centuries, not to speak of just the past 20 years, we should think we must be only part way on our journey. There will, for sure, be new development, most likely unexpected and, at first, rejected as deluded, unhealthy, impossible, or in the realms of science fiction, and then gradually – who knows – adopted.

There is no predestined, predetermined outcome, not now nor at any time in our history. It is easy to look back and think we can discern a foreordained destiny that set us where we are now – but human life *might* not have turned out as it has. The succession of "Imos" over the years might have invented different things, the innovation might not have been taken on, she might have perished before she could demonstrate it. Or, adopted for a while, it could have fallen by the wayside from lack of interest, disease or changing local or global conditions of climate, conflict, natural disasters. Or, another thought, the genius innovators might have been male and, though with an innovation just as good, perhaps better, not be in as good a position to pass on. For females, it is easier: to their children and grandchildren and around the gossiping female group while the males are off hunting or building things or fighting. Some innovations might have proved after all not to be very useful or – not the same thing – against the interests of those currently in power, and not survived. And there is always accident and the strong pull of the status quo. So, as I say, things might not have turned out the way they have.

For all that, here we are, astonishingly so, in fact, with many discoveries and inventions by a succession of clever forbears after something of the order of 300,000 years. And for all the twists and turns, we can be confident that the things that brought us here, that survived and worked through those long years, were those same tools as ever: the voice and, enabled by the hand, the pen and the lyre and then, beyond them, the unconscious pulls of consciousness, and beneath it all, human intelligence. It is striking that, for all the radical changes it is certain will surely have taken place in climate, in environment, in institutions, in gender relations, in settlement patterns, livelihood, political and religious revolutions over all those millennia, those key tools remained and were used – to many different purposes, no doubt, but used. They are here.

Can we doubt that we humans have been endowed with resources, many of them shared with other animals, to understand and relish our lives within the *oikoumene*, that beautiful Greek word (οἰκουμένη) that means the human inhabited world and our home. What new and unexpected arts and experiences, we must wonder, will human beings develop, reject, or destroy through the lengthening future millennia of unfolding human history?

The theme of human history has been change, but change amidst continuity. Change there has certainly been and, in many respects, but it has been gradual. And some changes have perished, not seldom by human hands; many have, by human will and intelligence, survived through the good use of the pen and the voice in coordination with the other tools, those of the lyre and the hand. Change is not necessarily destructive, even when it is unexpected and beyond human control. Even dinosaurs adapted to the cataclysmic changes in the earth's surface and vegetation; true, many perished, but many survived, changing their ways to become birds. We humans, a notably adaptable species, can surely cope with much less disastrous changes, many of them, indeed, brought about by our own will.

In this approach, human factors, not technology of itself, whether of "literacy" or "orality" or any other communication channel, are what count. Nor is the "information technology revolution" a pre-determined inevitability, for, as Burns sums up his account of the implications of new information technology, his comment, by now, some years ago but still much to the point:

> Ultimately, the way that the world we live in will look in the 21st century will be determined by the collective, accumulated choices of ourselves as individuals, and the directions taken by the corporate bodies whose actions determine the general shape of our society.
>
> *(Burns 1984: 234)*

In the last analysis, to see technologies of orality or literacy (or by extension computers) as the determinants of human choices or social arrangements does not fit the facts of human communicating history or of our variegated and rich uses of brush, pen, scroll, hand, and voice. These ways may not always have been what all would call "upward", but they have always been human, building on the human tools of pen and voice – tools that have come down from our ingenious inventive ancestors whose crafts of pen-brought literacy and of the voice, here with us through the ages, we have inherited. And, amidst those apparently all-encompassing results it is worth remembering that the pen's products can also be used to celebrate, to bring joy, to inspire.[2]

For how we have, so far, made use of these tools, we can look back and perhaps reflect. And for how we will make use of them in the future, time, of which there will be plenty of, will judge. Already, we accept electronic, radio, and sound waves and artificial intelligence, things if unimaginable magic to earlier generations. It could be that new waves of consciousness are hiding out there, awaiting only our acceptance of them as, in time, just a part of our everyday living. There will, doubtless, be many new concepts for understanding human communication, but they will surely be within the continuity of our human history and ancestry. It will go alongside, perhaps, a widening experience of the noosphere as something that has, in some, always been there: in the potential within humans that produced those strikingly similar patterns of caves painting across the globe and the independent developments, perhaps, of pictographic communicating and the working of metals; the wish to travel and – remarkable when you come to think of it – the preparedness to learn new ideas and ways from those who were once strangers. And through it all, the journeying of the mind.

This is what, ultimately, allowed the heritage from voice and pen of written, spoken and electronic language; visual imagery; dance; the many modes of communication technologies; of music and, allied to that and especially loved, of song. And then, emerging into our awareness at last, a shared consciousness that, again, has always, to an extent, been engrained in human life through trance, dream, and music, allowing – by whatever name – a glance of heaven.

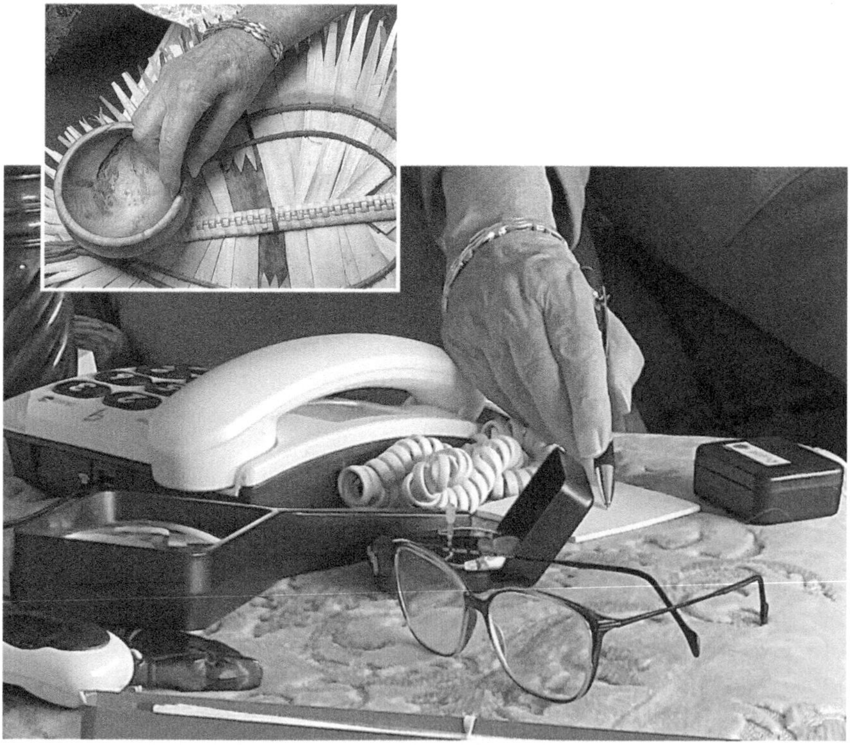

FIGURE 10.2 Tools photo.

The tools again and always

Maybe our suppositions about the earliest days of humankind are metaphorical and pleasing only in the same way as our stories of creation. It may be so. But they may still express something of deep analogical truth, communicating to ourselves something of who we think we are and where we might have come from.

However that may be, we humans, for sure, have much to celebrate.

First and again, there is always our human sociality – for good or bad, that is, both are there, but hopefully in larger part for good. In a theologian's conclusion to a key text on sociality (Sussman and Chapman 2004), Stephen Pope welcomes the outcome of primate studies that offer an alternative to the dominant Hobbesian paradigm of early humans living in small aggressive bands, red in tooth and claw, of the dominance of "the selfish gene".

> If other primates are prone to social behaviour more often than antisocial behaviour, perhaps pity, empathy, and other prosocial feelings do not have to be laid on top of a substrate that is essentially antisocial. If this is also the case for human beings, then perhaps our first person experience of caring for others is neither illusory nor derivative from self-concern. In this case social institutions have more to build on than atomistic individualism typically recognizes. Social life is not reducible to a ceasefire between antagonistic rivals.
>
> *(Pope 2004: 328–329)*

As he points out, an alternative position can be to build on the recent studies of primates to view human society not as warring individuals but as a network of communicating groups that, for the most part, make a positive contribution to well-being. It is a view that echoes Aristotle's concept of the human being as a social animal.

Finally, we have inherited and utilised fine tools that our ancestors used and developed, handed on, and sometimes enhanced to the next generations that we, in turn, use in our communicating among ourselves: with others, with our souls, with our intelligence, and our subconscious–consciousness. It is our nature.

The future be what it may, we can surely, as human beings, celebrate for now our human, social, communicating nature; the tools we exploit to achieve this; and the continuities of our past with nature, with other animals, and with the kingdom of all living creatures that dwell and communicate on our astounding, shared, sustaining earth. We have the multimodal singing speaking voice and all the arts of the hand – two different lines, but ones that, in our human continuous creation, cooperate and live

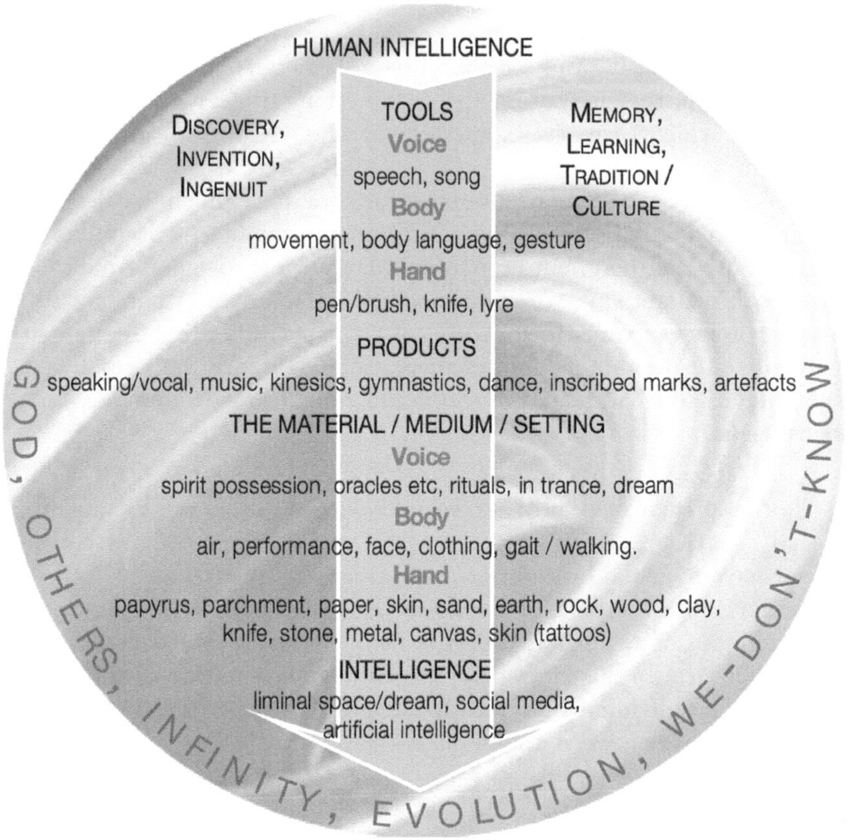

FIGURE 10.3 Tools diagram.

together: the voice, and the pen, and the lyre, implements of the hand. And behind these, again, we have human will and intelligence. We have ourselves.

Between them – other animals will, doubtless, disagree, and they might even be right –they, perhaps, make the greatest story that ever was.

Notes

1 "Only connect...": E.M. Forster.
2 The evidence is the whole of the world's literature. My own favourites are of poetry, Shakespeare's sonnets, Wavell's, *Other Men's Flowers,* and (of course) Homer; of prose, the writings of Darwin, Erasmus, and Thucydides.

APPENDIX

Equivalences

For convenience, the following terms for tools have been used as a shorthand for broader coverage:

- *Voice* – vocalising in speaking, singing, and non-verbally.
- *Pen* – all implements that meaningfully mark a surface (such as by inscribing, drawing, painting, engraving, cutting, piercing): thus including, for instance, brush, blade, knife, chisel, awl, needle, stylus for making marks on any material (e.g., wood, metal, bark, palm leaf, bones silk, paper, plastic, and a host of others).
- *Lyre* – tool for gesturing, manipulating, interacting, building, creating.
- *Mind, intelligence, consciousness* – as in "swarming", trance, intercommunication, and subconscious communicating.

BIBLIOGRAPHY

Abrahamsson, Hans (1951) *The origin of death: studies in African mythology*, Studia Ethnographica Upsaliensia, Uppsala.

Ahn, T. K., Janssen, Marco A., and Gushing, Bruce S. (2004) 'Signals, symbols, and human cooperation', in R. W. Sussman and A. R. Chapman (eds), *The origins and nature of sociality*, de Gruyter, New York, NY.

Aitchison, Jean (1996) *The seeds of speech: language origin and evolution*, Cambridge University Press, Cambridge.

Aldridge, David (ed.) (2008) *Music therapy in dementia care. International approaches*, Jessica Kingsley, London.

Alexander, Eben (2012) *Proof of heaven. A neurosurgeon's journey into the afterlife*, Piatkus, London.

Alexander, Eben (2020) 'Commencement address', online, http://ebenalexander.com/commencement-address-2020/

Allard, Olivier (2022) 'Anthropology of emotion', *Oxford Bibliographies Online*, https://doi.org/10.1093/obo/9780199766567-0161

Alpenfels, Ethel J. (1955) 'The anthropology and social significance of the human hand', *Artificial Limbs* 2/2: 4–21.

Amodio, Marc C. (2004) *Writing the oral tradition: oral poetics and literate culture in medieval England*, University of Notre Dame Press, Notre Dame IN.

Amodio, Marc C. (ed.) (2020) *John Miles Foley's world of oralities: text, tradition, and contemporary oral theory*, Arc Humanities, York.

Anderson, William (1990) *Green Man. The archetype of oneness with the earth*, HarperCollins, London.

Andrzejewski, B. W. and Lewis, I. M. (1964) *Somali poetry. An introduction*, Clarendon Press, Oxford.

Anon (2017) 'Your brain on music', *Pegasus, Magazine of University of Central Florida*, www.ucf.edu/pegasus/your-brain-on-music #:~:text="Professional%20musicians%20use%20the%20occipital,the%20auditory%20and%20language%20center/

Anon (n.d.(a)) 'The natural communicating of apes', online, https://www.pnas.org/doi/10.1073/pnas.0702624104#:~/

Anon (n.d.(b)) 'Hand function', online, https://www.sciencedirect.com/topics/biochemistry-genetics-and-molecular-biology/hand-function/

Aristotle (1962) *Politics*, English translation, Penguin, Harmondsworth.

Armstrong, David F. and Wilcox, Sherman E. (2007) *The gestural origins of language*, Oxford University Press, Oxford.

Ashby, Nina (2007) *Simply color therapy*, Zambezi Publishing, Plymouth, Devon.

Attenborough, David (1998) *The life of birds*, BBC Books, London.

Ayers, Roy (n.d.) 'The true beauty of music', online, https://allauthor.com/quotes/40746/

Barber, Karin (1991) *I could speak until tomorrow. Oriki, women, and the past in a Yoruba town*, Smithsonian Institution Press, Washington DC.

Barrere, Dorothy B. (1967) 'Revisions and adulterations in Polynesian creation myths', in G. A. Highland, R. W. Force, A. Howard, M. Kelly, and Y. H. Sinoto (eds), *Polynesian culture history. Essays in honor of Kenneth P. Emory*, Bishop Museum Press, Honolulu, HI.

Barron, Anne, Gu, Yueguo, and Steen, Gerard (eds) (2017) *The Routledge handbook of pragmatics*, Routledge, London.

Bascom, William R. (ed.) (1977) *Frontiers of folklore*, Westview Press, Boulder, CO.

Basso, Keith H. (1974) 'The ethnography of writing', in Bauman and Sherzer (eds), *Explorations in the ethnography of speaking*, Cambridge University Press, London.

Bates, Matthew W. (2015) *The birth of the trinity*, Oxford University Press, Oxford.

Bauman, Richard (1977) *Verbal art as performance*, Newbury House, Rowley, MA.

Bauman, Richard (1986) *Story, performance, and event*, Cambridge University Press, Cambridge.

Bauman, Richard and Briggs, Charles (2003) *Voices of modernity*, Cambridge University Press, Cambridge.

Bauman, Richard and Sherzer, Joel (eds) (1974) *Explorations in the ethnography of speaking*, Cambridge University Press, London.

Beattie, G. (2016) *Rethinking body language: how hand movements reveal hidden thoughts*, Routledge, London.

Becker, Howard S. (1982) *Art worlds*, University of California Press, Berkeley, CA.

Becker, Judith (2011) 'Exploring the habitus of listening: anthropological perspectives', in Justin and Sloboda (eds), *Handbook of music and emotion*, Oxford University Press, Oxford.

Beckwith, Martha Warren (1951) *The Kumulipo, a Hawaiian creation chant*, University of Chicago Press, Chicago, IL.

Bellos, Alex (2011) *Alex's adventures in numberland*, Bloomsbury, London.

Ben-Amos, Dan and Goldstein, Kenneth S. (eds) (1975) *Folklore: performance and communication*, Mouton, The Hague.

Benjamin, Arthur (2020) 'The original and universal language of ... MATH!', online, https://onlineacademiccommunity.uvic.ca/callmebog/2020/05/06/the-original-and-universal-language-of-math/

Berger, Harris M. (2007) *Stance, ideas about emotion, style, and meaning for the study of expressive culture*, Wesleyan University Press, Middletown, CT.

Berlin, Brent and Kay, Paul (1969) *Basic color terms. Their universality and evolution*, University of California Press, Berkeley, CA.

Best, Eldson (1923) *The Maori school of learning*, Dominion Museum Monograph, Wellington.

Blacking, John (1974) *How musical is man?* University of Washington Press, Seattle, WA.
Blacking John (1995) *Music, culture and experience*, University of Chicago Press, Chicago, IL.
Bloch, Maurice (ed.) (1975) *Political language and oratory in traditional society*, Academic Press, London.
Bloom, Howard (2000) *The global brain. The evolution of mass mind from the Big Bang to the 21st century*, John Wiley & Sons, New York, NY.
Bonabeau, Eric, Theraulaz, Guy, and Dorigo, Marco (1999) *Swarm intelligence, from natural to artificial systems*, Oxford University Press, New York, NY.
Boone, Elizabeth and Mignolo, Walter (1994) *Writing without words, literacies in Mesoamerica and the Andes*, Duke University Press, Durham, NC.
Borgo, David. (2005) *Sync or Swarm: Improvising music in a complex age*, A&C Black, London.
Bouwer, Fleur L. (2021) 'Rhythmic abilities in humans and non-human animals: a review and recommendations from a methodological perspective', *Philosophical Transactions of the Royal Society B*, online, https://doi.org/10.1098/rstb.2020.033/
Brown, Michelle (1998) *The British Library Guide to writing and scripts*, British Library, London.
Brown, Steven (2017) 'Joint prosodic origin of language and music', *Frontiers*, 8, online, https://www.frontiersin.org/journals/psychology/articles/10.3389/fpsyg.2017.01894/full/
Bruno, David (2017) *Cave art. World of art series*, Thames and Hudson, New York, NY.
Bulkley, Kelly and Bulkeley, Patricia (2005) *Dreaming beyond death. A guide to pre-death dreams and visions*, Beacon Press, Boston, MA.
Bulkley, Kelly, Adams, Kate and Davis, Patricia M. (2009) *Dreaming in Christianity and Islam, A guide to pre-death dreams and visions*, Rutgers University Press, New Brunswick.
Bulwer, John (1644) *Chirologia, or the natural language of the hand*, Thomas Harper, London.
Buren, Verena, Müllensiefen, Daniel, Roeske, Tina C., and Degé, Franziska (2021) 'What makes babies musical? Conceptions of musicality in infants and toddlers', *Frontiers in Psychology* 12, online, https://doi.org/10.3389/fpsyg.2021.736833
Burke, Peter (1978) *Popular culture in early modem Europe*, Temple Smith, London.
Burns, Alan (1984) *New information technology*, Wiley, Hoboken, NJ.
Burns, Alistair and Morris, Shelagh (2018) 'Music and dementia: a powerful connector', NHS England, online, https://www.england.nhs.uk/blog/music-and-dementia-a-powerful-connector/
Byrne, Richard W., Cartmill, Erica, Genty, Emilie, Graham, Kirsty E., Hobaiter, Catherine, and Tanner, Joanne (2017) 'Great ape gestures, intentional communication with a rich set of innate singles', *Animal Cognition* 20: 755–769.
Cain, Oliver and Finnegan, Ruth (2020) *One is One, or Green grow the rushes O*, Callender Press, Old Bletchley.
Callender, David Campbell (2023) *Birds and humans, who are we?* Callender Press, Old Bollingen Bletchley.
Campbell, Joseph (1949/2008) *The hero with a thousand faces*, Princeton University Press, Princeton, NJ.
Carey, John (2021) *A little history of poetry*, Yale University Press, NH.
Carey, James W. (1967) *Communication as culture. Essays on media and society*, Unwin-Hyman, Boston, MA.

Carpenter, Edmund and McLuhan, Marshall (eds) (1960) *Explorations in communications*, Beacon Press, Boston, MA.
Carocci, Max (ed.) (2022) *Art, observation, and an anthropology of illustration*, Bloomsbury, London.
Carter, Thomas F. (1925) *The invention of printing in China and its spread westward*, Columbia University Press, New York, NY.
Cavicchi, Daniel (1998) *Tramps like us. Music and meaning among Springsteen fans,* Oxford University Press, New York, NY.
Cengage (2019) 'Music and religion', online, https://www.encyclopedia.com/environment/encyclopedias-almanacs-transcripts-and-maps/music-music-and-religion#:~:text=p/
Chadwick, Hector M. and Chadwick, Nora K. (1932–1940) *The growth of literature,* 3 vols, Cambridge University Press, London.
Chaytor, Henry J. (1945) *From script to print*, Heffer, Cambridge.
Cherry, Kendra (2024) 'The psychological effects of color, does it affect how you feel? How color impacts moods, feelings, and behaviors', online https://www.verywellmind.com/color-psychology-2795824/
Chiang, Iris (2014) Personal communication.
Chomsky, Noam (1972) *Language and problems of knowledge*, MIT Press, Cambridge, MA.
Chrisomalis, Stephen (2010) *Numerical notation: A comparative history*, Cambridge University Press, Cambridge.
Christin, Anne-Marie and Bacon, Josephine (2002) *A history of writing: from hieroglyphics to multimedia*, Flammarion, Paris.
Cipolla, Carlo M. (1969) *Literacy and development in the west*, Penguin, Harmondsworth.
Clanchy, Michael T. (1970) *From memory to written record: England from 1066 to 1307*, Wiley-Blackwell, Hoboken, NJ.
Clark, Geoffrey A. and Willernet, Cathy M. (eds) (1997) *Conceptual issues in modern human origins research,* Routledge, New York, NY.
Clarke, Eric F. (2005) 'Creativity in performance', *Music & Science* 9: 157–182.
Clayton, Martin (2016) 'The social and personal functions of music in cross-cultural perspective', in S. Hallam, I. Cross, and M. Thaut (eds), *The Oxford handbook of music psychology*, Oxford University Press, Oxford.
Cohen, Sara (1991) *Rock culture in Liverpool. Popular music in the making*, Clarendon Press, Oxford.
Colenso, William (1881) 'Contributions towards a better knowledge of the Maori race', *Transactions and Proceedings of the New Zealand Institute* 14: 33–48.
Conversation, The (2021) 'How a handful of prehistoric geniuses launched humanity's technological revolution' online, https://theconversation.com/how-a-handful-of-prehistoric-geniuses-launched-humanitys-technological-revolution-171511/
Cook, Nicholas (2013) *Beyond the score: music as performance*, Oxford University Press, Oxford.
Cook, Nicholas and Everist, Mark (eds) (1999) *Rethinking music*, Oxford University Press, Oxford.
Cook-Gumperz, Jenny (ed.) (1986) *The social construction of literacy*, Cambridge University Press, Cambridge.
Cooke, Deryck (1959) *The language of music*, Oxford University Press, Oxford.
Corballis, Michael C. (1999) 'The gestural origins of language', *American Scientist* 87/2, online, https://doi.org/10.1511/1999.20.138/
Corballis, Michael C. (2002) *From hand to mouth: the origins of language*, Princeton University Press, Princeton, NJ.

Corry, Leo (2015) *Brief history of numbers*, Bishop Museum Press, Honolulu, HI.
Coulmas, Florian (2002) *The Blackwell encyclopaedia of writing systems*, Blackwell, Oxford.
Cox, J. Halley (1970) *Hawaiian petroglyphs*, Bishop Museum Press, Honolulu, HI.
Crapanzano, Vincent (1994) 'Reflexions sur une anthropologies des emotions', *Terrain, carnets du patrimoine ethnologique* 23.
Crosby, Ruth (1936) 'Oral delivery in the Middle Ages', *Speculum* 11/1: 88–110.
Crystal, David (1997) *The Cambridge encyclopedia of language*, Cambridge University Press, Cambridge.
Dale, Penny (2024) ' "Bipolar, colour and me" – an artist's spreadsheet of emotion', online, https://www.bbc.co.uk/news/articles/ce805y2z47jo/
Damour, Thibault, Darrigol, Olivier, and Rivasseau, Vincent (2005) *Einstein, 1905–2005: Poincaré seminar 1905–2005, Progress in mathematical sciences*, Birkhaüser, Basel.
Danesh, Kazem and Khazaie, Mohammad (2020) 'The symbolism of green color in Iranian-Islamic culture and art', *Paykareah. Journal of Art Faculty*, Shahid Chamran University of Ahvaz 9/19: 24–32, online: paykareh.scu.ac.ir/article_15725.html/
Darwin, Charles (1871) *The descent of man and selection in relation to sex*, Murray, London.
Daslia (2023) 'A brief history of art from prehistoric times to the present day', online: https://www.daslia.com/history-of-art#:~:
Dawkins, Richard (2004) *The ancestors tale*, Weidenfeld and Nicholson, London.
De Chardin, Teilhard (1955/2008) *The phenomenon of man*, Harper, London.
DeFrancis, John (1989) *Visible speech, the diverse oneness of writing systems*, University of Hawaii Press, Honolulu, HI.
DeJorio, Andrea (1832/2000) , transl and ed, Kendon, A., Indiana University Press, Bloomington
Delargy, James H. (1945) 'The Gaelic story-teller', *Proceedings of the British Academy* 31: 177–221.
Dementia UK (2023) 'Music and dementia', https://www.dementiauk.org/information-and-support/living-with-dementia/music-and-dementia/
Denora, Tia (2000) *Music in everyday life*, Cambridge University Press, Cambridge.
Desilva, Jeremy (2021) *First steps. How upright walking made us human*, Harper Collins, New York, NY.
Deutscher, Guy (2006) *The unfolding of language. The evolution of mankind's greatest invention*, Penguin, London.
Devere, Roland (2017) 'Music and dementia: an overview', online, https://practicalneurology.com/articles/2017-june/music-and-dementia-an-overview/
Diringer, David (1968) *The alphabet, key to the history of mankind*, 2 vols, Hutchinson, London.
Do Vale, Nilton Bezerra (2005) 'Serendipity in medicine and anesthesiology' [original in Portuguese], *Brazilian Review of Anaesthesiology* 55/2: 224–49, online, https://doi.org/10.1590/s0034-70942005000200010/
Dossey, Larry (2013) *One mind. How our individual mind is part of a greater mind and why it matters*, Hay House, Carlsbad, CA.
Du Bartas, Guillaume (1578) *La Sepmaine ou creation du mined*, trans Josuah Sylvester, Jacques Chouet, Geneva.
Dunbar Robin (1996) *Grooming, gossip and the evolution of language*, Faber, London.

Dunbar, Robin (2005) *The human story*, Faber, London.

Dundes, Alan (ed.) (1968) *Every man his way, readings in cultural anthropology*, Prentice Hall, Englewood Cliffs, NJ.

Duranti, Alessandro (1997) *Linguistic anthropology*, Cambridge University Press, Cambridge.

Duranti, Alessandro (ed.) (2004) *A companion to linguistic anthropology*, Blackwell, Oxford.

Duranti, Alessandro (2015) *The anthropology of intentions. Language in a world of others*, Cambridge University Press, Cambridge.

Duranti, Alessandro and Goodwin, Charles (eds) (1992) *Rethinking context, language as an interactive phenomenon*, Cambridge University Press, Cambridge.

Eastaway, Rob (2024) *Much ado about numbers, Shakespeare's mathematical life and times*, Allen and Unwin, London.

Edgar, Iain (1999) 'Dream fact and real fiction: the realisation of the imagined self', *Anthropology of Consciousness* 10(1): 28–42.

Edwards, Sean, J. A. (2000) *Swarming on the battlefield*, RAND Corporation, Santa Monica.

Eisenstein, Elizabeth L. (1979) *The printing press as an agent of change: communications and cultural transformations in early modem Europe*, Cambridge University Press, Cambridge.

Ekstut, Joann and Ekstut, Arielle (2013) *The secret language of colour: science, nature, history, culture. Beauty of red, orange, yellow, green, blue, and violet*, Black Dog and Leventhal, New York, NY.

Ellis, William (1829) *Polynesian researches*, 2 vols, Fischer, Son, & Jackson, London.

Eren, Metin I., Lycett, Stephen J., Tomonaga, Masaki (2020) 'Underestimating Kanzi? Exploring Kanzi-Oldowan comparisons in light of recent human stone tool replication', *Evolutionary Anthropology* 29/6: 310–316. https://doi.org/10.1002/evan.21858

Feld, Steven (1982) *Sound and sentiment: birds, weeping, poetics, and song in Kaluli expression*, University of Pennsylvania Press, Philadelphia, PA.

Feld, Steven (1986) 'Orality and consciousness', in Tokumara and Yamaguti (eds), *The oral and the literate in music*, Academia Music, Tokyo.

Feld, Steven (2012) *Jazz cosmopolitanism in Accra*, Duke University Press, London.

Feld, Steven, Fox, Aaron A., Porcello, Thomas, Samuels, David (2004) 'Vocal anthropology: from the language of music to the language of song', in Duranti (ed.), *A companion to linguistic anthropology*, Blackwell, Oxford.

Ferrara, Silvia (2023) *The greatest invention: a history of the world in nine mysterious scripts*, English translation, Farrar, Straus & Giroux, New York.

Finley, Victoria (2014) *The brilliant history of color in art*, Getty Museum, Los Angeles.

Finnegan, Ruth (1967) *Limba stories and story-telling*, Clarendon Press, Oxford.

Finnegan, Ruth (1970/2014) *Oral literature in Africa*, Clarendon Press, Oxford/Open Book, Cambridge.

Finnegan, Ruth (1977/1992) *Oral poetry*, Cambridge University Press, Cambridge/Indiana University Press, Bloomington.

Finnegan, Ruth (1988/2013) *Literacy and orality, studies in the technology of communication*, Callender Press, Old Bletchley.

Finnegan, Ruth (1989/2007) *The hidden musicians*, Cambridge University Press, Cambridge/Wesleyan University Press, Middletown.

Finnegan, Ruth (ed.) (2017) *Entrancement, the consciousness of music, dreaming, and the world*, University of Wales Press, Cardiff.
Finnegan, Ruth (2019) *Music and creation*, Callender Press, Old Bletchley.
Finnegan, Ruth (2023) *Communicating: the multiple modes of human communication,* 3rd edition, Routledge, London.
First Words Project (2019) 'Baby and toddler milestones: 16 gestures by 16 months', online, https://www.readingrockets.org/topics/developmental-milestones/articles/baby-and-toddler-mileston/
Fischer, Steven Roger (2020) *History of writing*, Reaktion, London.
Fisher, Len (2009) *The perfect swarm: the science of complexity in everyday life*, Basic Books, Lebanon IN.
Foley, John Miles (1985) *Oral-formulaic theory and research: an introduction and annotated bibliography*, Garland Publishing, New York, NY.
Foley, John Miles (2003) *How to read an oral poem*, University of Illinois Press, Champaign IL.
Foley, John Miles (2012) *Oral tradition and the internet, pathways of the mind*, University of Illinois Press, Champaign, IL.
France, Peter (1966) 'The Kaunitoni migration. Notes on the genesis of a Fijian tradition', *Journal of Pacific History* 1: 107–113.
Francos, Emily (2023) 'Meaning and symbolism of the number 3', online https://www.yourtango.com/2019328255/meaning-number-3-according-bible-numerology-astrology-tarot/
Frith, Simon (1988) 'Why do songs have words?' in S. Frith (ed.), *Music for pleasure*, Polity, Cambridge.
Geissmann, Thomas (2001) 'Gibbon songs and human music from an evolutionary perspective', in N. Wallin, B. Merker, and S. Brown (eds), *The origins of music*, MIT Press, Cambridge MA.
Gell, Alfred (1996) *Art and agency*, Oxford University Press, Oxford.
Gentili, Bruno and Paioni, Giuseppe (eds) (1985) *Oralita: cultura, letteratura, discorso*, Edizioni dell' Ateneo, Rome.
Gifford, Clive (2018) *The colours of history. How colours shaped the world*, Words & Pictures, London.
Gifford, Edward W. (1924) 'Tongan myths and tales', *Bishop Museum Bulletin* 8: 15–19.
Gill, Victoria (2023) 'Humans and wild apes share common language', online, https://www.bbc.co.uk/news/science-environment-64387401/
Gintsburg, Sarali (2018) 'Transitional texts', https://www.unav.edu/en/web/instituto-cultura-y-sociedad/discurso-publico/international-conferencd-transitional-texts/call-for-papers/
Gintsburg, Sarali (2019) Voice in a narrative: A trialogue with Ruth Finnegan, *Frontiers of narrative studies* 7/1: 1–20.
Glennie, Evelyn (2019) *Listen world!*, Balestier Press, Singapore.
Godzich, Wlad and Kittay, Jeffrey (1986) *The emergence of prose, an essay in prosaics,* University of Minnesota Press, Minneapolis, MN.
Goldin-Meadow, Susan (2003) *Hearing gesture. How our hands help us think*, Howard University Press, Cambridge, MA.
Goody, Jack (ed.) (1968) *Literacy in traditional societies*, Cambridge University Press, London.
Goody, Jack (1987) *The logic of writing and the organization of society*, Cambridge University Press, Cambridge.
Goody, Jack (2000) *The power of the written tradition*, Smithsonian Institution, Washington, DC.

Goupil, Louise, Saint-Germier, Pierre, Rouvier, Gaëlle, Schwarz, Diemo, and Canonne, Clément (2020) 'Musical coordination in a large group without plans nor leaders', *Scientific Reports* 10: 20377, https://doi.org/10.1038/s41598-020-77263-z

Graff, Harvey J. (ed.) (1981) *Literacy and social development in the west*, Cambridge University Press, Cambridge.

Graff, Harvey J. (2010) *Literacy myths, legacies and lessons*, Routledge, London.

Grant, Morag J. (2017) 'An angel of modernity: Karlheinz Stockhausen's musical vision', in R. Finnegan (ed.), *Entrancement, the consciousness of music, dreaming, and the world*, University of Wales Press, Cardiff.

Green, Toby (2019) *A fistful of shells: West Africa from the rise of the slave trade to the Age of Revolution*, University of Chicago Press, Chicago, IL.

Greenfield, Patricia M. (1972) 'Oral or written language: the consequences for cognitive development in Africa, the United States, and England', *Language and Speech* 15/2: 169–178.

Grey, George (1854) *Nga mahinga a nga tupuna Maori*, George Willis, London.

Grey, George (1855) *Polynesian mythology*, J. Murray, London.

Griffiths-Lynch, Kristen, Greenfield, Patricia M., Feng, Y, Savage-Rumbaugh, Sue, and Lyn, Heidi. (2013) 'A cross-species study of gesture and its role in symbolic development: implications for the gestural theory of language evolution', *Frontiers in Psychology* 4, https://doi.org/10.3389/fpsyg.2013.00160

Grimm, Jacob (1851/1984) *On the origin of language*, English translation, Brill, Leiden.

Griswold, Martin (2012) 'Are inventions, inevitable? simultaneous invention and the incremental nature of discovery', online, *The Long Nose: Technology and Economy*. November 25

Guggenheim, Bill and Guggenheim, Judy (1995) *Hello from Heaven*, Bantam, New York, NY.

Hall, Edward T. (1959) *The silent language*, Fawcett Publications, New York, NY.

Hammond, Norman (1986) 'New light on the most ancient Maya', *Man* 21: 399–414.

Hanks, William F. (1996) *Language and communicative practices* Westview Press, Boulder.

Harris, Roy (1986) *The origin of writing*, Duckworth, London.

Hauser, Mark D. (2001) 'The sound and the fury: primate vocalizations as reflections of emotion and thought', in N. Wallin (ed.), *The origins of music*, MIT Press, Cambridge, MA.

Havelock, Eric A. (1982) *The literate revolution in ancient Greece and its cultural consequences*, Princeton University Press, Princeton, NJ.

Havelock, Eric A. and Hershbell, Jackson P. (1978) *Communication arts in the ancient world*, Hastings House, New York, NY.

Hayward, Guy (2013) 'Chanting as one, the synchrony of sonorous community', PhD thesis, University of Cambridge.

Heaney, Nicholas (2007) *The silence at the song's end*, Songsend Books, New York, NY.

Heelas, Paul (1996) *The New Age movement: Religion, culture and society in the age of postmodernity*, Wiley-Blackwell, London.

Helmenstine, Anne Marie (2019) 'Why mathematics is a language', online, https://www.thoughtco.com/why-mathematics-is-a-language-4158142/

Hemingway, Annamaria (2008) *Practicing conscious living and dying: stories of the eternal continuum of consciousness*, O Books, New Airesford.

Henige, David P. (1971) *The chronology of oral tradition*, Clarendon Press, Oxford.
Herz, Robert (1960/2008) *Death and the right hand*, Routledge, London.
Hewes, Gordon W. (1996) 'A history of the study of language origins and the gesture primacy hypothesis', in Lock and Peters.
Hirata, Satoshi, Watanabe, Kunio, and Masao, Kawai (2008). 'Sweet-potato washing revisited', in Matsuzawa, T. (eds) *Primate origins of human cognition and behavior,* Springer, Tokyo, online, https://doi.org/10.1007/978-4-431-09423-4_24/
Hofmeyr, Isabel (2004) *The portabl Bunyan. A transnational history of The Pilgrim's Progress*, Princeton University Press, Princeton, NJ.
Hogben, Lancelot (1989) *Mathematics for the million*, 4th edition, Merlin Press, London,
Hogben, Lancelot and Bodmer, Frederick (1943) *The loom of language*, Allen and Unwin, London.
Honour, Hugh and Fleming, John (2002) *A world history of art*, Laurence King, London.
Horton, Robin and Finnegan, Ruth (eds) (1973) *Modes of thought: essays on thinking in western and non-western societies*, Faber, London.
Houseman, Barbara (2002) *Finding your voice, a step-by-step guide for actors*, Nick Hern Books, London.
Houston, Stephen (ed.) (2004). *The first writing*, Cambridge University Press, Cambridge.
Howes, David (ed.) (2011) *The sixth sense*, Berg, Oxford.
Howitt, Alfred W. (1889) 'Notes on Australian message sticks and messengers', *Journal of the Anthropological Institute of Great Britain and Ireland* 18: 314–332.
Huang, Rachel (2017) 'Scientists study music's effects on brain with fMRI', online, https://www.jhunewsletter.com/article/2017/04/scientists-study-musics-effects-on-brain-with-fmri/
Humphrey, Nicholas (1984) *Consciousness regained,* Oxford University Press, Oxford.
Hurford, James R. (2014) *The origins of language, a slim guide,* Oxford University Press, New York, NY.
Hurford, James R., Studdert-Kennedy, Michael, Knight, Chris (eds) (1998) *Approaches to the evolution of language,* Cambridge University Press, New York, NY.
Huxley, Julian (1942) 'Origins of human graphic art', *Nature* 149/3788: 637.
Hymes, Dell (1964) (ed.) *Language in culture and society*, Harper & Row, New York, NY.
Innis, Harold A. (1950) *Empire and communications*, Clarendon Press, Oxford.
Innis, Harold A. (1964) *The bias of communication*, University of Toronto Press, Toronto.
Institute of Semitic Studies (2016) 'About the alphabet', Institute of Semitic Studies, Princeton, NJ.
Iverson, Jana M. and Goldin-Meadow, Susan (2005). 'Gesture paves the way for language development', *Gesture and Language Development* 16/5: 367–371, online, https://doi.org/10.1111/j.0956-7976.2005.01542.x
Izen, Sarah C., Cassano-Coleman, Riesa Y., and Piazza, Elise A. (2023) 'Music as a window into real-world communication', *Frontiers of Psychology,* 14, online, https://doi.org/10.3389/fpsyg.2023.1012839/

Jeffries, Keith J., Fritz, Jonathan B., and Braun, Allen R. (2003) 'Words in melody: an H2 15O PET study of brain activation during singing and speaking', *Neuroreport* 14: 749–754.
Jung, Gustav (2001) *Dreams*, Routledge, London.
Juslin, Patrick N. and Sloboda, John (eds) (2011) *Handbook of music and emotion*, Oxford University Press, Oxford.
Kagan Eugene and Ben-Gal, Irad (2015) *Search and foraging, Individual motion and swarm dynamics*, CRC Press, Taylor and Francis, New York, NY.
Kahraman, Ferruh (2022) 'The birth of communication: the origin of language and the diversification of languages', *Marife Dini Araştırmalar Dergisi* 22/1, online, https://typeset.io/papers/the-birth-of-communication-the-origin-of-language-and-the-1w1uw22f/
Kallberg, Jeffrey (1996) *Chopin at the boundaries. Sex, history and musical genre*, Harvard University Press, Cambridge, MA.
Kamei, Nobutaka (2004) 'The sign languages of Africa', *Journal of African Studies* (Japan Association for African Studies) 64: 43–64.
Kelber, Werner (2013) *Imprints, Voiceprints, and Footprints of Memory: Collected Essays of Werner H. Kelber*, Society of Biblical Literature, online, https://doi.org/10.2307/j.ctt5hjh34.3/
Kelber, Werner and Byrskog, Samuel (2009) *Jesus in memory: traditions in oral and scribal perspectives*, Baylor University Press, Waco, TX.
Keller, Helen (1903/2020) *The story of my life*, Callender Press, Old Bletchley.
Kelly, Piers (2019) 'Australian message sticks: old questions, new directions', *Journal of Material Culture* 25: 1–20.
Kendon, Adam (1994) 'Do gestures communicate? A review', *Research on Language and Social Interaction* 27/3: 175–200 https://doi.org/10.1207/s15327973rlsi2703_2/
Kendon, Adam (2001) 'Gesture as communication strategy', *Semiotica* 135: 191–209.
Kendon, Adam (2004) *Gesture. Visible action as utterance*, Cambridge University Press, Cambridge.
Kendon, Adam (2017) 'Reflections on the "gesture-first" hypothesis of language origins', *Psychonomic Bulletin & Review* 24/1: 163–170, online, doi:10.3758/s13423-016-1117-3/
Kennedy, Lesley (2024) 'The Prehistoric Ages: how humans lived before written records', online, https://www.history.com/news/prehistoric-ages-timeline/
Knight, Chris, Studdert-Kennedy, Michael and Hurford, James (eds) (2000) *The evolutionary emergence of language, social function and the origins of linguistic form*, Cambridge University Press, Cambridge.
Knoblauch, Hubert and Kotthoff, Helga (eds) (2001) *Verbal art across cultures*, Narr, Tubingen.
Koelsch, Stefan, Fritz, Thomas, Cramon, D., Yves V., Müller, Karsten, Friederici Angela D. (2006) 'Investigating emotion with music: an fMRI study', *Human Brain Mapping* 27/3: 239–250.
Kohli, Krishleen Kaur (2023) 'Which is the world's most loved number?', online, https://krishleenkaurkohli.medium.com/which-is-the-worlds-most-loved-number-41f48d53fbe2#:~:text/
Kotthoff, Helga (2001) 'Aesthetic dimensions of Georgian grief rituals', in Knoblauch and Kotthoff (eds), *Verbal art across cultures*, Narr, Tubingen.
Ladinsky, Daniel (1999) *The gift, Poems by Hafiz the Great Sufi*, Penguin, London.
Laslett, Peter (1965/2021) *The world we have lost*, Routledge, London.

Lease, Emory B. (1919) 'The number three, mysterious, mystic', *Classical Philology* 14: 56–73.
Lee, Nylah (2023) 'Message sticks: Australia's ancient unwritten language', online, https://www.bbc.com/travel/article/20230811-message-sticks-australias-ancient-unwritten-language/
Lehman, Lotte (2017) *My vocal craft. How to sing*, Callender Press, Old Bletchley.
Lenin, Vladimir (1920/2017) 'The tasks of the Youth Leagues' in *Collected Works*, Volume 31, Verso Books, London.
Leonhardt, David (2019) 'Speechwriting three', online, https://thgmwriters.com/blog/speechwriting-tip-power-of-three/
Leppert, Richard (1993) *The sight of sound*, University of California Press, Berkeley, CA.
Levetin, Daniel (2008) *This is your brain on music*, Atlantic Books, London.
Levman, Bryan, G. (1992) 'The genesis of music and language', *Ethnomusicology* 36/2, online, https://doi.org/10.2307/851912/
Lock, Andrew and Peters, Charles R. (eds) (1996) *Handbook of human symbolic evolution*, Clarendon Press, Oxford.
Lohmann, Heidemarie and Tomasello, Michael (2003) 'The role of language in the development of false belief understanding: a training study', *Child Development*, 74(4): 1130–44. online doi: 10.1111/1467-8624.00597.
Lord, Albert (1960/2019) *The singer of tales*, Harvard University Press, Cambridge MA.
Lord, Albert (1965) 'Oral poetry', in A. Preminger (ed.), *Encyclopedia of poetry and poetics*, Princeton University Press, Princeton, NJ.
Lord, Albert (1968) 'Homer as an oral poet', *Harvard Studies in Classical Philology* 72: 1–46.
Lowie, Robert H. (1925) 'Five as a mystic number', *American Anthropologist* 27: 578.
Luomala, Katherine (1949) *Maui-of-a-thousand-tricks: his Oceanic and European biographers*, Bishop Museum, Honolulu, HI.
Luomala, Katherine (1950) 'Melanesian mythology', 'Micronesian mythology', 'Polynesian mythology', in M. Leach (ed.), *Funk and Wagnalls standard dictionary of folklore, mythology and legend,* II, Funk & Wagnalls, New York, NY.
Luomala, Katherine (1955) *Voices on the wind. Polynesian myths and chants*, Bishop Museum, Honolulu, HI.
Luty, Jerzy (2017) 'Do animals make art, or the evolutionary continuity of species: a case for uniqueness', *Avant* 8/1: 107–116.
Lutz, Catherine A. and Abu-Lughod, Lila (eds) (1990) *Language and the politics of emotion*, Cambridge University Press, Cambridge.
Lutz, Catherine and White, Geoffrey M. (1986) 'The anthropology of emotions', *Annual Review of Anthropology*, 15, 405–436.
MacDonald, Margaret R. (2001) *Mabela the clever*, Albert Whitman & Co, Park Ridge IL.
Madden, Joah R. (2008) 'Do bowerbirds exhibit cultures?', *Animal Cognition* 11: 11–12.
Magowan, Fiona (2007) *Melodies of mourning. Music and emotion in northern Australia*, James Currey, Oxford.
Malein, Flora (2012) 'Bonobo ape Kanzi creates flint tools to prise open logs' online, https://www.theguardian.com/science/blog/2012/aug/22/bonobo-kanzi-flint-tools-logs/

Marabito, Maria (2024) 'The incredible science behind starling murmurations', *Treehugger*, online, https://www.treehugger.com/the-incredible-science-behind-starling-murmurations-4863751/
Marler, Peter and Slabbekoorn, Hans (2004) *Nature's music: the science of birdsong*, Academic Press, Cambridge, MA.
Marini, Stephen A. (2003) *Sacred song in America: religion, music, and public culture*, University of Illinois Press, Urbana, IL.
Martinet, Lison, Sueur, Cédric, Hirata, Satoshi, Hosselet, Jérôme, Matsuzawa, Tetsuro, and Pelé, Marie (2021) 'New indices to characterize drawing behavior in humans (Homo sapiens) and chimpanzees (Pan troglodytes), 11/3860 online, https://www.nature.com/articles/s41598-021-83043-0#citeas/
Matsuzawa, Tetsuro (2015) 'Sweet-potato washing revisited: 50th anniversary of the Primates article', *Primates* 56, 285–287, online, https://doi.org/10.1007/s10329-015-0492-0/
Mayer, Jon (2023) 'The interesting etymologies of 71 everyday words', *Words*, online, https://www.mentalfloss.com/posts/interesting-etymologies-everyday-words/
McGilchrist, Iain (2009) *The Master and his emissary: The divided brain and the making of the western world*, Yale University Press, New Haven, CT.
McGinn, Colin (2015). *Prehension: the hand and the emergence of humanity*, MIT Press, Cambridge, MA.
McGlynn, Terence (2010) 'How does social behavior evolve?' *Nature Education Knowledge* 3/10, online, https://www.nature.com/scitable/knowledge/library/how-does-social-behavior-evolve-13260245/#:~:text=/
McLuhan, Marshall (1962) *The Gutenberg galaxy: the making* of *typographic man*, Routledge & Kegan Paul, London.
McLuhan, Marshall (1967) *Understanding media, the extensions of man*, Sphere Books, London.
McNeill, David (2005) *Gesture and thought*, University of Chicago Press, Chicago, IL.
McNeill, David (2012) *How language began: gesture and speech in human evolution*, Cambridge University Press, Cambridge.
McNeill, David (2015) *Why we gesture the surprising role of hand movements in communication*, Cambridge University Press, Cambridge.
McPherson, Sarah (2023) 'Humans can understand the gestures of other great apes', *BBC Wildlife Magazine*, online, https://www.discoverwildlife.com/news/humans-can-understand-the-gestures-of-other-great-apes/
Meggitt, Mervyn (1968) 'Uses of literacy in New Guinea and Melanesia', in Jack Goody (ed.), *Literacy in traditional societies*, Cambridge University Press, London.
Mehr, Samuel A., Krasnow, Max M., Bryant, Gregory A., Hagen, Edward H. (2021). Origins of music in credible signaling, *Behavioral and Brain Sciences* 44: 643234. https://doi.org/10.1017/S0140525X20000345/
Mellas, Andrew (2020). *Liturgy and the emotions in Byzantium. Compunction and hymnody*, Cambridge University Press, Cambridge.
Meltzoff, Andrew N. and Moore, M. Keith (1977) 'Imitation of facial and manual gestures by human neonates', *Science*, 198, online, doi:10.1126/science.897687/
Merker, Björn, Wallin, Nils L., and Brown, Steven (eds) (2000) *The origins of music*, MIT Press, Cambridge MA.
Merriam, Alan P. (1964) *The anthropology of music*, North Western University Press, Evanston.

Merton, Robert K. (1961) 'Singletons and multiples in scientific discovery', *Proceedings of the American Philosophical Society* 105: 470–486.
Meyer, Kuno (1906) *The triads of Ireland*, Hodges Figgis and Co, Dublin.
Meyer, Leonard (1956) *Emotion and meaning in music*, University of Chicago Press, Chicago, IL.
Milton, Kay and Svasek, Maruska (eds) (2005) *Mixed emotions, anthropological studies of feeling*, Berg, Oxford.
Miri, Adhid (2024) 'Ancient Mesopotamian music', *Chaldean News*, online, https://www.chaldeannews.com/culture-and-history/2022/11/1/ancient-mesopotamian-music/
Mitcalfe, Barry (1974) *Maori poetry. The singing word*, Price Milbum for Victoria University Press, Wellington.
Mithen, Steven (1996) *The prehistory of the mind*, W&N, London.
Mithen, Steven (2006) *The singing neanderthals: the origins of music, language, mind, and body*, W&N, London.
Moore, Kimberly (2012) 'Which came first: music or language. A theory that language evolved as a subset of music', *Psychology Today*, online, https://www.psychologytoday.com/gb/blog/your-musical-self/201209/which-came-first-music-or-language#/
Morphy, Howard (ed.) (2006) *The anthropology of art*, Blackwell, Oxford.
Morris, Desmond (1962) *The biology of art: study of a picture making behaviour of the great apes and its relationship to human art*, Methuen Young Books, London.
Morris, Desmond (1977/2002) *People watching, the guide to body language*, Vintage, London.
Moss, Robert (2010) *The secret history of dreaming*, New World, Library, Novato.
Müller, Max (1862) *The science of language*, Scribner, New York, NY.
Müller, Max (n.d.) (ed. Georgina Adelaide Müller) *Thoughts on life and religion*, Edinburgh University Press, Edinburgh.
Muller, Raymond (1903) 'Die Zahl 3 in Sage, Dichtung, und Kunst', *Jahresbericht der K.K. Staats Oberrealschule* 1901–1902: 1–23.
Mursell, Ian (2021) 'Maya colour symbolism', online, https://www.mexicolore.co.uk/maya/teachers/resource-colour-symbolism/
Nedjah, Nadia and Mourelle, Luiza de Macedo (eds) (2006) *Swarm intelligent systems*, Springer, Berlin.
Ngata, Apirana T. (1959) *Nga Moteatea. The songs. Scattered pieces from many canoe areas*, Part 1, Polynesian Society, Wellington.
Ogede, Ode (1993) 'The role of the Egede poet, *African Languages and Cultures* 6: 49–68.
Okpewho, Isidore (1983) *Myth in Africa*, Cambridge University Press, Cambridge.
Olrik, Axel (1909) 'Epische Gesetze der Volksdichtung', *Zettschrift fur Deutschland Altertum* 51: 1–12.
O'Mara, Shane (2020) *In praise of walking*, Vintage, London.
Ong, Walter J. (1967) *The presence of the word*, Yale University Press, New Haven.
Ong, Walter J. (1977) *Interfaces of the word*, Cornell University Press, Ithaca.
Ong, Walter J. (1982) *Orality and literacy: the technologizing of the word*, Methuen, London.
Opland, Jeff (1983) *Xhosa oral poetry: aspects of a black South African tradition*, Cambridge University Press, Cambridge.

Opland, Jeff (1986) 'World epic: on heroic and epic traditions in oral and written literature', in E. S. Shaffer (ed.), *Comparative criticism* 8, Cambridge University Press, Cambridge.
Oriono, Nduka and Akoma, Chiji (eds) (2021) *Oral literary performance in Africa, beyond text*, Routledge, New York, NY.
Ostler, Nicholas (2006) *Empires of the word: a language history of the world*, Harper Perennial, New York, NY.
Otiono, Nduka and Akoma, Chiji (eds) (2023) *Oral literary performance in Africa: beyond text*, Routledge, New York, NY.
Ottenheimer, Harriet (2013) *An anthropology of language* Cengage Learning, London.
Ottenberg, Simon (1996) *Seeing with music. The lives of three blind African musicians* University of Washington Press, Seattle.
Pacey, Arnold, (1974/1994), *The maze of ingenuity*, MIT Press, Cambridge MA.
Parkinson, Neil (2023) *The history of colour*, Frances Lincoln, London.
Parry, Milman and Lord, Albert B. (1954) *Serbocroation heroic songs. Novi Pazar*, English translation, Harvard University Press and Serbian Academy of Sciences, Cambridge, MA and Belgrade.
Parsons, Elsie Clews (1916) 'The favourite number of the Zuni', *Scientific Monthly* 3: 596–600.
Pashchevskaya, Sonya, Fruth, Barbara, and Hohmann, Gottfried (2024) 'Water scooping: tool use by a wild bonobo (Pan paniscus) at LuiKotale, a case report', *Primates* 65/3: 145–150, online, https://doi.org/10.1007/s10329-024-01121-z
Pastoureau, Michael (2009) *Black: the history of a color*, Princeton University Press, Princeton NJ.
Pastoureau, Michael (2014) *Green: the history of a color*, Princeton University Press, Princeton NJ.
Pastoureau, Michael (2017) *Red: the history of a color*, Princeton University Press, Princeton NJ.
Pastoureau, Michael (2016) *Blue: the history of a color*, Princeton University Press, Princeton NJ.
Pastoureau, Michael (2019) *Yellow: the history of a color*, Princeton University Press, Princeton NJ.
Pastoureau, Michael (2023) *White: the history of a color*, Princeton University Press, Princeton NJ.
Peralta, Lia (2023) 'How does music affect society?' online, https://easysociology.com/sociology-of-media/sociology-of-music/the-sociology-of-music-how-music-reflects-and-shapes-social-structure/#/
Pilkey, Dav (2017) *Dogman*, Scholastic, Witney Oxon.
Pinker, Stephen (2015) *The language instinct: how the mind creates language*, Penguin, London.
Poe, Marshall T. (2011) *A history of communications: media and society from the evolution of speech to the internet*, Cambridge University Press, Cambridge.
Pollick, Amy S. and de Waal, Frans B. M. (2007) 'Ape gestures and language evolution', online, https://doi.org/10.1073/pnas.0702624104/
Pope, Stephen (2004) 'Primate sociality natural law theory', in R. W. Sussman and A. R. Chapman (eds), *The origins and nature of sociality*, de Gruyter, New York, NY.
Prieure, Jacques, Barbu, Stéphanie, Blois-Heulin, Catherine, and Lemasson, Alban (2019) 'The origins of gestures and language: history, current advances and proposed theories', *Biological Reviews*, 95(3): 531–554. https://doi.org/10.1111/brv.12576

Propp, Vladimir (1958) *Morphology of the folktale*, English translation, Indiana University Press, Bloomington, IN.
Provasi, Joëlle and Bobin-Bègue, Anne (2003) 'Spontaneous motor tempo and rhythmical synchronisation in 21/2- and 4-year-old children', *International Journal of Behavioral Development* 27: 220–231, online, 10.1080/01650250244000290/
Putnam, Hilary, Putnam, Ruth A., and Macarthur, David (2017) *Pragmatism as a way of life: the lasting legacy of William James and John Dewey*, Harvard University Press, Cambridge, MA.
Radin, Dean (2006) *Entangled minds*, Pocket Books, Chicago, IL.
Radin, Dean (2009) *The conscious universe. The scientific truth of psychic phenomena*, Harper Collins, London.
Radin, Paul (1957) *Primitive man as philosopher,* Dover Publications, New York, NY.
Raimondi, Teresa, Di Panfilo, Giovanni, Pasquali, Matteo, Zarantonello, Martina, Favaro, Livio, Savini, Tommaso, Gamba, Marco, and Ravignani, Andrea (2023) 'Isochrony and rhythmic interaction in ape duetting', *Proceedings of the Royal Society B*, online, https://doi.org/10.1098/rspb.2022.2244/
Ransome, Hilda M. (1937) *The sacred bee in ancient times and folklore*, Allen and Unwin, London.
Reggiani, Enrico (2023) 'What is sound? Gerald Manley Hopkins's poetic acoustics', in M. Canani and A. E. Soccio (eds), *The language of science in the long nineteenth century*, Edizioni Solfanelli, Chieti.
Robinson, Andrew (2007) *The story of writing: alphabets, hieroglyphics and pictograms*, Thames and Hudson, New York, NY.
Roffman, Itai, Savage-Rumbaugh, Sue, Rubert-Pugh, Elizabeth, Ronen, Avraham, and Nevo, Eviatar (2012) 'Stone tool production and utilization by bonobo-chimpanzees (Pan paniscus)', *Proceedings of the National Academy of Sciences* 109/36: 14500–14503, https://doi.org/10.1073/pnas.1212855109/
Rogers, Nala (2018) 'The greatest scientists are artists too', https://shiningmountainwaldorf.org/the-greatest-scientists-are-artists-too/#:/
Romanes, George (1891–1892) 'Thought and language', *The Monist* 2: 3, online, https://www.jstor.org/stable/27896915?seq=1/
Root-Bernstein, Michele Robert (2010) 'Einstein on creative thinking, music and the intuitive art of scientific imagination', *Psychology Today*, online, https://www.psychologytoday.com/gb/blog/imagine/201003/einstein-creative-thinking-music-and-the-intuitive-art-scientific-imagination/
Saaty, Thomas (2016) 'Seven is the magic number in nature', *Proceedings of the American Philosophical Society,* 160/4: 335–360.
Sanders, Rob (2011) 'Lists, the Duke of three, and repetition', online, http://robsanderswrites.blogspot.com/2011/05/lists-rule-of-three-and-repetition.html/
Sapir, Edward (1949) *Language. An introduction to the study of speech*, Harcourt, Brace, New York, NY.
Schimmel, Annemarie (1993) *The mystery of numbers*, Oxford University Press, New York, NY.
Scholderer, Victor (1963) *Johann Gutenberg. The inventor of printing*, British Museum, London.
Schutz, Alfred (1951) 'Making music together, a study in social relationship', *Social Research* 18: 76–97.
Schwartz, Stephan A., Woollacott, Marjorie H. and Schwartz, Gary E. (eds) (2020) *Is consciousness primary?* Academy for the Advancement of Postmaterialist Sciences, online, https://www.aapsglobal.com/

Schwartz, Theodore, White, Geoffrey M., and Lutz, Catherine A. (eds) (1992) *New directions in psychological anthropology*, Cambridge University Press, Cambridge.
Scribner, Sylvia and Cole, Michael (1981) *The psychology of literacy*, Harvard University Press, Cambridge, MA.
Seddon, Frederick A. and Biasutti, Michele (2009) 'Modes of communication between members of a string quartet', *Small Group Research* 40: 115–137, online, https://doi.org/10.1177/1046496408329277/
Sell, Karen (2005) *The disciplines of vocal pedagogy, towards an holistic approach*, Ashgate Publishing, Farnham.
Shaw, John (2001) 'Turn thrifty lectures into rich jazz recitals', *The Times Higher*, 21 September.
Seeger, Anthony (1987) *Why Suya sing. A musical anthropology of an Amazonian people*, Cambridge University Press, Cambridge.
Simmons, David R. (1966) 'The sources of Sir George Grey's *Nga Mahi a Nga Tupuna*', *Journal of the Polynesian Society* 75/2: 177–188.
Smelser, Neil J. (2001) 'Evolution of sociality', in Neil J. Smelser and Paul B. Baltes (eds) *International encyclopedia of the social & behavioral sciences*, Elsevier, New York, NY.
Smith, Deirdre Madeleine (2023) 'The origins of animal art', *Configurations* 31/1, online, https://muse.jhu.edu/article/885566/
Steele, Philippa and Boyes, Philip J. (eds) (2022) *Writing around the ancient mediterranean*, Oxbow Books, Barnsley.
Stevens, John (1986) *Words and music in the Middle Ages*, Cambridge University Press, Cambridge.
Stewart, Ian (2024) 'Number symbolism', online, https://www.britannica.com/contributor/Ian-Stewart/4535
Stolz, Benjamin A. and Shannon, Richard S. (eds) (1976) *Oral literature and the formula*, Center for the Coordination of Ancient and Modern Studies, University of Michigan, Ann Arbor, MI.
Street, Brian V. (1984) *Literacy in theory and in practice*, Cambridge University Press, Cambridge.
Stubbs, Michael (1980) *Language and literacy: the social linguistics of reading and writing*, Routledge & Kegan Paul, London.
Sun, Hongkai (1983/2009) 'The Ersu Shaba pictographic writing system', *Asian Highlands Perspectives* 1: 159–186.
Suroweicki, James (2004) *The wisdom of crowds*, Little Brown, Boston, MA.
Sussman, Robert W. and Chapman, Audrey R. (eds) (2004) *The origins and nature of sociality*, de Gruyter, New York, NY.
Tannen, Deborah (ed.) (1982) *Spoken and written language: exploring orality and literacy*, Ablex, Norwood, NJ.
Tanner, Nancy M. (1981) *On becoming human*, Cambridge University Press, Cambridge.
Tavenner, Eugene (1916) 'Three as a magic number in Latin literature', *Transactions of the American Philological Association* 47: 117–143.
Taylor, Hollis (2018) 'Can George dance? Biosemiotics and human exceptionalism with a lyrebird in the viewfinder', *Social Semiotics* 28/1: 60–76.
Tedlock, Dennis (1977) 'Toward an oral poetics', *New Literary History* 8: 513–523.
Tedlock, Dennis (1983) *The spoken word and the work of interpretation*, University of Pennsylvania Press, Philadelphia, PA.
Thaut, Michael (2006) *Rhythm, music, and the brain*, Routledge, London

Titze, Ingo R. (2008) 'The human instrument', *Scientific American* 298/1: 94–101.

Tokumaru Yosihiko and Yamaguti Osamu (eds) (1986) *The oral and the literate in music*, Academia Music, Tokyo.

Tomasello, Michael (2008) *Origins of human communication*, MIT Press, Cambridge MA.

Tomasello, Michael and Call, Josep (2019) 'Thirty years of great ape gestures', *Animal Cognition* 22: 461–469, online, https://doi.org/10.1007/s10071-018-1167-1/

Toynbee, Arnold (1978) *A selection of his works*, Oxford University Press, Oxford.

Tracey, Karen (ed.) (1999) *Language and social interaction at the centuries turn, special issue Research on language and social interaction* 32/1, 2.

Treitler, Leo (2003) *With voice and pen. Coming to know medieval song and how it was made*, Oxford University Press, Oxford.

Tufte, Edward R. (1990) *Envisioning information*, Graphics Press, Cheshire.

Turner, Victor and Bruner, Edward (eds) (1986) *The anthropology of experience*, University of Illinois Press, Champaign, IL.

UNESCO (1966) *World congress of Ministers of Education on the eradication of illiteracy (Teheran 1965): speeches and messages*, UNESCO, Paris.

Ustinova, Yulia (2009) *Caves and the ancient Greek mind: descending underground in the search for ultimate truth*, Oxford Academic, Oxford.

Van Leeuwen, Edwin J. C., DeTroy, Sarah E., Haun, Daniel B. M., and Call, Josep (2024) 'Chimpanzees use social information to acquire a skill they fail to innovate', *Nature Human Behaviour* 8: 891–902, online, https://doi.org/10.1038/s41562-024-01836-5

Van Leeuwen, Theo (1999) *Speech, music, sound*, MacMillan, Basingstoke

Van Zyl, H. J. (1941) 'Praises in northern Sotho', *Bantu Studies* 15/2: 119–156.

Waterman, Christopher A. (1990) *Juju: a social history and ethnography of an African popular music*, Chicago University Press, Chicago, IL.

Wavell, Archibald P. (ed.) (1944/1992) *Other men's flowers*, Pimlico, London.

Weber, Max (1958) *The rational and social foundations of music*, English translation, Southern Illinois University Press, Carbondale.

Whiten, Andrew, Goodall, Jane, McGrew, William C., Nishida, Toshiada, Reynolds, Vernon, Sugiyama, Yukimaru, Tutin, Caroline E., Wrangham, Richard W., Boesch, Christophe (1999) 'Cultures in chimpanzees', *Nature* 399: 682–685.

Whorf, Benjamin L. (1964) *Language, thought and reality*, MIT Press, Cambridge MA.

Yan, Hektor (2013) 'Can animals sing? On birdsong, music and meaning', *Social Science Information* 52.2: 272–286.

Zamm, Anna, Palmer, Caroline, Bauer, Anna-Katharina R., Bleichner, Martin G., Demos, Alexander P., Debener, Stefan (2021). Behavioral and neural dynamics of interpersonal synchrony between performing musicians: a wireless EEG hyperscanning study. *Frontiers in Human Neuroscience* 15: 717810. https://doi.org/10.3389/fnhum.2021.717810

Zangrilli, Quirino (2012) 'Dreams and telepathy', online https://www.psicoanalisi.it/english-1/dream-and-telepathy/1770/.

Zentner, Marcel R. and Kagan, Jerome (1998) 'Infants' perception of consonance and dissonance in music', *Infant Behavior and Development* 21: 483–492.

INDEX

For Product Safety Concerns and Information please contact our EU representative GPSR@taylorandfrancis.com Taylor & Francis Verlag GmbH, Kaufingerstraße 24, 80331 München, Germany